Praise for Chris Grosso and *Dead Set on Living*

"Chris's books have been a significant source of inspiration in my own healing journey, and his newest work, *Dead Set on Living*, is no exception. Anyone looking for something real—something raw, ragged, and authentic—won't be disappointed. I believe anyone who reads Chris's honest and unabashed words will truly benefit. This is very, very real shit."

—Bam Margera, professional skateboarder,
actor (*Jackass/CKY*), musician (Evesdroppers)

"Chris Grosso's *Dead Set on Living* is an awesome work, the totally honest account of a man seeking the realities of life and death, compassion and indifference, sorrow and joy—as if they really mattered. He tells his own moving story, holding nothing back, consults with many amazing people who work with depression, addiction, etc., and shares with us his process of integrating their teachings and advice in a vivid and beautiful way. If you and your loved ones struggle with life in an existential way, you will love this noble book—it will bring you courage and many blessings."

—Robert A.F. Thurman, coauthor of *Man of Peace:
The Illustrated Life Story of the Dalai Lama of Tibet*

"Chris Grosso is a Warrior of the Heart. With humility, honesty and courage as his weapons, he does battle with the shadows in the dark corners of our hearts."

—Krishna Das, Grammy-nominated kirtan musician

"Chris Grosso, like myself, is a searcher. He is on a quest. He is thirsty. For what, you might ask? Wisdom! It is so rare these days to want to know truth that people who seek it are thought of as odd, out of the norm, or naive. Hunter S. Thompson once said, 'When the going gets weird, the weird turn pro.' We are well beyond weird now. We are in the Twilight Zone of reality. We need the Chris Grossos of the world to tell us what they've seen and where we are. Read it!"

—Bob Forrest, author of *Running with Monsters*,
TV personality (*Celebrity Rehab/Sober House*), RehabBob.com

"Chris Grosso comes at us with a deeply intense and personal sharing of his life journey, reminding us that you don't have to be a goody-two-shoes to seek goodness and a spiritual life. It is often working through our darkest depths that we learn to become the light. Laying out some really easy practices we can all apply to our daily lives and advice from notable teachers of all lineages for all levels, this is a must-read."

—Jessica Pimentel, actress on *Orange Is the New Black*, Tibetan Buddhist, singer of Alekhine's Gun

"*Dead Set on Living* gets down to earth in dialogues that bring light to depression, addiction, and journeys through the dark night of the Spirit. Chris Grosso is an authentic voice of a new generation of meditation teachers. If you're ready for a book that does not shy away from important issues that are not often addressed by spiritual teachers, read this one."

—Loch Kelly, author of *Shift into Freedom: The Science and Practice of Open-Hearted Awareness*

"What a read! What a ride! Chris Grosso shares his journey and brings in a team of others who tell the truth and give us hope, light, and direction. This is spirituality in action. Thank you for this valuable contribution."

—Raghunath (aka Ray Cappo), international yoga teacher, speaker, singer of Youth of Today and Shelter

"Chris Grosso has assembled a team to help aid in solving the addiction crisis in America. It's not a new drug czar, an expensive ad campaign aimed at the youth, or resuscitating the half-century-long War on Drugs. The solution is an integrated treatment plan in which each individual is a participant in their own inner and outer healing. We have suffered too long through the darkness and despair of mental illness, trauma, material craving, and spiritual emptiness. Thankfully a new recovery community has surfaced with a road map to personal and social wholeness."

—Eben Sterling, *Thrasher Magazine,* practicing yogi, recovered addict of twenty-one years

"Chris Grosso comes from a place of compassion to bring hope to people who are suffering. He's been through it all, and the result is a quality of empathy that makes *Dead Set on Living* such a valuable book. We need a fresh view on the way to recover, and this remarkable gathering of voices from all sorts of perspectives—traditional to innovative to experimental—opens myriad doors to integrated healing as it guides readers toward their individual path to wholeness. I've personally seen Chris work with many of the young adults at one of my facilities over the last three years, and he has a special way of making deep and authentic connections quickly. I believe this book will create a similar experience with its readers."

—Jamison Monroe, founder and CEO of Newport Academy, Youth Mental Health and Healing Centers

Additional Praise for Chris Grosso

"Chris Grosso is an honest and engaging young teacher, and his work is both clearly expressed and inspiring."

—Andrew Harvey, bestselling author of *The Hope*

"You awaken your True spirit by way of the broken heart: ragged, vulnerable, fierce, and finally compassionate. Chris trod this rough way and shows honestly how it can be done."

—Jack Kornfield, bestselling author of *A Path with Heart*

"It is too easy to assume that America's young rockers and hipsters are all casually nihilistic, but Grosso taps into the deep yearning for authentic spirituality—questions allowed."

—*Library Journal*

"[Grosso] writes with refreshing wit and candor, deeply and broadly reflecting on what it means to be human, personally and collectively."

—*Publishers Weekly*

BOOKS BY CHRIS GROSSO

Everything Mind

Indie Spiritualist

BOOKS BY ALICE PECK

Be More Tree

Bread, Body, Spirit

Next to Godliness

DEAD SET
ON LIVING

MAKING THE DIFFICULT
BUT BEAUTIFUL JOURNEY FROM
F#*KING UP TO WAKING UP

CHRIS GROSSO
WITH ALICE PECK

GALLERY BOOKS

New York   London   Toronto   Sydney   New Delhi

G

Gallery Books
An Imprint of Simon & Schuster, Inc.
1230 Avenue of the Americas
New York, NY 10020

First Gallery Books trade paperback edition March 2018

GALLERY BOOKS and colophon are trademarks of Simon & Schuster, Inc.

For information about special discounts for bulk purchases,
please contact Simon & Schuster Special Sales at 1-866-506-1949
or business@simonandschuster.com.

The Simon & Schuster Speakers Bureau can bring authors
to your live event. For more information or to book an event,
contact the Simon & Schuster Speakers Bureau at 1-866-248-3049
or visit our website at www.simonspeaks.com.

Interior design by Bryden Spevak

Illustrations on pages 30–34 by Duane Stapp

Manufactured in the United States of America

10 9 8 7 6 5 4 3 2 1

Library of Congress Cataloging-in-Publication Data is available.

ISBN 978-1-5011-7397-4
ISBN 978-1-5011-7399-8 (ebook)

For Mom, Dad, and Jay.
None of this would be possible if it weren't for you.
Forever grateful and I love you so much.

Keep true to the rare music in your heart, to the marvelous and unique form that is and shall always be nothing else but you. Keep to that and you can do no wrong, which I realize is easier said than done.

—Mark Z. Danielewski, *House of Leaves*

It is impossible to explain the way God wounds the soul or to exaggerate the agony this causes. It makes the soul forget herself entirely. Yet this pain carries such exquisite pleasure that no other pleasure in life can compare to that happiness. The soul longs to die of this beautiful wound.

—Teresa of Ávila: *The Book of My Life*
(translated by Mirabai Starr)

There ain't nobody to be pretty for.
Fuck it, let it rattle.

—P.O.S ("Let It Rattle,"
from the album *Never Better*)

CONTENTS

The dragonfly, in almost every part of the world, symbolizes change and change in the perspective of self-realization; and the kind of change that has its source in mental and emotional maturity and the understanding of the deeper meaning of life.

—dragonfly-site.com

PREFACE

SEA OF HEARTBREAK

I can't breathe. Fuck. Fuck. *Fuck. I can't breathe!* My eyes pop open as a full-body panic attack sets in. Through my haze, I see my hands strapped to the bed. "Oh, *fuck*. Not again. I—" I'm gasping for air. There are tubes coming out of my mouth—*This is new.* I raise my head and realize I'm in a hospital. But where? How did I get here? What the fuck happened? That's when I see my parents sitting in chairs at the end of my bed, near a window. The heartbreak and despair in their eyes are unmistakable. To their right stands a nurse. She's telling me to calm down and let the tubes do the breathing for me, but I'm too panicked. I begin thrashing in the bed, trying to break the woven nylon straps that are keeping me from ripping the tubes out of my mouth. Later I'll find out this is the reason I was restrained in the first place.

I do my best to communicate with the nurse with my eyes. I'm pleading with her to take the tubes out, but to no avail. If my eyes could have screamed, they would have been saying, *"I can't force myself not to breathe! Please, for the love of whatever piece-of-shit god you believe in, get these fucking tubes out of me!"* Unfortunately, the nurse was not fluent in eye language, but luckily my parents figured it out and advocated on my behalf.

A doctor arrived and the tubes were removed. My memory is blurry, but I do recall it was painful, so painful that my mother had to leave the room. One of the tubes was in my lungs, breathing for me; the other was in my stomach, soaking up the alcohol, pills, and whatever other ugliness was down there.

It may have looked like a suicide attempt, but it wasn't. This was the result of a twenty-four-hour relapse that began with me sitting on a bus ride from Hartford (where I'd been visiting with family) back home to Ottawa, where my wife and stepdaughter lived. It started with a couple of Percocet, which I'd been prescribed after a root canal, and escalated during a layover at a depot in Vermont, when I bought a bunch of small wine boxes and poured them into a Powerade bottle so I could drink on the bus, which I did until I reached Montreal. There, on another layover, I found a liquor store and bought a fifth of vodka. I consumed most of it on the last leg of my ride to Ottawa, but decanted some into a plastic water bottle to save for later.

I don't remember arriving in Ottawa that night. I don't remember hailing a taxi and stumbling into the apartment and somehow managing not to wake up my sleeping wife and stepdaughter. What I do remember is waking up the next morning sick to my stomach and walking out into the kitchen, where my wife was preparing my stepdaughter's lunch for school. I gave her a kiss, and she could smell the mints I'd put in my mouth just moments before. She immediately had a panicked look on her face, thinking I'd been drinking. I lied and told her it was just mints. I walked into the living room, where my stepdaughter was watching TV as she ate her breakfast. I gave her a kiss on the forehead and told her I loved her so much. I had to vomit and I was trying desperately to hold it in for what would have been roughly fifteen minutes, since I knew that's when my wife would be taking my stepdaughter to school. As hard as I tried, though, I just couldn't. I was too sick. The devastated expression on my wife's face as she entered the bathroom while I clung to the toilet and vomited will haunt me forever. She held the water bottle I'd hid in my dresser; it still had a little bit of vodka in it. As her eyes filled with tears, my heart filled with self-loathing. Neither of us spoke, but it was in that moment we both knew our marriage was over.

When I finished throwing up, I took my last two Percocet and logged onto my computer to book a plane ticket back to Connecticut. I called my parents to let them know what had happened and that I'd need a ride from the airport. They were heartbroken and worried, but said they would be there—they'd been through this before. Luckily for me, my suitcase was still packed.

During the taxi ride to the airport I felt so physically and emotionally ill that I asked the cabdriver to stop so I could buy a bottle of vodka. Then I went to a grocery store and bought a bottle of Gatorade. (What is it with me and sports drinks? They contain electrolytes, which can help with hangovers—or maybe that's just some urban legend I've bought into for all these years.) I took my first swig of vodka in the grocery store bathroom and then poured the rest into the Gatorade bottle, leaving just enough so that the color stayed purple (a very diluted purple, but purple enough for my purposes). I got back into the taxi, and we headed to the airport. I was extremely nauseated. My hope was that the swig of vodka I'd taken in the bathroom would help settle me, but it had the opposite effect—for the duration of that thirty-minute ride it was all I could do to not throw up in the backseat of the taxi.

I made it to the airport terminal, found a bathroom, and puked there. Then I drank more vodka and sat in a waiting area to let things settle, but they wouldn't, so back to the bathroom I went for another round of vomiting. I followed that with another drink. I finished the bottle and this time didn't throw up. The nausea was starting to subside, but the emotional pain was still there, and it took everything I had not to burst into tears in the middle of Ottawa International Airport.

Once I got through security, I found a restaurant near my gate, ordered a double shot of vodka, and ate a breakfast sandwich. After finishing both, I ordered another drink, and the nausea was finally gone. When I called my parents to check in, I couldn't hold back my tears. I was in so much pain about so many things, not the least being the fact that here I was again, putting my parents through the hell of having to watch me relapse. As I descended into the nightmare of my own making, it began to sink in that my marriage was over. My entire world was about to be upended—I'd built my life, my career around advocating for healing, spirituality, and recovery, and here I was returning to substances. I was broken and lost in a way I had never been before, and if you've read my previous two books, you know that, like many of us, I'd already been through my share of vodka-and-pill-induced wake-up-and-vomit marathons.

After I got off the phone with my parents, I had an odd moment of clarity (odd in that it happened while I was a total shit show in every sense of the word and in every possible way). I knew that even though I'd taken Percocet and had a lot to drink, I was not going to travel all the way back down the road of an extensive, full-blown relapse as I had so many times in the past. I'd come too far and worked too hard on myself and in my life to do that.

Knowing in my heart I would not return to the chaotic, self-destructive, and all-consuming cycle that is addiction, I called my mentor in Refuge Recovery (a Buddhist approach to recovery from addiction, which I'll get into later) and let him know what had happened. I also told him that although I would drink a bit more throughout the day, I was not going to succumb after that. While he didn't want me to keep drinking, he understood where I was at with things and wished me safe travel home, letting me know he'd be there for me when I was ready. I also called my old college professor, who'd since become a close friend in recovery, and let her know the situation as well. She was very sad to hear from me, especially because she had spent time with my wife and knew how much we meant to each other. She, like my Refuge Recovery mentor, wished me safe travel and asked me to connect with her when I was back.

I boarded the first of two planes back to Connecticut. When we landed in Toronto, I made my way through border security and headed straight to the airport bar. I ordered another double shot of vodka and a sandwich. I was feeling much better physically, but emotionally, no amount of alcohol could ease the hell blazing within me.

From there, I sought out a duty-free shop and bought another liter of vodka. I went into a newsstand and purchased two big bottles of water. I went into the bathroom and replaced the water in the bottles with vodka. I took a big swig and proceeded to find my gate for the final flight. I gave my parents one last call to let them know I was all right. They could tell that I'd been drinking, but I was still coherent and, all things considered, doing okay. I boarded the plane and took my seat in the empty last row. I kept drinking.

I remember landing in Hartford and meeting my parents at the baggage claim. I must have been visibly drunk at this point. I pulled out one of the water bottles of vodka and told my parents I had some left that I planned on drinking, but would stop after that. They told me they felt it best if I stopped drinking *now*. It wasn't a forceful request, just one of care and concern. Since I still had a second bottle of vodka in my bag, I agreed and handed them the one in my hand. Then I told them I had to go to the bathroom, where I proceeded to drink down the entire second water bottle of vodka.

No surprise that I passed out on the ride home. My parents didn't think twice about that, because in years past they'd seen me like this plenty of times. What *was* different was that when we made it back to their place, roughly forty minutes from the airport, I was completely unresponsive. They couldn't get me to stand on my own. They noticed my breathing was labored. That was when they knew they had to take me to the hospital. The ER staff thought I'd overdosed on heroin because I was still completely unresponsive, so they gave me Narcan (an emergency treatment used for opiate overdose) and tested my blood to see what else was in my system. Aside from the Percocet I'd taken more than twelve hours earlier, and the copious amount of vodka that left me with a blood alcohol content level of .47 (anything above .30 to .35 can be fatal for many people), there was nothing to be found.

It was at this point that they had to intubate me, as I was unable to breathe on my own, and the machines would have to do it for me. They also inserted a urinary catheter into the tip of my penis so I didn't end up pissing myself and the bed all night. This was not a first, but it's the kind of thing you never get used to, and it hurts like hell when it's removed. (Have I mentioned how glorious addiction is yet?)

The hospital kept me under observation for a day and then sent me on my way the following morning. I barely had the strength to walk back to the car. The combination of the alcohol I'd consumed and the medications they'd pumped into me left my body a wreck. And it would continue to be so for the next several days.

Within a week or so, I was back to about 70 percent and even running a few miles a day. During one of those runs where all that could be seen in every direction was trees and sky, I realized that even though my heart was shattered, even though I despised myself for what had happened, I would persevere. I would use the experience to double my efforts toward personal healing so that I could continue my work in helping others heal as well.

That promise began with this book—an exploration of the myriad ways we humans stumble and fall and, no matter what our circumstances, can stand back up and live bold, passionate, and empowered lives. The pages that follow hold words and conversations that have meant so much to me in my healing—ones I believe will help support and complement whatever practices or prayers, fellowships or sanghas, satsangs or congregations you travel through or reside in on your own way. At least that's my sincere and humble intention.

May we all know true peace, contentment, freedom, and happiness, and share it joyously with others in need.

INTRODUCTION

SOMETIMES ALL I AM IS
A DARK EMPTINESS

Because I have lived so many years caught in a cycle of addiction, recovery, relapse, repeat, a quote from Zen master Ikkyū Sojun— *Sometimes all I am is a dark emptiness*—sums up and shadows much of my experience. I'm no stranger to relapsing and the pain, shame, guilt, confusion, and heartbreak that come along with it. Nor am I a stranger to detoxes, rehabs, emergency rooms, jail cells, and psych hospitals. What is strange for me is that after my last relapse, I began to *care* about relapsing. In the past, when I found myself in a place where I was willing to pick up a bottle or succumb to depression, I didn't give a damn about the consequences. Fights, handcuffs, lies, withdrawals, self-cutting, hospitals, vomiting, and pissing blood— none of it mattered. I meant nothing to me.

Today things are different. Over the past several years, I have worked incredibly hard on my sobriety, my spiritual life, and my physical and mental health. That said, I am not here to make excuses. I have fucked up, recovered, staggered, stumbled, and recovered again in countless ways, and not just with drugs and alcohol. My introversion has made it hard for me to reach out for help when I needed it most. For years, books and music, words and the computer were my only sources of comfort during times of isolation and hopelessness. In them, I sought solace and connection, something I couldn't find with another living being. I know that wasn't healthy; nothing about me during those times was. I did all I could to hang on, to survive. If you're reading this, I'm guessing you know the feeling.

That's why I want to share these words with you. The spiritual teachers, poets, scientists, psychologists, punk rockers, hip-hoppers, and skaters I've met in my quest to understand healing and relapse have taught me that the decisions we make today and each day moving forward are what determine whether we're going to show up for ourselves or numb the fuck out, be of service or be a menace, destroy illusions or inhabit them, live or die. And today, I'm not ready to die. I'm dead set on living. My hope is that you are, too.

"Cunning, baffling, powerful"—these are the words used to describe addiction in the twelve-step fellowships, but we don't need to be addicted to drugs or alcohol to have experienced the impact of these adjectives on our lives. There are all sorts of self-destructive behaviors we deal with as human beings that are cunning, baffling, and powerful. Food addictions; meaningless sex; countless hours spent in front of the television, playing video games; unhealthy eating—all means of dropping out for a while, avoiding unpleasant feelings and emotions.

In my case, it's been predominantly drugs and alcohol, although I could just as easily put a check mark next to pretty much all the addictions and behaviors I listed above. Throughout the years, I've found myself returning to the place of brokenness that results from using substances to numb out, but the question that resounds is *Why?*

As I dedicated more attention to this question, I began thinking about all the talks and workshops I've given on addiction, recovery, and healing over the last several years, and all the beautiful people I've connected with along the way. Some of them were more than just beautiful; they were what I would call tragically beautiful, barely able to string together more than a couple of days of sobriety or to consider an act of self-care. Their pain, despair, and frustration resonated for me—not only did I know them, I *was* them.

It was in that resonance with tragic beauty after my last relapse that I wondered why I, and so many others like me, return to things we know will ultimately destroy us—mentally, emotionally, physically, and spiritually. Why do we put the bottle to our lips, the unhealthy food in our mouth, the powder up our nose, the chips on the blackjack table, the needle in our arm, or engage in risky sexual behavior when we absolutely know better? I didn't have an answer then, nor do I have a definitive one now, but I understand the question. After speaking with friends and colleagues in various fields of psychology, spirituality, and neuroscience, I realized it's okay to not have one single answer, because the number of right answers is equal to the number of people who engage in self-destructive behaviors. We each have a set of circumstances in our lives that shape who we are, filter our experiences, and motivate our actions.

I've learned a lot about myself throughout years of recovery, and while I don't recommend relapsing, I can say that I have gratitude for the lessons those experiences have taught me. That, and the somewhat deeper understanding I have of this triumphantly fucking weird thing called life (which is basically just that it's triumphantly fucking weird, but hey, at least I understand that now). If we make the effort, we can learn how to navigate our paths with greater skillfulness, composure, and ease, and I believe that this book can help you to do just that. However, it's not simply a matter of reading the following pages. To create significant and lasting change, you will need to engage in plenty of practices and take a number of action steps, but if you're reading these words right now, that in and of itself means you can do it. It means that you're alive and breathing, which leads me to believe that you've got to be a goddamn fucking warrior for having made it this far in life.

So being your warrior self, *you* can find true recovery. You've found hell on numerous occasions, right? The healing process, while not easy, is a piece of cake compared to that. I say that with confidence because I've done it—in fact, more than once—and I know for damn sure there's nothing special about me. I just did it. That's how it gets done. As I'll remind you many times throughout this book: Show up and do the fucking work. *Period.*

No matter how deep your experience of pain, despair, and emptiness is (or has been), I get it. I've wanted to fucking die. I've tried to fucking die. I've been hopeless and broken beyond what I believed I could (or would) ever return from, but with time, patience, anger, acceptance, heartbreak, and persistence, I'm still here, and I'm a stronger, better person today because of it. I've shared this quote from Henry Rollins before, but fuck it, I'm going to repeat it once more: "Scar tissue is stronger than regular tissue. Realize the strength, move on." That's what we do. We show up, find what strength we can in this moment (and sometimes that means leaning on someone else to begin with), and move on.

Let's get this shit started.

DEAD SET
ON LIVING

THE TRANCE OF UNWORTHINESS

CONVERSATION WITH TARA BRACH

When I was just beginning to get interested in spirituality and meditation, I stumbled upon Buddhist teacher Tara Brach at my local library. I checked out her book *Radical Acceptance* during a time when the only thing I was willing to radically accept was deep self-loathing and an overall feeling of discontent with the world. Thanks to Tara's insights, I began to awaken from what she calls the "trance of unworthiness." The process was (and continues to be) daunting, but is much more accessible thanks to how she approaches meditation and self-healing practice.

There's a passage in her book *True Refuge: Finding Peace and Freedom in Your Own Awakened Heart* that I've always loved:

> When the Buddha was dying, he gave a final message to his beloved attendant Ananda, and to generations to come: "Be a lamp unto yourself, be a refuge to yourself. Take yourself to no external refuge."
>
> In his last words, the Buddha was urging us to see this truth:

*although you may search the world over trying to find it, your ulti-
mate refuge is none other than your own being.*

*There's a bright light of awareness that shines through each of us
and guides us home, and we're never separated from this luminous
awareness, any more than waves are separated from ocean. Even
when we feel most ashamed or lonely, reactive or confused, we're
never apart from the awakened state of our heart-mind.*[1]

Poetic, right? I was psyched to get Tara to elaborate on it. When we
spoke, she started our conversation by explaining the idea of a trance,
which is how we spend most of our lives—not paying attention to the
moment, not "being here now," as spiritual teacher Ram Dass would
put it. The self is in us and the world is out there, and there's generally
a story involved about what we need to do to be okay and what we perceive as a threat.

She went on to say, "We are also in a trance about spiritual awakening," in which we say to ourselves "It's down the road" or "It probably
can't happen to us." Tara maintains that "the most liberating perspective that we can have, and we can choose, is to begin to sense, 'Oh, that
awakened state is intrinsic to what I am. I just need to relax into it.'"
She described it as being like riding a bicycle—you've pedaled and pedaled up a hill, and there's that moment when you stop pedaling, relax,
and glide—letting go.

"The big delusion in trance is that we're on our way somewhere
else, and the freedom of teachings like 'Be a lamp unto yourself' is to
understand that the light we're seeking, the love we're seeking, and the
truth we're seeking are all right here." We have the answers within us
the whole time—kind of like Dorothy and the ruby slippers, right?

Tara went on to explain that we must be careful, because there's a
way our spiritual ego can misunderstand "I am a lamp unto myself."
This self is the one that "mistakenly believes it owns the spirituality and
thinks that we can't look toward and find truth in our engagement with
others, when in fact as much as we're a lamp unto ourself, we're a lamp
unto each other." So we do our best to stay on this path, trying to be a

light unto ourselves and letting our light out and the light from others in—letting it be, if you will. The passage can be a complicated one. The Buddhists have a name for one of the complications. In their cosmology, the torment of intense desire that can never be satisfied is depicted as the realm of Hungry Ghosts—a place where we're driven by emotional needs rooted in trauma, addiction, or both. As someone in recovery, I know all too well about these kinds of desires, but have found the practice of "letting be," which is to say, just allowing this moment to be however it is without any resistance or struggle, to be helpful. As hard as I try, there are still times when I've completely sucked at "letting be," as when I've relapsed with alcohol or screwed up a relationship. What did Tara have to say about the attachments and addictions that so many of us struggle with?

"I want to honor what you're saying about 'letting be,' because in a way, the most profound meditation is just letting everything be as it is—allowing our life to unfold. Because we're so caught in grasping and resisting and struggling and controlling, there are some ways of training our heart and mind that create the atmosphere that allows for letting be." You can't be caught in an addiction or a destructive relationship and the excruciating suffering that comes with it and just say, "Okay, I'm just going to let be"—it just doesn't work. Tara pointed out the different ways of understanding the suffering of desire.

"Desire itself is not only normal and natural, it's a necessary, essential part of existence. We wouldn't be here if it weren't for desire. That is not the problem. The problem is that our sense of self gets organized around wanting and 'having to have' in a way that makes what is in the present not okay. There's no capacity to be happy with the moment." This starts when our basic needs—like nurturing, security, positive reinforcement—aren't met and we try to fill the emptiness within with substitutes, and the substitutes can't satisfy—like drinking, misusing sexuality, or overeating. I know from experience that these things *feel* like they help for a while.

Tara had a great example. "Let's say the substitute is 'Let's get approval because we don't feel loved.' Getting approval is a temporary fix.

We feel good for ten minutes until we need to go and get our next fix of approval. Similarly, if it's a drink or bingeing on food or whatever, there's a temporary sense of self-soothing, but we end up suffering because we believe we must have it again and again. Not only that, we end up feeling shame about being hooked. The Buddha described that as the second arrow. The first arrow is this unquenchable thirst, and the second arrow is the shame about it. We bring the second arrow to ourself when we feel needy or out of control, and so part of the pain of strong desire and grasping and addiction is the sense of being a bad person."

Tara opened my eyes with what she said next: "It's not until we begin to let go of the second arrow, it's not until we begin to forgive that the addictiveness is there, that we can begin to heal the actual wound that's underneath it."

Powerful words. How do we go about it?

The first step is to let go of the shame. Other people can help us with this, like a recovery support group, a therapist, a congregation, or a sangha. When we do that, we come to see that it isn't *my* addiction or *your* addiction or even *our* addiction, it's just addiction—conditioned behavior in response to an unmet need. This helps us to loosen the grip of addiction on our hearts and our spirits so we can start to look at what's underneath it. We don't *have* to abuse drugs, overeat, or constantly seek attention. Tara encourages us to go deeper: What's the real yearning?

To find this out, we must get past what she calls "if only" mind. This is the part of us that says things like "I'd be okay if only I could get that job" or lose ten pounds or meet the right person. We need to disconnect from that by paying attention to the source of wanting itself.

So many of us experience life as a constant battle within ourselves. We're plagued by thoughts of unworthiness and dissatisfaction. In some cases, these thoughts are so loud they can force people to inflict harm on themselves or even take their own lives. In other cases, these thoughts are subtler, resulting in a relentless underlying sense of dis-ease in life, often unrecognizable to people because they've become so used to it. I still struggle with this, even after many years of meditation and other practices. Why is it that so many of us end up in this place of constant battle with ourselves, and how can we begin to lay our weapons down and cultivate inner peace?

To find the answers, I went back to Tara's book *Radical Acceptance*, which came out of her own experience of realizing how far she was from being her own best friend. Even after working with clients and students for years, she was still so harsh with herself that she came to see what a pervasive form of suffering these struggles within ourselves are. She brought it back to the trance of unworthiness. "We might know we judge ourselves, but we don't often get how much that squeeze of 'something's wrong with me' is a part of everything, so that in every interaction on some level, we're not free to be as spontaneous or play-ful or alive, because we're afraid we're not going to be the person who's accepted by another. Even when it's not the deep 'I'm damaged goods,' there's still a sense of not enough." She pointed out that "the deepest truth is the one we forget, which is that if we're not kind toward our-self, if we don't feel love toward the light that's within, we can't embrace others fully. We're always going to be guarded. We all have parts of our being where we feel vulnerable, where we don't trust that if others knew us, they'd respect us anymore. And it takes a big commitment to love ourselves back into wholeness. To me, if there's any one commitment right at the front, the center of the spiritual path, it's the commitment to embrace the parts of ourselves that we've pushed away."

What Tara said made me think of a time about ten years ago when I was in a treatment center and realized I had been getting heavily tattooed up to that point in my life because I wanted people to look at my tattoos instead of at me. I believed the tattoos would distract peo-ple from who I was. After having that realization, and taking about five years off from getting any new ink, I'm back to getting tattoos again, but from a different place, a place of appreciation. I've always loved the artwork of tattooing, even when I was getting them as a distraction from myself. I don't want anyone to misunderstand what I'm saying here, or to think that I'm trash-talking tattoos, because I've always loved them and I'm probably about 70 percent covered now—but understanding my relationship with them helped me understand something about myself.

Tara calls experiences like that false refuges. "When we're feeling bad about ourselves, we all have a set of strategies on how to feel better, how to impress people or ourselves, or do more, and what happens is that the false refuge locks us into a smaller identity. We still feel like a small, deficient person, but we're more defended. The hard part is that we generally fix our attention on where we think we're doing things wrong. We're always monitoring and noticing where we're falling short. For any of us who have hurt other people, or find that we're caught in habits that are hurting ourselves, it's very hard to forgive and embrace ourselves."

She explained that we need to step out of thoughts, step out of all the negative self-talk, and just sense what's within us. What we'll find is pure and good. "There's an innate wakefulness right within each of us, a wakeful awareness. There's a quality of openness. There's no center or anything that's solid. There's a tenderness, a warmth, which intrinsically loves whatever we encounter." I could get behind that: The more we let go of the bullshit, the more we can move toward who we are— our essence. Once we find that best part of ourselves, we can live from it and reconnect to it in our spiritual practices.

So how do we learn to genuinely heal and forgive ourselves and others?

"When it comes to forgiveness," Tara said, we need to "look at the evolution of consciousness." To do this, we need to move from an ego-driven state where we default into judgment of ourselves and others and reach a sense of belonging or connection that she calls "we-ness." We both agreed that forgiveness is the truest way to get there. Tara told me she often uses the phrase "unreal other." What it means is that "when we're in an egoic state, you and I perceive each other as a kind of two-dimensional being that we hope approves of us, or likes us, versus sensing the light and awareness that's looking through both of our eyes and realizing that it's both the same. The work is where that's not happening. Each one of us has somebody or some group of people that we have created into 'other' who is in some way bad or wrong."

This made me think of Martin Buber's book *I and Thou*:

The basic word I-You can be spoken only with one's whole being. The concentration and fusion into a whole being can never be accomplished by me, can never be accomplished without me. I require a You to become; becoming I, I say You.[2]

The places the differences lie are where the work needs to be done. As Tara put it, "Most people have this idea that forgiving is a good idea until they must forgive something, and then it gets hairy. So one of the metaphors that have been most helpful to me when we're caught in an 'unreal other'—perhaps a situation where we think this person should be different—is to imagine we're walking in the woods and we see a little dog by a tree, and we bend over to pet it and it lunges at us. Its fangs are bared, it's aggressive, so we go from being friendly to being angry. But then we see that one of its legs is caught in a trap, and we shift to feeling pity and maybe even compassion. That's what it's like when we're having a hard time forgiving someone. How in some way there are unmet needs—sorrow, fear, insecurity—that are causing that behavior."

When Tara works with forgiveness, she clarifies that the first step when we've been injured by someone is *not* to try and forgive them! The first step is to bring self-compassion to the place that feels hurt. If we skip that step, it won't be real forgiveness. We must acknowledge the hurt, bring kindness toward ourselves, and then find the opening to move through and see that the creature's leg is caught in that trap. "When we're lashing out, it's a lazy way of trying to cover the wounded place." Tara gave me a new phrase to work with: Vengeance is a lazy form of grief. Let's sit with that for a minute—*vengeance is a lazy form of grief.*

And it's bigger than just you and me. Tara put it in the context of the planet so we "don't make Earth an unreal other." We need to "recognize that the Earth is our living body and that we sense our compassion to the Earth—that's carrying forward the teachings. We need to recognize that we have implicit racism and be willing to face it and wake up from it because we can't be whole on this planet if we have one entire domain of people who aren't considered part of our being that's carrying forward the teachings. Each generation needs to bring the teachings alive in a way that's most relevant to the planet in that time."

When I teach at rehabs or recovery centers, I'm always inspired by younger people stepping up. Even if it's not specifically in a spiritual context, they're showing up and being of service toward one another as humans and learning to be more loving in the world. However, I do speak with many younger people who feel jaded and who are cynical toward the notion of spirituality, something I experienced as well. I think that can be healthy to a certain extent, but we can also go overboard and completely close ourselves off to some people. On one hand, a new tolerance is blossoming in much of our youth—they are rejecting things like racism, sexism, and homophobia, and they are being more adamant and vocal that those things should never be acceptable. They're expressing more love, more understanding, more compassion toward one another, but many of them are still closed to the idea of spirituality. I believe spirituality, healing, and forgiveness can be very strong foundational blocks upon which the next generation of truth seekers can build a more caring and nurturing world for all beings, starting right *now*. What would Tara tell the cynics and the naysayers?

"What I would do is ask them, 'When is it that you feel most fulfilled or gratified, or what is it that you most enjoy or take pleasure in? What do you want?' I think that inside the jadedness there's an intelligence, which is not wanting to get carried away on a current of delusion. Just as I honor truth seeking, I honor jadedness. I think it's also important to ask, 'Where do you feel most sincere? Where do you feel that you want to unfold the best of yourself? What is most important to you?' Start with that, because spirituality isn't something out there. Every one of us has our own version of unfolding into the best that we can be. That's because we each have a deeper capacity to care, to speak truth, to hear truth, to see truth, and to live from wholeness."

PRACTICE

Tara Brach's RAIN

Anyone familiar with Tara's teachings has probably heard about RAIN (an acronym coined by Vipassana teacher Michele McDonald). It's one of her signature practices, and it has a powerful resonance for both beginning and seasoned meditators. It can take us to that place of living with wholeness as we enhance our ability to care, hear truth, speak truth, and see truth. It's especially useful when working with our habits and addictions because it's a practice that allows us to redirect and regulate our experiences. It's a great one, too, because if you get stuck or lost, there's the acronym to keep you on track:

> **R:** Recognize what is happening.

> **A:** Allow life to be just as it is.

> **I:** Investigate inner experience with kindness.

> **N:** Nonidentification.

It may seem trivial, but I most recently used RAIN meditation to help me get through losing an apartment I was excited about moving into. Here's what the process looked like:

R: I checked out the apartment, and it looked great. Then I went back and did thirty minutes' worth of paperwork, only to find out at the very end of the process that my shit credit could stand in the way of me getting it. It was upsetting because I was feeling good about finally finding the perfect place to live after moving back to Connecticut, once again a single man not sure if I'd ever find "the one." I didn't want to get wasted or anything over this, but I *recognized* that it bummed me the fuck out and that I'm a person for whom things as seemingly minor as not getting the apartment I wanted could, under the right circumstances, trigger a relapse.

A: Instead of fighting my feelings of sadness and disappointment, I *allowed* them to be just as they were. I observed my mindset and the disappointment I felt, and simply let it be there as it was happening. I also reminded myself to be grateful because today I was at least in a healthy enough place (mentally, physically, spiritually, and financially) that I could look at this incredible apartment. I wasn't sick or hungover or caught in some mental/emotional space of self-loathing. In the words of Ice Cube, "It was a good day."

I: I began to *investigate* the energies located predominantly in my stomach and shoulders and saw that they, just like any other positive or negative feelings, were temporary energies hanging out in my body for a bit. The "with kindness" part is tricky because I'm so prone to beating myself up, but I kept recalling impermanence in relation to the investigation step and eventually felt ready to move on to N.

N: Through *nonidentification*, I gradually realized that my issue with disappointment over potentially not getting the apartment was symbolic of infinite moments in life: Some situations bring us what we want, while others do not. I could let go and accept that, without being cliché about it. If this is meant to be, it will be, and if not, I'll find another place. It's not the end of the world, and it certainly wasn't worth enduring with Narcan or a urinary catheter.

When it comes to N—nonidentification—sometimes Tara will simply say, "It's okay, sweetheart," or repeat Vietnamese Buddhist teacher Thich Nhat Hanh's message, "Darling, I care about this suffering," or the words of Hawaiian Ho'oponopono teacher Dr. Ihaleakala Hew Len: "I'm sorry. And I love you."[3] I, too, appreciate the teaching of Ho'oponopono and found myself reciting his words as I drove home, my head hanging a little lower than usual from disappointment, but not as low as it's been because of the mess of addiction I've lived through. "I'm sorry. Please forgive me. Thank you. I love you." But that's just me. You use the phrase that comforts *you* and brings you to a place of nonidentification with the fucked-up things you're struggling with.

As Tara reminded me, "The key moment is to notice what happens after we do the steps of RAIN. Just like after a gentle rainfall, the flowers can bloom. Just sense who you are when you're no longer the thing inside the thoughts and beliefs and feelings of a bad self. If you're no longer believing that anything is wrong with you, who are you? Rest in that spacious, tender awareness, your larger sense of being. When you're ready, take a few more full breaths and open your eyes . . . and here we are again."

2

THE PRIMARY PROBLEM

CONVERSATION WITH GABOR MATÉ

I first learned about Gabor Maté through his groundbreaking book *In the Realm of Hungry Ghosts*, which explores his work with addicted individuals living on Vancouver's skid row, as well as being an exceptionally comprehensive delineation of just what the hell addiction is, its causes, its effects, and so, so, so much more. Aside from that, Dr. Maté is a renowned speaker and bestselling author, highly sought after for his expertise on a range of topics, including addiction, stress, and childhood development.

I'd heard that Gabor believes addiction is not the problem but rather a person's attempt *to solve a problem in his or her life*. I reached out to him because I wondered, among other things, how he would define addiction and what his perspective was on people using addiction to solve their life problems.

When I posed my questions, he answered them with a question: "You're very open about your own addictive history. What did *you* get from it?"

While I was thinking about my answer, Gabor gave me his definition of addiction:

> *Any behavior—substance-related or not—that a person craves, finds*
> *temporary pleasure or relief in, and suffers negative consequences as*
> *a result of, but can't give up despite those negative consequences.*

Check, check, and check. His definition summed up the experiences
I (and countless others I've met) have had with drugs and alcohol—and
I could add food and many other substances in here, too, for good
measure.

So, pleasure, craving, relief, negative consequences, inability to let
it go . . . What does our addictive relationship to these substances *give*
us? For many—myself very much included—it provides a sense of relief from self-loathing, depression, and dissatisfaction with the world
(among other things). It's a way for us to get release from our emotional
pain and just drop the fuck out of our heads for a while. As I looked
back on my own life, I saw that addiction was everything to me, a
means of making it through the day.

Gabor was just getting started. He echoed my internal dialogue,
noting that *everyone* wants relief from pain. And he was right. Who
doesn't?

"What you were after was a perfectly normal human aspiration.
Your problem was the emotional pain, and the addiction came along
as an attempt at a solution. Addiction is never the primary problem. It
creates problems—that's why we talk about it so much—but it's not the
primary problem. The primary problem is: Why are we in such emotional pain? What happened?"

Gabor went on to present addiction in a way I'd never quite heard
before, taking it out of the context of disease and willpower and
putting it into a Buddhist framework—the realm of suffering. Addic-

tion "has to do with how you suffered at a time in your life when you couldn't avoid the suffering—and that means childhood. It doesn't matter what form addiction takes—sex, gambling, drugs, alcohol, shopping, or eating—it's always an attempt (in one way or another) to compensate for or escape from intense suffering in childhood. When I say 'intense suffering,' I don't necessarily mean terrible things, but a child who suffers ends up having more pain than they can handle— hence the escape into addiction. In other words, the addiction is an attempt to solve a problem."

I found his perspective so interesting and sensible. Several years ago, I'd done an internship in substance abuse counseling at a rehab facility in Connecticut. I noticed the biggest common factor among many of the patients was an obvious childhood trauma or traumas— like sexual or physical abuse or a lack of love and affection. In my case, when I looked back at my own childhood, in comparison to many of these patients, growing up for me was not so bad. I hadn't endured a trauma that you could label atrocious.

As I started talking about this, Gabor stopped me. He believes that this kind of comparative thinking is what prevents people from understanding their own life experience and addiction. He asked me not to compare myself to others but to tell him one thing about my childhood that made me unhappy.

This was hard for me to answer. The first things that came to mind were from when I was a teenager. I was never bullied as a kid or sexually harmed. My parents didn't abuse alcohol or each other. They argued, of course, but not any more than what I believe happened in most households (shit—there I go comparing again), and neither of them suffered from a major or minor mental illness. I had a hard time tapping into my own experience. I was kind of stuck. It took some digging, but Gabor helped me realize that when I became a teenager, I pretty much stopped talking to my parents—or anyone—about my feelings because I felt like my ideas and experiences were so outside the norm that I didn't want anyone sending me to a shrink. In retrospect, my ideas and experiences weren't that crazy, but in the rural community where I grew up, anything slightly different was very much frowned upon. I'd traded a childhood of athletics and listening to pop music for teenage years playing in punk/hardcore bands, watching David Lynch and Quentin Tarantino films, and reading books by William S. Burroughs, Charles Bukowski, and Jack Kerouac, all of which served to fuel my experience of feeling separate from others, apart from a few friends who were also interested in this weirdo shit. That disconnection was a scary and very lonely experience, even though I didn't recognize it as such at the time, but it still didn't seem like that big of a deal—I mean, don't all adolescents isolate to some degree?

Then Gabor asked a question that helped me shift my perspective and begin to see what he was getting at: "If a six-year-old said to you, 'When I'm sad and lonely, I have nobody to talk to,' would you say to them, 'Oh, come on, it's not so bad. Think of the kids who are being beaten or sexually abused or starved.' Is that what you would say to a child?"

Of course not!

"That's what you're saying to yourself. When you say 'Not like others' or 'It's not so bad,' you're simply dismissing your own experience—it's a disconnection from yourself." He explained that I survived my childhood through disconnection, which is the basis of trauma. *Webster's Unabridged Dictionary* defines trauma as "a psychological or emotional stress or blow that may produce disordered feelings or behavior," and that disorder is what Gabor was getting at.

"That's what happens in trauma—as soon as you start comparing your experience with anybody else's, and as soon as you say it wasn't *as* bad, that's a sign of the disconnect. And *that's* the problem you're trying to solve through your addiction. You were trying to resolve *your* pain—that you had nobody to talk to."

Holy shit!

I began to understand that it wasn't that I didn't have anybody to talk to—my loving parents were there, after all—but that when it came to my emotions, I didn't know how to talk to my parents or to anyone else. And I know I'm not unique in this. How many of us felt awkward in communicating, in expressing ourselves—not just with family but also with friends, teachers, coaches, religious authorities, and so on. In our formative years, we desperately want approval and to fit in. We want to find our place in the world and to be liked and loved, and this is what matters most. In a way, it's our full-time job as adolescents.

Once I saw how I had disconnected myself in this way, my next question to Gabor was, How can we begin to reintegrate the disconnected parts of ourselves and start healing them? I've talked a bit in this book about the twelve-step fellowship work I've done and its value, but what became clear to me with my relapse was that this work doesn't address the underlying traumatic event. Twelve-steppers help you get clean and sober, ask for forgiveness, and move forward with your life, but they don't clearly help you address the various traumas of the past.

Gabor agreed with me. "It may come up, it may not come up, but there's nothing structurally present in the twelve-step programs that allows people to deal with their trauma. It's all behavior related and substance related. That reconnection or reintegration is what is missing. Unfortunately, rehabilitation centers, medical education, and addiction counseling programs, for the most part, leave out the trauma element. And even when they focus on the trauma, it's only overt or extreme, not the actual experience of a child who is 'just' in emotional pain." Though, in all fairness, it does seem that this is beginning to shift, thanks in part to the work that Gabor and others like Peter Levine and Bessel van der Kolk are doing.

So how can we integrate trauma and reconnect?

"Before you can heal a disconnection, you have to realize that there *is* a disconnection. Before you can integrate childhood pain, you must recognize that childhood pain. It shows up every day in people's lives; they just don't see that it's showing up."

If we become more aware of this dissociated material daily and the ways it might be manifesting in our relationships, what did Gabor recommend next? I'd learned that trauma can be held in our bodies on a cellular level and even influence our genes, so how would we address the mind-body connection?

Once again I was creating a schism where Gabor saw none. He explained, "There's no distinction between working with the mind and working with the body. Mind and body can't be separated. Bessel van der Kolk's book *The Body Keeps the Score*, or my book on physical illness *When the Body Says No*, or Babette Rothschild's book *The Body Remembers* all show trauma is in the body, so at some point the attention must be brought to the body. There are many ways of working in both mind and body, but it should be in a unified manner. Trauma has psychological aspects and physiological aspects, and you can't separate the two."

If you're reading this, and it's new for you, because perhaps you're rooted in the twelve-step fellowships—which, as Gabor says, for the most part don't cover the trauma aspect—what can you do to take that unitive step forward, bringing mind and body together to uncover and release trauma?

Gabor's advice is not to rush into things, but to build a deep foundation of understanding—not just intellectually but the nitty-gritty in relation to our own lives. He suggested more resources: his book *In the Realm of Hungry Ghosts*, Peter Levine's *Waking the Tiger* and *In an Unspoken Voice*, and Bessel van der Kolk's books and videos.

Once we understand the foundation of our addiction, then we can move forward and decide what works for us. "There are many modalities out there, but it's got to begin with the recognition that 'I'm traumatized, and that traumatization results in a disconnection from myself and all kinds of emotional pain that I don't know what to do with. That trauma is not my fault, it's not my parents' fault.' Even if parents did their best, their best was conditioned by what they received in childhood. It's not about blaming anybody or saying it's anybody's fault, but if we want to heal, we have to recognize what happened and how that affects us now so we can integrate and heal."

Gabor suggested techniques to facilitate that healing. Maybe it's therapy, maybe not. Maybe it's a trusted friend or a structured meditation practice. Maybe it's bodywork, somatic experiencing, yoga, or eye movement desensitization and reprocessing (EMDR), or maybe it's a psychedelic modality—

What the fuck? I did psychedelics like they were going out of style in my younger addicted years, but never in any sort of healing or spiritual context. Psychedelics then were about having fun, or maybe they were an escape and I just didn't know it at the time. But psychedelics to work through addiction? *Fascinating.* I wanted Gabor to tell me more, and he did, but first he gave me a serious warning.

"Psychedelics *are not for everybody.* They're probably not even for *most* people, because most people won't be able to access the right context and guidance to do them. The last thing that I want to advocate is that people start taking psychedelics as a form of self-treatment. That's *not* the way to go."

Then he got to the interesting part. "I understand the argument that 'I was substance addicted and now I don't want to do another substance to change my consciousness.' Okay, then don't. *But* here's the reality—it all involves context, guidance, and intention."

That phrase bears repeating: *context, guidance, and intention.*

He explained that when I was younger and tripping my brains out on acid and mushrooms while watching *Blue Velvet* or listening to the Dillinger Escape Plan, I had no guidance and no context. "It's very different when you do something in a traditional context where there's a real culture behind it. Where there's compassionate and experienced guidance to help you through the difficulties and surprises that may show up. Where there's clear intention, then it's not an escape, but a path to realization. Then psychedelics become a way of mind-manifesting—psyche to mind. Our minds are very deep. They are multilayered. There's a lot of unconscious material. Psychedelics just help you get to it. That's all.

"By the way, psychedelics are not the only way to get there. They just happen to provide, with the right context, guidance, and intention, a very quick way to get there. They're not a requirement for recovery, and ultimately I never talk anybody into that kind of thing. Either you're called to it or you're not called to it. In terms of addiction, I've seen extremely good results, results like you don't see anywhere else. For example, psilocybin mushrooms in the treatment of nicotine addiction. MDMA in the treatment of PTSD. Ibogaine and the treatment of opiate addiction. Ayahuasca and the treatment of all kinds of addiction. These results are indisputable and certainly not simple panaceas, because the outcomes are considerably better than what you usually get with the normally available treatment."

I got where he was coming from. I'm friends with a group of people who've been doing ayahuasca explorations—which is to say, ingesting the medicine under the guidance of a shaman in a sacred context—for several years now. One of these friends specifically comes to mind. Before participating in these ceremonies, he was depressed to the point that I feared he might kill himself. This group of friends engage in the ceremony four times a year, and over the course of his first year, I saw a profound change in this particular friend. It was incredible. I kind of wanted what he had, and I've been invited to participate, but I'm afraid of relapse, reactivating the pleasure center in my brain and using a substance to treat substances. Alcohol was always my drug of choice, though I loved pretty much everything, and some of my relapses began with pills or marijuana. So if I ingested ayahuasca, would it revive my addiction? Would it reactivate the pleasure center in my brain?

Gabor reminded me that the brain's pleasure, reward, incentive, and motivation centers and the circuits in the brain that regulate impulses are physiological entities that don't function properly in people who are addictive. These centers are dysfunctional because the brain develops via interaction in a specific childhood environment, and when that childhood environment does not provide the responsiveness that the child needs, these circuits will not develop properly. "Therefore,

when addiction comes along and it motivates you and it gives you pleasure, those centers are feeling, 'Oh boy, now I've got what I want.'"

He understood my fear and proceeded to shed some very interesting
light on ayahuasca in relation to the brain's pleasure center. "The last
thing you'd say about an ayahuasca experience is that it's pleasurable.
First, the stuff tastes awful. Second, it makes you puke. That's not a bad
thing. It's a purging of whatever you need to purge. But 'pleasure' is not
a word you'd ever ascribe to an ayahuasca experience."

All this got even more interesting. Gabor pointed out that in countries where the ayahuasca plant is legal and has been studied in con-
trolled groups and used by hundreds or thousands of people, the risk
of addiction, depression, and mental illness decreases. "I've done ayahuasca, and I work with it. I don't crave the experience. I don't look
forward to it at all. I shudder at it because of the taste and sometimes
the nausea, but that's not what it's about. It's about learning to do something important for myself. Don't do it because you feel like doing
it—that's not a good reason. Don't do it if you're afraid, because then
you're not ready. Do it or don't do it, but don't *not* do it for the wrong
reasons, like because you think it's going to somehow activate your
pleasure center."

When it comes to the pleasure center of the brain, what's the difference between someone like me who has struggled with addiction and
someone who hasn't? When some of my friends are eating, for example,
they stop when they're full, even if there's still food on their plate. It's
hard for me to understand that ability to stop, especially when there's a
sugary dessert involved. Or when I go out to dinner and someone leaves
the table with wine or beer still in their glass—I just don't get that.
For addicts, it's consume, consume, consume—drugs, alcohol, food,
whatever—until there's nothing left. What's happening there with our
brains?

According to Gabor, our earlier circumstances and perhaps some
degree of genetic sensitivity prevented our pleasure centers from developing adequately. "They are unsatisfied. The impulse regulation of your
brain that says, 'I'd like a bit more chocolate cake, but I've already had

two pieces, and that's enough for me'—that part of your brain didn't develop properly, and giving yourself pleasure that way brings tremendous activation of the incentive circuitry. 'I want it. I have to have it right now.' It's a setup. You can overcome that. You can heal that, but it takes time."

He explained that there's a difference between abstinence and sobriety. Abstinence is self-restraint or self-denial with regard to using something. Sobriety is not *having the impulse* (or not having more than a mild impulse, one that can easily be dealt with) to use something. Although Gabor has never been addicted to drugs or alcohol, I was intrigued to learn that he had dealt with other addictive patterns, even one that was close to my heart—purchasing music.

"It's not that I was addicted to music—that's not an addiction, that's just a love of music. The purchasing is what I was addicted to. It was having to get one thing and immediately having to go back to the store to get a bunch more, and as soon as I got home, I was already thinking about the CDs I didn't buy, and then I'd go back the next day and get them. So there was a preoccupation with the acquisition—a preoccupation that took me away from being emotionally present with my children or my spouse, that led me to lie about it and spend much more money than was reasonable. That's the addiction. For me it had to do with not feeling alive enough. It was a kind of deadness that had to do with my childhood. The way I survived my childhood trauma was to suppress my feelings. When you separate from your feelings, life feels empty, purposeless, and kind of boring. I'd found something to excite me and to live for outside of me—the motivation centers of my brain were highly activated by the thought of purchasing music. For some people, they'll be activated by the thought of compulsive sex, shopping, drugs, or food."

Food—even now that I'm sober, food still comes up for me. I do my best to eat well, but let's say there's a day I allow myself to have a little treat, and I then say to myself, "Well, you already had that, so why not have more?" Totally addictive, compulsive thinking similar to that I manifested when I was using drugs. The only difference is that I can stop those eating behaviors the next morning and start over, whereas if I have a sip of alcohol, I'll be off to the races and drinking again.

Gabor pointed out that although we make distinctions between types of addictions—alcoholic, heroin addict, shopaholic, gambler—the basis of addiction is all the same. The same brain circuits are involved in all. Physiologically, it's that same discomfort in the body. Psychologically, it's the same emotional pain and emptiness. Spiritually, it's the same disconnection. Historically, it's some variation of trauma. "In other words, there's a *universal addiction* process, which is characteristic of every addicted human being on the planet. So to think that there's one kind of addiction here may be true in terms of the outward behavior, but it's not true in regard to the underlying dynamics."

What about a drug addict who has been abstinent for ten, fifteen, or twenty years and then goes back to using? I'm talking now not just about those who take drugs, but about anyone who has struggled with some form of self-defeating behavior, been free from it for several years, and then returned to it. And let's say that these are people with ways of coping—a meditation or yoga practice, a psychotherapist, or a spiritual teacher—but they return to behaviors fully aware of the harm they can cause. What's happening there?

Gabor reminded me that one of the circuits in the brain that doesn't develop well under adversity is the stress regulation circuitry. Stress happens, but by the time we reach adulthood, our brains need to be able to process it. An infant's brain cannot deal with stress, but the adult brain should have learned to handle it through healthy development and adaptation. That regulation does not develop fully for an addict, so when we're stressed, we're prone to relapse. He said, "The default setting is to go back to the addictive escape from the stress."

That made sense. We pick up a drink, binge on ice cream, or return to whatever behavior harmed us; we're back in detox or rehab, or we're back to an old eating disorder. Then what? Many of us have recovered and relapsed again and again. And each time there's more shame, stress, self-loathing, and other negative feelings. How is a person supposed to deal with this?

Gabor reminded me of something that many other spiritual teachers I spoke with emphasized: *compassion*. He employed a phrase that was new to me: compassionate curiosity. He used my relapse as an example. "I could say to you, 'Why did you relapse?!' or I could say to you, 'Hey, Chris, let's inquire. Why do you *think* you had a relapse?' Do you notice a difference between the two questions?" As he mentioned this, it made me think of Tara Brach's RAIN process. I found it pretty cool to see how the insights and teachings from people with different backgrounds and viewpoints were already complementing one another.

In other words, rather than condemning me with the first question, he was asking me to explore what had happened in a gentler and more open way. The first way is not a question, it's an accusation. The second way is just an exploration. When you relapse, you need to approach yourself not with "Why did I do this?!" which is a statement that you're an idiot, you're faulty, you're morally weak, you're unworthy. Instead, you can approach it like, "Hmm. Here I am, committed to recovery, committed to sobriety. I've suffered a lot because of my addictive behavior, and despite my commitment and all that I've learned in the past, I relapsed. Huh. I wonder what happened. What is it that this relapse came along to teach me? There's still something about myself that I don't know yet, that clearly, some part of me needed to show me. Huh. Well, let's look at that." Isn't that an interesting question? And once you ask it in that way, then the answers will start coming, because the reality is that each relapse can be interpreted as a learning experience. Not that one chooses it deliberately—"I'm going to relapse so I can learn." Don't worry about that. Life will bring it along when you need it. But once such an incident does come along, it's a learning experience. Purely and simply. A learning experience that will help you recover more completely.

"The word 'recover' is one I never get tired of saying. It means to find something you've lost. And what is it that people recover once they're recovered? *Themselves.* That's the disconnection, and it's healing. A relapse helps you find yourself."

We weren't quite finished yet. I wanted to know about family members who are dealing with addiction. What can they do for a loved one who's caught in the grips of *active* addiction? Because when people are that deep in addiction, they've lost themselves—they're gone in a way. I know I was. I know there was nothing my family could have done no matter how much they wanted to.

Gabor didn't agree with me. "You don't know that. What you do know is what they tried didn't work, but you don't know that there's nothing they could have done. In one sense, you are 100 percent right: There's nothing they can directly do to change your mind. There's nothing they can directly do to change your mental status. There's no way that they can talk to you, advise you, control you, beg you, accuse you. That does not mean there's nothing they could have done. Imagine if your family had come and said, 'Chris, here's how it is. We recognize that your addiction is not your primary problem. Your primary problem is that you're in a lot of pain. And that pain is not yours alone. That pain has been carried in our family for generations. And we're as much a part of that pain as you are. You're just the one who's soothing it with that behavior. In fact, you're the one whose behavior shows us how much pain there is in our family. Thank you for showing that to us. So we're going to start working on you, because we realize that we're as much a part of it as you are. We're going to take on the task of healing ourselves. We invite you to be there if you feel like it. And if you're not ready, sweetheart, then just do what you need to do right now.'"

Fuck. That's so beautiful. I can't say with complete certainty that if my family had said those things, I would have reacted differently, but the hopeful and optimistic part of me believes I would have. If nothing else, I can see how taking that approach shifts the conversation away from being accusatory and toward an attitude of compassion, acceptance, and unconditional love, and if there's one thing I know, those are the most potently powerful things in life.

Gabor wasn't blaming my parents. He recognized that they loved me and did their best. He was just showing me that there *is* something those who love us can do when we're in the throes of addictive behavior. "Families also have to decide, can I have this person in my life, or can I not? If I want them in my life, there must be certain rules, like they can't steal from me and so on, but if I can have them in my life, I must accept them exactly as they are, exactly where they're at, and 100 percent accept that right now they're using because they feel they need to. I'm not going to nag them, cajole them, advise them. I'm not going to say a thing that they didn't ask me about. I'm just going to accept that this is who they are and I'm just going to love them. That's a rational decision to make. It's equally rational to say, 'You know what? It's too painful for me. I can't handle it. I can't stand to see you do this to yourself. It's too stressful. I can't be with that, so I'm sorry, I love you very much, but I can't be with you.' That's legitimate, too.

"What is completely nonsensical—and unfortunately the pitfall for most families—is to try to be in the addict's life and try to change them all the time. That's the one thing you cannot do. So either accept or lovingly distance yourself, but don't try to stay in there with the intent of altering the other person. To the addict, that signals only one thing: 'They don't love me the way I am.' That's my advice to families. I do believe that addiction in a person can be a healthy wake-up call for them and for everyone in their lives."

PRACTICE

Mahasati Hand Meditation

Mahasati hand meditation is a practice that can be particularly useful during times of excessive stress or emotional upheaval, or when our minds just won't shut the fuck up no matter how much yogic breathing or how many rounds of mantras we've done. And yeah, I speak from experience.

I learned this practice at my most rock bottom of rock bottoms. I was at a rehab facility, three days into a seven-day stay in detox from alcohol. My body was still squeamish, my brain still racing, my hope nonexistent, and my self-loathing at an all-time high. As I lay in bed aware of the physical battle going on between withdrawal and the benzodiazepines I'd been given to help relax me and keep me from having a seizure, my thoughts raced—I'd just lost my job, my car was about to be repossessed, I had a court date and jail time awaiting me, and last but (definitely) not least, I was going to miss my brother's wedding, the one where I was supposed to be his best man. *Yeah,* I was in rough shape.

Later that morning I stumbled into our group session, where a young, prayer-bead-wearing, bald-headed man announced we were going to practice meditation. Grunts and grumbles filled the room, and the corner I'd staked out as my own was no exception. I'd been meditating for several years already and knew that I was in no place mentally or emotionally to sit quietly and let my mind cause me even more trouble than it already was.

In all fairness, yes, those are often the times when meditation can be extremely beneficial. I'm all about gently and compassionately leaning into the pain and allowing it to teach us what it can, but I also believe that there are times in life when the pain is too great and it's counterproductive to lean into it. There's no such thing as a spiritual superhero; no trophies are awarded to those who can endure the heaviest shit, so please, honor what you can and can't do in the moment and go from there. Only you can know for sure, so be honest with yourself.

That being said, I find a nice side effect of meditation is that we become much more in harmony with our intuition, so you shouldn't have much of a problem knowing what's right for you in the moment. I love the Buddhist example of a musician tuning the strings on her instrument. If the strings are too tight, they'll break; if they're too loose, no sound will come out. Our meditation practice should be like those strings: not too tight, not too loose, and right in the middle. What I like about Mahasati hand meditation is that it's an excellent middle ground between states of excessive mental and emotional pain and fostering attention and compassion. So that's where this young, bald-headed Buddhist counselor at the detox came into play.

After the objections quieted down, he said he'd be teaching us a fifteen-part hand meditation. Admittedly, my curiosity was piqued— I'd never encountered a hand meditation in my years of practice. The counselor went on to tell us how he'd learned this technique while studying with a monk who had lived in a cave in Laos for many years, and that it was one of the root practices they had worked with. He had my attention.

Knowing that many of us were in bad shape in that detox, he went easy and had us practice for only five minutes, but once those five minutes were up, I knew that this was something I'd carry with me for a long time. The beauty of the experience was that as he led us through the fifteen hand movements (described in detail below), we were forced to pay attention to what we were doing (well, those of us who participated, anyway). While you are doing Mahasati, a core part of the practice beyond just the gestures themselves is focusing on the slow and rhythmic pattern of your hands and arms as they move, which was exactly what I needed to help me get out of my head, if only for five minutes. After I had the order of movements down, a process that takes about a minute, I could bring my full awareness to the practice. I wasn't thinking about my hands or arms, nor was I thinking about all the other shit that had been bouncing around in my head. I was simply there, aware of my arms and hands, though that's not even quite accurate. The experience was more of a knowledge of motion; my hands and arms weren't even mine anymore. Just movement and awareness, awareness and movement, and it was beautiful . . . though brief.

The next day we did Mahasati hand meditation for ten minutes, and I had another powerful experience. But the times between sessions were still terribly rough. I would periodically do the practice on my own in my room, and it helped, but it was hard to keep myself sitting upright for very long. The sedatives I was being given were powerful and left me in a groggy state, one in which I was just awake enough to be cognizant of my incessant thoughts about the total nightmare my life had once again become. Despite everything, I finished my time in detox, then finished my time in rehab, and life got better. Much better. In part, I believe, because of this practice, which I still use frequently and hold dear.

The intentional practice of the hand movements described below helps facilitate that awareness in our daily lives. What follows is the formal version, but the practice can be engaged in any time we're aware of what we're doing or simply present in the moment.

Here are a few things to know before starting:

- When practicing, sustain a steady motion or flow with your hands—motion and pause, motion and pause.
- You can close your eyes, but if you keep them open, focus on

something that won't distract you. The floor approximately three feet in front of your gaze works well.

- While moving your hands and arms, be aware of your body in space.

You can sit in any position that feels right for you—on the floor, in a chair, or even standing up or lying down.

- Whichever body position you choose, do your best to allow the movements to be natural, performing one at a time while being aware of each as you're doing it.
- Be comfortable and relaxed. Try not to go into this practice with expectations for results.
- The joy is in the doing and the being. Try it out and see for yourself.

1. Rest your hands palm down on your thighs.

2. Turn your right hand onto its side, with the awareness of what you're doing. Make the movement mindfully and slowly, then stop. Do not think about turning your hand but rather be aware of the movement as it happens.

3. Mindfully raise your right hand up. Stop.

4. Lower your right hand down to your abdomen, allowing it to rest. Stop.

5. Turn your left hand onto its side Stop.

6. Raise your left hand up. Stop.

7. Lower your left hand down on top of your right hand, which is resting on your abdomen. Stop.

8. Move your right hand up to your chest. Stop.

9. Move your right hand out. Stop.

10. Lower your right hand onto its side on your thigh. Stop.

11.   Turn your right palm down. Stop.

12.   Move your left hand up to your chest. Stop.

13.   Move your left hand out. Stop.

14.   Lower your left hand onto its side on your thigh. Stop.

15.   Turn your left palm down. Stop.

3

GOD IS NOT YOUR BITCH

CONVERSATION WITH LISSA RANKIN, MD

My explorations led me from potentially mind-bending psychedelic journeys to another pioneering practitioner of medicine, my longtime friend and mentor Lissa Rankin, a doctor I've found to be inspirational through her real and raw approach to transformational work. We discussed how stress becomes normalized. Before I got to my questions about the mind and its addiction to certainty, and how understanding this can help us to begin removing our self-defeating behaviors, I wanted to talk about stress and fear. In her book *The Fear Cure,* Lissa wrote, "According to the Centers for Disease Control and Prevention, 80 percent of visits to the doctor are believed to be stress-related."[1] Stress in its many forms—fear, anxiety, and worry—is often the excuse we give for addictive behaviors.

Lissa had some great things to say about this. She maintains that we've normalized stress to the point where it has become almost a badge of honor in our culture, as well as a defense. To say we're stressed is to put on a suit of armor that makes us feel more socially acceptable, because now we're important, contributing, productive. Lissa shared an example from her life. "I'm probably the only person you'll meet who winds up in therapy with friends and lovers within three months of meeting them. I was in therapy with one of my friends, and we were the perfect trigger for each other's core wounds. Me being me would trigger his mommy issue, because Mommy put him in an orphanage when he was nine, and him being him would trigger my daddy abandonment wounds from when my dad died ten years ago. What our therapist said was, instead of going into a triggered state of anger, blame, criticism, judgment, whatever, we could recognize the moment when the energy of that trigger is coming up in us and have the presence to say 'I'm scared.' Then it can de-escalate. We started doing that and discovered we could *feel* threatened instead of *responding* to the threat. Instead of going on the defensive, we could go into the vulnerability of 'I'm scared . . . scared you're going to leave.' If everybody could say 'I'm scared,' then we could have compassion instead of lashing out in petty and even horrific ways. She helped me see that underneath all our posturing, there's a tremendous softness in our wounded child. We can begin to heal if we access that place."

Man, did that ever ring true for me: I get scared and act out in my own unskillful ways. Before my last relapse, I had a moment when I was deciding whether to drink. Something had shifted within me. It was as if an old version of Chris appeared and I lost the conviction to care for myself. That's when I went to the liquor store, bought a bottle of vodka, and drank it all down, fully cognizant of the ramifications it would have on my life, my loved ones, my everything, yet still saying "Fuck it!" because I couldn't have given less of a shit in that moment. (It's what twelve-steppers call "playing the tape through," but I'd pressed the mute button.) It was as if a force had come over me, and that force was propelled by fear. No matter how much I knew a part of me didn't want to drink, it felt like that force greater than myself had taken charge. Why do we respond to fear in that way? Our bodies are naturally equipped with what's known as either the acute stress response or the fight-or-flight response. The phrase "fight or flight" has been around for a while; it's used to describe how our brains prepare our bodies for action in reaction to a stressful or potentially dangerous situation. Walter B. Cannon, a physiologist, brought this term into the vernacular in his book *The Wisdom of the Body,* which was published in 1932.[2]

This made me think about a connection between flight and using. Was there a connection between self-destructive actions and this physiology of fear? In other words, getting drunk, bingeing on episodes of *The Walking Dead,* or burying our emotions in salted caramel ice cream are also a kind of flight, a running away from whatever it is in front of us (or within us) in the moment that we don't want to face or deal with it. And so for many of us, we engage in the behaviors that make us temporarily high, from sugar to sex to heroin, to take us out of the unpleasantness of the moment and give flight to our feelings . . . until they crash to earth in a burning mass of regret and dysfunction.

When I once spoke with an old professor of mine who specializes in addiction, she mentioned how there can be a strange wisdom for an addict when he or she picks up drugs or alcohol, because there is a safety equated with those substances—a way to take flight, if you will. She wasn't saying relapsing or using drugs or alcohol is the right thing to do, but that there is a strange wisdom. There are many paths to healing.

Lissa seemed to agree with this, and illustrated her understanding with another story from her therapy experience. "I was in a session with my friend, and he was coming at me aggressively. I knew he loved me. I knew I was safe. But my physiology went into full-on fight or flight. I could feel it. I could feel everything in my body wanting to flee, because I'm not a fighter, I'm a fleer. My nervous system felt threatened, like there was a tiger coming at me. In retrospect, if I examine the thought, it goes back to the wound of my dad dying, feeling like my safety got shattered and how I would be at risk. If this friend left, I'd be unsafe. It's in my physiology. It's in my body. When I rationalize and pull out all the mental tricks, like questioning my thoughts, it doesn't do a thing for my body, because my body is in full-on fight or flight. What happens is that when fear is triggered, it activates the amygdala in the limbic brain, flipping on the sympathetic nervous system and activating the stress response. The limbic brain overpowers the rational mind every time, so we can argue with our limbic brain, but our body is still in that state. The limbic brain is not rational. It's the primal lizard brain, and it can't tell the difference between a thought like 'He's going to leave' and one like 'A tiger is about to eat me.' "

She likened it to a light switch—either on or off. When we flip the switch to fear, the body has a physiological response, which is "the stress response, or fight or flight, or the sympathetic nervous system. A whole cascade of stress hormones gets triggered that puts you into that recognizable adrenaline rush that threatens your relaxation response, which is the parasympathetic nervous system, the kind of homeostatic, peaceful state of the nervous system.

"In *The Fear Cure*, I talk about true fear versus false fear. We want true fear. The spiritual teachers might argue that we don't even need true fear, but true fear is there to protect the survival of the organism, so true fear is what you feel when the tiger is coming after you, or you're standing on the edge of the cliff looking over it and thinking, 'I'm afraid to jump.' True fear is there to keep the physical body safe. Some children have disorders where they're born with no fear; they don't last very long. They'll walk out into the street right in front of a car because they're not afraid of anything. Survival mechanisms are there for a reason, but our nervous system and our brain, our limbic brain, have not caught up with the evolution of how we live our lives and how our minds work. The problem is that we're in stress response about 70 percent of the time in modern culture. I was up at sixteen thousand feet in the Andes with the Q'ero tribe in Peru and discovered that this is not the case for them. Society is so different there, but in our culture, we're in stress response more than fifty times per day. You can call it fear, anxiety, worry—whatever it is, it's triggering that same thing in the nervous system, and it can't tell the difference between an anxious thought and a tiger attack.

"False fear is what I call an imagined fear. You're imagining you're going to run out of money or your wife is going to leave you or your friend is going to abandon you. Those things may happen, but they're not *definitely* going to happen, so until there's a threat to the survival of the organism, it's not technically a true fear."

The key is to distinguish between false fear and intuition. How do we go about doing that?

A lot of it is working through our misconceptions. Lissa explained that "we think we need false fear to protect us. We think that we need to be afraid of running out of money to make sure that we don't run out of money. We think we need fear to keep us from drinking, to keep us from overspending, to keep us from cheating, to keep us from doing things that will get us in trouble. That's how our culture operates. Look at the media. Many of the messages are fear based, and our society uses fear to control us. It's damaging our health, our longevity, our quality of life. When I talk to people about fear, I always have to overcome the resistance that people have, the idea that 'I need my fear, because if I'm not afraid of losing money, then I'm going to go broke.'"

That's when Lissa brings in the idea of intuition. "What about the part of us that isn't afraid at all, but is here to guide us? It's here to protect us, here to give us insights and epiphanies and to help us make aligned decisions *without fear*. We don't have to trigger the nervous system into stress response to have a dropped-in download that says, 'Here's a good financial plan for this year.' It doesn't have to come from fear. Intuition feels different in the body. It's very calm. It comes in as a very neutral thing. I've come to recognize that it has a flavor. It tastes like basil. Like, once you know what basil tastes like, it's like, 'Oh, it's basil.' And it's different from paranoia or the fear thoughts."

There's a mystery to intuition. Lissa gave some amazing examples of people who are protected by their intuition. "Like the woman who's walking out the door and suddenly gets the 'Don't trust the babysitter' download. Her mind will argue and say, 'You're being paranoid. That's crazy. She comes highly recommended.' The woman goes back and cancels her plans and finds out the babysitter has a criminal record. Or another woman who got the intuition to check on her baby. The baby's room was on fire! An electrical wire had sparked this fire." Lissa has come to think about intuition as a "stealthy way the unseen world communicates with the seen world."

The more we quiet our minds through things like meditation and prayer, the more we can recognize the voice of intuition. There have been so many people I've spoken with who've had glimpses of this and have called it by many different names—Christ consciousness or Buddha Mind, stillness, big Self, or Divine nature. There have been times when I've been connected to that intuition, as when I married my ex-wife (a decision I'll never regret and one for which I'll forever be immensely grateful). It was an absolute knowing beyond comprehension. Yet more than once I have found myself back in a place where drinking seemed to be the only viable option, in that desperate moment when that switch in my mind flipped to the old Chris who wanted to escape pain and revert to drinking, even though I knew better. I found myself locked in that mental place of fear, of fight or flight, even after having had tastes of the Divine through my spiritual practices and work with meditation and non-dual awareness. If one is in that place of fear, how does one not act out? How can one turn up the volume on their intuition? I wondered if it was even possible.

Lissa believes it is. "Be aware that you're triggered. Notice it in your body, notice the fight or flight. Notice what's happening in your mind. Step into that witness consciousness if possible. Then use that trigger as a cue to pause, get silent, and surrender." Sometimes it's as simple as removing yourself from the situation. That's when she pointed out something fascinating: Sometimes it helps to flee *temporarily*. Remove yourself from the immediate threat. "Go to the bathroom or outside for a walk and try to calm down. Sometimes it's fifteen minutes and sometimes it's an hour, but I do it so I can relax my nervous system, using various techniques.

"When I'm able to calm my nervous system down a little bit, that's when I'll get emotional. I'll start crying or I'll feel angry. I'll notice what's coming up. I try to do it in silence and breathe through it and then allow myself—and this is a big thing for me—to recognize the part of me that's triggered. It may be seven-year-old me, so I try holding this seven-year-old the same way I'd hold my daughter. Can I visualize this part of me being held in the benevolent arms of an angel or Jesus or the universe, Mother Earth holding the part of me that's feeling scared or sad or angry with complete nonjudgment? I let myself comfort myself, and by this point my nervous system has calmed down and I know there's no tiger. I'm feeling tender. I'll hold my arms around myself like I'm giving myself a hug. Then I'll look at what's happening in my mind. I can't go straight into the mental inquiry when my nervous system is triggered. I'm in fight or flight. I'm not rational, so there's no point trying to employ a rational process until I've expressed the emotional."

Lissa showed me how the process of dealing with triggers can be broken down into three consecutive parts: the physiological, the emotional, and the spiritual inquiry. As was true with Tara Brach's RAIN, when we reach the point of spiritual inquiry, we can ask, "What is the thought that's causing me pain right now?" Then we can put the mental inquiry into "Is that a true thought? Is there a way to turn that thought around? Is there a thought that can be truer than this?" That's often where I get deep insights that take me out of a judging and blaming place and into a place of greater compassion for myself and for whoever or whatever triggered me.

Lissa has always been very careful not to use this process as some kind of spiritual bypass. Spiritual bypassing is a term I encounter a lot in my work and study, and it's important to this book. It was coined by Buddhist teacher and psychotherapist John Welwood in the early 1980s and describes a "tendency to use spiritual ideas and practices to sidestep or avoid facing unresolved emotional issues, psychological wounds, and unfinished developmental tasks."[3] I think many of us who've had issues with addiction or relapses fall into this. I know I have. We believe our lives can be "fixed," and in spiritual bypassing we feel that we've done that, at least at first. We meditate, pray, do yoga, and whatever else our healing program might prescribe, but instead of digging into our issues, we're circumventing them and perhaps burying them and allowing them to fester.

So when it comes to bypassing and triggers, Lissa said, "This doesn't mean that I don't then go back to the situation and set a boundary or make a request or attempt to come to an agreement. I see a lot of people using these kinds of techniques as a way of having blind compassion and neurotic tolerance of unacceptable behavior. This is not a technique for tolerating abuse; however, I can come *from* that place to one of compassion. I can put myself into the other's shoes. I can find that place of oneness, and then I can return to 'What do I need to do to protect this human in this dualistic realm?' What do I need to do to protect this organism? Then I'm able to come back from that with inspired action, an undefended, nonreactive response that comes from a calm, compassionate—albeit fierce—loving place that can say, 'No, that's not acceptable.'"

Lissa had more to say about triggers. "I also want to acknowledge that I get very triggered by the self-help industry in general because it sticks needles in people's 'not enough' wounds. We all have 'not enough' wounds, so the last thing we need is for people to poke at the spot that we're always trying to heal, that's always a little tender. The disclaimer I would like to make is that we're always looking for a tool we can use so that we never need to go back into a dark place—like, for example, your relapse—but I don't think it works that way. We're always looking for how we can control life. When people ask me what the fear cure is, I tell them the name is sort of a misnomer, because it's about letting fear cure you. If I had to say there is a fear cure, I would say it's coming into right relationship with uncertainty."

Cue the record-scratch sound effect: *coming into right relationship with uncertainty.* That was something I wanted to know more about, and Lissa did not let me down. "It's related to control. When we have a painful experience, our minds try to figure out, 'How can I keep that experience from ever happening again?' For example, asking, 'How can I make sure I don't end up with a bottle in my hand and drinking from it? What can I do to make sure that never happens again?' But what if that's impossible? What if there's nothing we can do to make sure that never happens again? What if there's nothing we can do to make sure people we love don't die? We are not in control."

I'm going to repeat this statement, because it's really important in terms of any spiritual process or return to self-damaging behavior, and I think it will strike a nerve for others as well: *We. Are. Not. In. Control.* Lissa took it further. "Yes, we co-create in the world. Yes, we participate. Yes, we have a Divine spark within us. I like to think of it like I get a vote and God gets a vote, and if we disagree, then God gets the tiebreaker. It's not that we're powerless; it's not that we're victims."

Then Lissa got into something I'd been thinking about a lot as well: the Law of Attraction. If you don't know what the Law of Attraction is, go online, and you'll find a ton of stuff, from books to videos—it's a whole industry. Here's the short version: a belief that by focusing positive thoughts on something while energetically imagining that you already have that thing, you can manifest it, bring it into being. Lissa notes, "I have a difficult relationship with all the Law of Attraction teachings, but I've come to think of it as a sort of spiritual puberty. Maybe one of the early phases is that we believe we are victims of a hostile universe that we can't control, that we are at the mercy of chaotic forces that do not have our best interests at heart, and that life is terrifying. That's where so many people in modern culture live. That's their steady state. If we're comparing this maturity to adolescence, let's say that they are eight. And then maybe they turn twelve and realize, 'Oh my goodness! I can visualize and say affirmations and make wishes and interface with this force and manifest things into reality . . . and I can get what I want!' It works—some of the time, at least. It's empowering to read things like 'dimensionalize a yellow butterfly' and all of a sudden there are yellow butterflies everywhere and you're, like, 'Oh my god! I did that. I am God. I am a creator.' It's exciting, except you're wondering why the Ferrari isn't showing up. 'Why can I manifest the butterfly but not the Ferrari?'

"People grow disillusioned with this Law of Attraction teaching, which says you can have everything you want if you only try harder, visualize more, affirm more, because they're trying to dimensionalize what their *ego* wants. There's a deeper level of spiritual maturity. That's when you don't attach to needing to get what your ego wants, because your ego isn't the wisest part of you. It's not that you don't have preferences, but even more than your preferences, you become interested in allowing something larger to guide your life. You're willing to live in a place of spiritual yielding where all desires become an offering to the Divine as a devotional act.

"I've been very influenced by the teachings of Tosha Silver, who wrote *Change Me Prayers: The Hidden Power of Spiritual Surrender*. A lot of the spiritual teachings are so patriarchal in their leanings, and I so appreciate the feminine devotional approach she offers. She sees spiritual surrender as an act of love. We can take our desires and our problems and our decisions and all the things the ego perseverates over and we can surrender them to a force of love and ask for help. For example, if I have a desire or something I'm meant to do, one of my regular prayers is to say, 'Here's what I'm inclined to do, and if this is motivated toward the highest good, please help me, and if not, please stop me.' To be genuinely and equally grateful for the cosmic yes as well as the cosmic no is critical. This is not another sneaky way to get what you want. It's not another way to manipulate the Law of Attraction. As Tosha said, 'God is not your Costco. God is not your bitch.' You don't give God a shopping list and say, 'Here's what I want.'

"The side effect of this way of operating is that it puts the nervous system into relaxation. Think about how many stories you've heard of addicts who are in that moment of despair or of people who are on the verge of suicide and something breaks. There's a level of surrender that is so profound that suddenly it opens a portal for love to rush in. One of the keys to this—and Tosha teaches it in a very lighthearted and sweet way—is saying, 'Surrender your desire to find a parking spot in San Francisco on a Saturday night to the Divine and wait and see what happens.' If you're meant to go to this event, you'll find a parking spot, and if not, you're not meant to go. Part of the reason she teaches that is because it develops into a habit. If you're surrendering your small desires, when it comes to the big and difficult things that the ego is grasping or resisting, then it's already part of your practice. That practice has helped me to come into right relationship with uncertainty, because then I can relax into it."

What Lissa said brought to mind my experience when I was newly married and waiting for my paperwork so that I could live in Canada. I was in a dark place of not knowing anything when it came to untangling the red tape of the application and approval process for residency. The crux of the problem was that I had two old DUIs—felony offenses in Canada—on my record, and for all intents and purposes, immigration probably shouldn't have allowed me into the country at all. I was at a point of despair and surrender when my caseworker took the time to read my entire file, including the letters of reference I'd included. She said she'd looked online and saw that I was in a place where service was a top priority for me in my life, and because of that she helped me get permission to come into the country.

"Everything in our culture teaches us to avoid uncertainty at all costs. The unknown is dangerous, but we can reach a place where we stop being afraid and become simply curious about it—a place of wonder. It starts to get exciting, because if we don't know what the future holds, anything can happen. We can have a spontaneous remission from a seemingly incurable illness. Or Oprah could call. We never know. Tomorrow is a mystery. I look out my window at the beach and think, 'You know what? I could look out my window and see a band of angels one day. I've seen all kinds of curious, awe-inspiring things, but I've never seen that, and it would be cool.'"

I laughed to myself when Lissa said this, because it reminded me of my last detox and treatment program, one during which I'd pissed myself because I was so out of it. When I finally came to, I felt like I was dying for real this time—I mean it, I was honestly unsure whether I was going to survive this one, let alone go on to write books about healing. That's when I met an incredible clinical director at the inpatient program I was in and saw yet again that life is fucking crazy and certainly awe-inspiring at times, but like Lissa said, we must *show up* so life can *show us*.

Lissa continued, "We can reach a place with uncertainty where it almost becomes seductive, which can be a risky phase because we can become reckless, almost as if we're chasing uncertainty. Anything that feels too much in our comfort zone starts to feel boring, and we're constantly on the edge, chasing after the next mystical experience or the next extreme sport or the next dangerous relationship. But there's a phase of spiritual maturity beyond that when we're not resisting uncertainty and we're not grasping at uncertainty. That's when we're in right relationship with uncertainty—where we're no longer trying to control life. We're not trying to get what we want. We're not trying to resist what we don't want. We're in agreement with life."

This made me want to chant Lissa's mantra: "I'm in agreement with life, and I resist nothing." Although for her, "it was a hard thing to take into my heart and make a practice, because I'd lost five people in six weeks. It's hard not to resist when you're in that much grief. And I had a painful romantic breakup. When you're grieving and you're heartbroken, there's that instinctual, limbic part of you that wants to protect you from having to go through that ever again because it hurts so much. I was trained as an OB/GYN, so here's an apropos example: When a woman is laboring, she is going to have pain, so to resist pain is pointless, and when she resists the contraction, it hurts more. All the midwives and skilled doulas and such know that the coaching is around softening into the pain and relaxing into it, which is counterintuitive, but the more you can relax into the pain, the more you let it sweep through you, the less it hurts.

"For me, it's the same thing with emotional pain, heartbreak, or grief. I feel it as a physical contraction of the heart. My heart hurts, but if I don't resist it, if I don't have a story that says life should be different than it is right now, then that wave of heart pain can sweep through me, and it usually lasts only the length of a uterine contraction—about ninety seconds. Ironically, that's about how long a stress response lasts if you don't attach mental stories to it. There's something about ninety seconds. If I can let that contraction sweep through my heart, then it passes and I get a reprieve. I may have another contraction, like labor, but over time, the contractions space out, and then they don't hurt so much."

Then Lissa did something that touched me in a profound way—she put this in context of my relapse. "What if there was nothing wrong with your falling off the wagon? Why was this bad? Why make a story that says, 'I made a mistake, I did something bad'? What if that's the next phase of your soul's journey?"

I was so grateful to her for saying that. I have seen that growth can come from relapse. It showed me a lot of areas I was stuck in that I wasn't aware of, but there's also the part of me that says, "Well, you're in recovery, and since you fucked up, you're bad. You should be punished and feel shame and guilt." And there is some of that, but I can't deny that relapse was something that happened to me, it was an internal, shitty experience. I didn't drive drunk or try and fight people in public, but I've been carrying a lot of stress and guilt and shame, particularly over how my marriage ended. I guess it's because of my ingrained belief that relapse is a failure. I did bad, and now I must get back up and start all over again, but I refuse to let that one experience—that twenty-four-hour contraction in my sobriety—define who I am as a person and negate all the hard work I've put into my life and my path over the years.

Lissa reminded me that "taking away the shame and the judgment and almost adding some levity to it makes it such an act of self-love. It's an act of self-care to be gentle with the part of us that continues to do the things we feel embarrassed or guilty or ashamed about." At some point in our spiritual maturation, we start caring about ourselves so much that we don't want the cigarette or the drink or the food. "We *really* don't want it. It's not like we need to beat ourselves into not having the cigarette; we don't want it because we've come into a different kind of relationship with this precious vessel—our body—that holds the spirit with which we've developed a relationship. It's a very gentle, compassionate relationship with the physical, emotional, mental, and spiritual self. All those pieces have become integrated, and from that place of integration, the natural impulse to eat better, to drink less, to quit smoking, or whatever becomes a side effect of that tremendous self-tenderness."

Lissa nailed it with her comments on applying self-tenderness toward ourselves and our lives as we move forward. As I'm finishing this chapter, I find myself missing my ex-wife and stepdaughter in ways I haven't in a while. That's life, right? Things ebb and flow, but in this moment, I can hold myself and these feelings of sadness and distance in self-tenderness. It's quite beautiful and comforting. (The flip side is that I'm holding myself in said tenderness while listening to Bloodlet, an exceptionally brutal hardcore band, so I guess it all balances out, right?)

PRACTICE

From Fear to Freedom

After we spoke, Lissa sent me an excerpt from her book *The Fear Cure* that she said could be the foundation for a practice:

> *When we're willing to view life as the teacher, even in the midst of uncertainty, a journey begins. This journey—some might call it the spiritual path—challenges us to shift from fear of uncertainty to trusting life in the face of that which we can't know and don't understand. After interviewing many people about what they'd learned on their own spiritual journeys, I discovered that the journey from fear to freedom, which is all about coming into right relationship with uncertainty, is a predictable journey, one that many have traveled before you and many will travel after you. . . . It is a map of sorts and can help you assess where you are on your path.*

Here are Lissa's five phases:

1. *Unconscious Fear of Uncertainty:* "Better safe than sorry."
2. *Conscious Fear of Uncertainty:* "The only thing certain in life is uncertainty."
3. *Uncertainty Limbo:* "I'm curious about the unknown, but I have my reservations."

4. *Uncertainty Seduction:* "The flip side of the fear of uncertainty is the excitement of possibility."

5. *Surrender:* "The only way to experience life's richness is to surrender to the unknown."

Here's how I navigated these phases when I began my divorce:

1. I became aware of my *unconscious fear of uncertainty* about my relationship when I thought about my experience with addiction and relapse and how that could create insecurity for my ex-wife and her daughter. I dug into how I tend to cling to safety and certainty in a relationship and questioned whether this relationship had been working for me.

2. This helped me touch my *conscious fear of uncertainty* and recognize how my need to be sure limited my possibilities, generating a predisposition toward what that exactly needs to look like in my life, especially when it came to my relationship with my ex-wife. I tried to get to a place of self-compassion.

3. As I engaged in the *uncertainty limbo*, I looked at this situation and my fears and doubts with curiosity. I tried my best not to judge or "know" the answers, but it wasn't easy! There's a natural inclination to squirm away from the discomfort of the unknown.

4. By being aware of the *uncertainty seduction*, I could avoid stumbling, and discriminate between reasonable fear and experiencing the unknown with integrity—except in this instance, that wasn't the case. I hadn't utilized Lissa's From Fear to Freedom Practice. (Let this be a lesson for you kids . . .)

5. *Surrender* was the part of this practice I couldn't commit to. I would shove the feelings of uncertainty, fear, loneliness, and lack of self-worth deep down as they arose. I'd worked with surrender practices in other areas of my life prior to this, and since then, even using Lissa's formula, but this time around I

chose not to, and the results, well . . . you read the preface to this book.

Lissa reminded me that it's a process! "You may leap forward from one phase to the next, only to find that you regress in times of loss or trauma. Because we're often more comfortable with uncertainty in some areas of our lives than in others, you may not be in the same phase in all aspects of your life. There is no right or wrong phase, and you should trust your own timing. The reason to identify where you are in your development is not to trigger your 'not good enough' story, but simply to help guide you as you walk your own path. Be extra gentle and compassionate with yourself as you navigate from fear to faith. Trust the process!"

4

DRINKING, DRUGGING, OVERSPENDING, AND SEXCAPADES
CONVERSATION WITH ANNE DAVIN

L issa Rankin turned me on to Anne Davin, an incredible woman! Anne spent several years living on a Native American reservation in New Mexico, and her later work with Southeast Asian Indochinese refugees inspired her exploration of the intersection of psyche, culture, and the marginalized voice of the feminine. She is a licensed psychotherapist and the cofounder of the Imagin-NATION Academy, offering a pathway to wisdom and healing using the ancient tools and practices of earth-based indigenous cultures.

Anne's background in depth psychology is based on an understanding that the world itself is "ensouled," or inclusive of the cosmos, the natural world, and the unseen forces beyond what is visible. "The pervasive symptoms of dis-ease—depression, anxiety, and addictions—are an invitation to deeper inquiry and a remembering of ourselves as who we are. When we find the courage to look closely and inhabit our whole self, meaning, joy, and coming home to our highest purpose become abundantly available." See what I mean about incredible?

When we spoke, I shared the story of my relapse. I told her about sitting on that long bus ride back to Ottawa and taking the pills that led to the wine that led to the vodka, all within several hours, and how it ultimately left me intubated in the hospital while knocking on heaven's door. (Or hell . . . who knows?) I asked Anne what we can do when we struggle not to pick up that drink, not to eat that second piece of cake, or not to buy yet another pair of sneakers we don't need.

Anne had four responses to my question, each focused on a facet of the whole person. That's because Anne's perspective is to look at an individual as an amalgam of four different bodies. "There's the *spiritual* body, the *emotional* body, the *physical* body, and the *mental* body."

She started with the spiritual. "In relation to the spiritual body, the cycle of addiction is a crisis of imagination and faith. If we look at the metaphor, there's a reason why alcohol is called spirits. We're embodying a substance that can put us in a state of alternative consciousness. In a historical context, this was done to reach states of rapture. When you're in a cultural context in which there is a creation mythology that gives value and meaning to an organized, highly constructed environment, where substances are used to personify the spirit within the human form and to connect with other forms of intelligences and realities that surround us in a quantum universe, you can see what a substance like a bottle of vodka or a gram of cocaine in the traditional indigenous sense would have looked like. Ayahuasca and other kinds of sacred herbs or substances would have been ritually harvested, cultivated, prayed for, and then embodied in a conscious way to achieve a specific outcome. That heritage is in our spiritual DNA.

"When we experience states of extreme suffering—whether that suffering is not knowing our sense of purpose in the world, not feeling loved and located in our marriage, or feeling displaced in our own physical body because we can't control something—these modern-day realities impress upon a spiritual DNA metric that's inside of us. This spiritual DNA understands what it is to be located, what it feels like to be embodied in our aliveness as souls having a human experience where it is safe to move in the environment via its understanding of the natural world. When, spiritually speaking, we become separated from that, we can see it manifesting in our desire to caffeinate ourselves to get out of bed, to slow ourselves down at night through a permissive culture of addiction, where three glasses of wine for a woman at night as she's relaxing is considered okay.

"Our modern suffering and our ancient spiritual DNA go hand in hand. Therefore, it was possible for me to live in an indigenous community where there were actual traditional spiritual practices occurring alongside some of the highest addiction and death rates due to addiction in the nation. There was a huge trauma that had occurred to the spiritual culture, and even those people who are living what's left of an indigenous tradition are suffering this same dis-ease of the soul as those who don't know anything about that. In other words, a Western person moving around in our culture with their own sense of indigenousness usually will not know what or how to manage that." That was her perspective of the spiritual body—the modern pain yearning for the ancient healing.

Next came the emotional body. "There are very specific life events that help shape our brains. It starts with early childhood experiences that shape the brain, which then creates a flood of hormones into the body based on the event that's happening. These are transmitted into the body through neural pathways developed in response to the environment. Inside each of us is a whole neural network that's been formed as an imprint in response to the social environment that influenced us in our developmental years. Those tracks inside of us start to change when we start to ask those larger questions as we become young adults: Who am I? Why do I get angry every time a person does this? Why am I responding to my wife in this way and sounding just like my father? It's when we start to make those associations, asking those deeper questions, that we discover that we are our past in the present."

I found that fascinating, as it's something I've contemplated at great length, especially when it came to my experience of addiction. By this

I mean everything I've experienced in my life—including those god-damn psych wards and dingy basement detoxes—has culminated in the person I am today, just as my actions today will create the person I am tomorrow, ad infinitum. That's why teachings such as Ram Dass's "Be here now" are crucial. They help take us off autopilot and enable us to live a more conscious and skillful life, resulting in a better tomorrow not only for ourselves but for our loved ones and the entire planet as well.

The roots of this are deep. As Anne went on to say, "If you've had early childhood trauma, how do you restore your body, the nervous system, if it's in the subtle body? How can you be effective in healing what may cause an addiction *now* that's related to something that happened to you when you were sexually abused as a child? We know that women are more likely to become addicts if they have experienced sexual assault or domestic violence, or were abused as children.[1] There have been many studies that have demonstrated we end up self-medicating later in life because we don't know how to manage trauma in the body.[2] That's one area to attend to from the emotional body. What were those early childhood experiences that are now guiding and informing a person's life as an adult? What needs to be tended to in the nervous system? Was the person sexually abused? Were they hit? Were they forgotten on the side of the road? Did they experience an alcoholic parent? All those things impress not only into the feeling state but also into the physical state of the body. We know now because of all the research in brain elasticity that this can be changed."

Anne turned me on to a remarkable methodology called eye movement desensitization and reprocessing (EMDR). "What this does is help remove a traumatic event from the part of the brain that has the stress response. Generally, it helps to relocate it to the part of the brain that has the relaxation response in the body. If one of the ways in which a person is triggered is that they were hit as a child and therefore they have a difficult time trusting that they won't be at risk of being hurt in an intimate relationship, when they get into an intimate relationship, they experience a lot of anxiety and symptoms. Their drinking might increase or they might get strung out. But an EMDR therapist will analyze and ask questions: What happened? How did it feel in your body?

"Then the therapist will create a different experience for the body. They will ask a client if there was someone in their environment who was a wise person, a protector, someone who stood up for them. Was there someone in their environment who loved them and created a sense of warmth? When the patient speaks about the traumatic event, while it's alive in their nervous system, the EMDR therapist has them think about and meditate on one of those restorative figures. In effect, they're dosing the body with the relaxation response we get when we think about that nurturing figure and how protected and safe we felt."

Using a bilateral stimulation device, the "therapist will create a bilateral stimulation in the ears with a beeping sound that goes from the right to the left ear. Often they'll put electrical vibrators in your hands that you'll also feel going left to right, right to left. And sometimes the EMDR therapist will have you tap it left to right on certain points of your body. What all that sort of mad science does is to start to move your experience out of trauma into the relaxation response, because you're messing with all those neural pathways. The trigger becomes less intense and less frequent, and you're able to manage it better. This is an example of the mind-body connection that science is tracking. It's not just a bunch of woo-woo—there's something happening with the biochemistry of the body."

This sounds incredible, but a lot of my friends and the people I work with—myself included—don't have insurance that covers therapy or specialists such as those who facilitate EMDR. I would love to try EMDR with a trained professional, but it's not an option for me. What do people without insurance or the money to pay out of pocket do to explore therapies such as this? I asked Anne if she had an alternative practice or method she could suggest.

Fortunately, she did. "The wonderful thing about all the restorative therapies modern science is now pointing us toward is that we were doing them in ancient times—when we were running around in villages and tribes. Science is catching up with timeless indigenous traditions that don't cost a dime. There's a practice I do if I have anxiety. Maybe I have a speaking engagement and I'm having performance anxiety that is linked to when I was a child and had a negative experience of being bullied by other children. I have all that operating. I have normal performance anxiety, and it's being amplified by the fact that I was bullied as a child. What I'll do is take a walk around the block in a meditation, swinging my arms and repeating, 'I am safe. I am loved. I am safe. I am loved.' I'll repeat that over and over for up to an hour if I need to. What happens is that I create a bilateral motion in my body by swinging my right arm and swinging my left arm, and I'm effectively mimicking what EMDR does with the bilateral simulation of the ears and the energy in the hands. It's my way to dose my nervous system with the energy of 'I am safe. I am loved.' Usually my anxiety is lessened, and I'm more able to be in possession of myself and feel more comfortable and relaxed going into my presentation. I do that practice a lot, because I have a lot of generalized anxiety.

"Another way that people can do this is through movement—something like Nia cardio-dance or another form of structured movement. These kinds of exercises are brilliant articulations of what we used to do when we were in ritual or ceremony, which is moving and allowing our nervous system to align with the music, the motion, and the direction of the room. If we choose to hold on to a positive intention in our minds, just as I was doing on my walk, we can begin to soothe the nervous system through motion."

I could relate to this fully. Even though I'm currently not formally in a band, I've played drums for many bands throughout my life, and even when I wasn't part of a group per se, I'd often sit down at the kit and relax into the rhythmic relation that naturally occurs while playing. (As a matter of fact, I was feeling a little stressed while working on this chapter, and you can bet your ass I took a twenty-minute drum break to work through the stress and frustration I was holding. I feel much better now.)

The techniques Anne shared connected the emotional body directly to the physical body, and she brought it back to my original question about relapse and addiction. "Everything is all tangled up with one another. In addition to that, there's all the neuroscience that talks about the brain structure and everything that gets set into motion when we become habituated to a substance. There's substance abuse—what used to be called addiction—and all the research around what happens to our brains when we develop a habit that becomes a dependency. There's a biological corollary, and when we stop doing that, there are very specific things that go on within the biology that manifest in cravings. Those things create a rumination in the form of obsessive thoughts. It's as if our biology begins to drive what's going on in the mind, and then our mind starts to have a conversation with the body. Soon we end up back in front of a bottle."

That brought us to the mental body. "When someone has experienced early childhood trauma and the neural pathways in the brain imprint on that, it's not just a feeling experience that gets stuck there, it's also supported by a mental decision that the child made in that moment—a decision about themselves and the world. That negative core belief starts running in the background like a CD that's on replay, and it stays on replay for that person's entire life. It's usually buried in the unconscious. I have read—and I have no idea how scientists measure this—that we have something like sixty thousand unconscious beliefs in a twenty-four-hour period. How do they even know that? Most of those unconscious beliefs are coming from the limbic brain, which is the part of our brain that is the fight-or-flight response. The reason that they're firing those images is because the limbic brain is trying to keep us safe from a real or perceived threat. When we have a negative experience as a child, that message goes right into that sound wave.

Unless we're conscious of it, we can unconsciously organize our life around that negative belief. We can choose people, places, and things that will create an emotional environment in which that belief can stay intact. Our inner life will start to picture itself in our outer reality until we start to take steps to change that—whether that's to read a great self-help book, have a deep conversation with a friend, or get sober and start engaging in a restorative community. All those things contribute to spiritual, emotional, and physical change."

Then Anne returned to my question. "If it's that easy, if that's all it takes, why does relapse happen? Why relapse? In the eighties, there was a wonderful person named Terence Gorski who was on the front end of the addiction and recovery movement. I asked Terry to come and speak at a program I was managing for the University of California because he had written or cowritten a series of books, one of which stood out for me: *Staying Sober: A Guide for Relapse Prevention*. It's been around since the eighties, but I still think it's the go-to text for understanding the psychology of relapse.[3] Basically, what Terry brought to the conversation at that time was that relapse doesn't happen at the bottle—it happens days, weeks, and even months before the decision to drink."

I could certainly relate to that. I could pinpoint the instant my last relapse began, the moments when I would feel unhappy about my marriage and would know my wife shared similar views. I'd quickly suppress those thoughts with ruminations about work or food or something, *anything* else. I'd pretty much repeated this pattern over the course of a couple of months every time I picked up a drink. I also became aware that I would pay more attention to liquor stores as I drove by them, noting what neon signs were lit up in the window or making a mental note that they were open in the evenings. Seemingly innocent thoughts in and of themselves—that is, unless you have a history of alcoholism or addiction.

Anne broke it down, noting that we each have a unique core set of triggers that set off a relapse. "They're specific to our orientation in the world and how we manage love, being a householder, getting up and going to work, and the stresses of life. From that perspective, relapse starts to show itself well in advance of the action to drink or use. In that way, it's one more layer of understanding and knowing ourselves. It requires a high degree of self-awareness, which takes time and effort to develop, but once we have it, it becomes a useful tool in helping us see the signs early and start to mitigate them more effectively and more immediately."

What I've learned from personal experience is that it's not enough to have the awareness of these triggers; instead, it's necessary to be proactive in telling on ourselves when they begin to activate. What I mean is to let a friend or sponsor or someone we trust in our recovery circle know what's coming up for us. As they say in the twelve-step programs, we're only as sick as our secrets, and I'll be goddamned if that isn't some serious truth. (Well, I'm probably goddamned for plenty of other reasons, but let that not be one of them!) I shared with Anne that when I think about my relapses, the one thing I always remember feeling is a sense of freedom once I'd ingested the alcohol. I grew up as a punk-rock-loving skateboarder in a rural town; I had many experiences of being judged and not feeling free to be myself. But in later years, I came to realize that after I do relapse, a sense of freedom comes with it. Because when I'm not drinking, it's not that I dwell on it, but there is the feeling that *I'm not free to drink.* The catch-22 is that once I begin to drink again, although I feel that initial sense of relief and freedom, it always leads to a bondage to the alcohol. There is no real liberation in it because I'm the kind of drinker who starts drinking as soon as I wake up, before withdrawal kicks in and I start feeling sick. Even when my relapse only lasted twenty-four hours, I started with one pint, then two pints, and before the week was over, I was drinking mouthwash. On the one hand, I was experiencing a sense of relief and freedom in drinking; on the other, I was right back to being a slave to it. In my case, when I go back to drinking, it's not just that I'm drunk, it's the mental stuff that comes with it—all the old, ingrained stuff. The horrible self-talk.

Anne picked up on something interesting. "This is the place where agreement, acceptance, and approval can be most powerful as you explore your relapse triggers. That becomes a meditation versus something that is preventing the monster from coming back. It becomes a moving prayer for you. You are a person with a tremendous life force. There's tremendous aliveness inside of you. It's what has driven you to create on the scale that you have, and even as a child, to operate outside of the conditions of your world. There is a tremendous drive inside of you to feel that sense of interconnectivity, that sense of quantum correlation.

"I grew up like you. Running as hard and fast as I could in my body, trying to chase my brothers down. Why did I do that? I was trying to keep up with them, but the real reason I did it is because when I'm in a state of emotion within myself, I enter a zone that is much bigger than human. It was no surprise that during the years I was an adolescent and a young adult I was using very heavily, because that was a part of the paradigm that got me *there*. Now the task for me as an adult—and perhaps you share in this—is, 'How do I achieve that sense of quantum correlation, that flow of life force, as a sober person? How do I get to those states of rapture through intimate contact with my beloved? With my sense of purpose and work in the world?' Even in the moment when I respond to someone who has pissed me off in traffic. It's like the world is now our ashram, so that you're always on your skateboard. I'm always running on Taos Mountain. I could be thrown into the category of an adrenaline junky, but I don't believe that's it at all. There's nothing more grounding and more enlivening to me than to be in that sense of correlation, which is why I love indigenous cultures, because everything about them was cultivating and sustaining the correlation."

Then Anne told me I struck her as a person who's addicted to correlation. I found that to be a fair and accurate assessment. She said it was a healthy desire. "You have come so far in your own personal development that when you reached for the old habit, you discovered that it no longer correlates you. Not in your head—you already knew that. I'm talking about in your nervous system. It was like, 'Nah, this isn't it.'

Now the burn is in the sobriety for you. It's in daring to be beholden to other humans. That's the temple. That's it. That's the burn."

That's a big part of why I do what I do. I've worked very hard on myself over the course of the past several years, but there's still more to be done. Now I'm trying to look under those rocks that I've yet to turn over to see what I can find. My conversation with Anne opened doors that I wanted to walk through and explore. During my relapse and active addiction stages, I kept journals, the underlying theme of which was anger toward God. I'd often write about wondering where God was. Why was I empty and hurt? I was trying to fill that pain with alcohol and drugs, but now I see how that doesn't serve me at all.

I'm piecing it all together. Drinking doesn't serve me in any way, shape, or form; it's just horrible. It's a horrible thing, and it's sad for me to see countless people lose their lives to this. It's tragic. I told Anne that in rural Connecticut, where I live, there's a huge opioid epidemic, as there is across the nation. Conversations like this one make me grateful to be in a place to help people, even while working through the guilt of relapsing again, because I know better. It's just part of what I live with.

Anne told me she appreciated my creative courage, and that meant a lot. Then she turned me on to Anne Wilson Schaef, who wrote *When Society Becomes an Addict*.[4] "She provided the most brilliant commentary on patriarchy, its consequences, the rise of the industrial world, and what happened to soul within that, even though she doesn't use this language. She also talked about one of the consequences of this—the sense of dis-ease across an entire culture being the rise of addictive behaviors. What your work collectively speaks to is that condition, and it is part of how the culture is both destroying itself and remaking itself at the same time, which is exactly what happens in the cycle of addiction. In my opinion, your most recent relapse is an indicator of your growth. It's not a signature that you're still at risk. It's a signpost indicating how much you're not at risk any longer because of how you handled it. I give you the highest praise for being willing to live it and to then rise on the other side of it, because that moment is now guiding and informing everything you do in a way that you weren't being guided and informed before. It's taken you to the next level."

This was high praise coming from someone like Anne. It inspired me even more to do my work and share hers.

PRACTICE

Thank Your Habit

Anne taught me an exercise that worked for her when she quit smoking. It's a way to get into agreement with an addiction, ultimately accepting that you're not in control.

1. Draw a simple picture of your habit.

I chose to draw a cookie, representing my periodic sugar problem.

2. Label it.

I wrote the words "cookie/sugar" and added how it made me feel: fat and weak.

3. Turn the page over and draw two columns. Label them + and –.
4. Under the minus sign, write eleven reasons this habit is a problem.

I wrote: "weight gain, trouble sleeping (if eaten in the evening), form of aversion, unhealthy, zits (poor complexion), feelings of shame, high blood pressure, increased uric acid levels (which have already been an issue for me since my early twenties, when I was di- agnosed with gout due to my drinking), bad for my teeth, potential for diabetes, and, like many things in this world, increased chances of cancer." That wasn't so bad.

5. Under the plus sign, write eleven positive consequences of the habit.

WTF? This was harder than a double kickflip on a board with shitty bearings. I finally listed four: "comfort, safety, temporary relief (from whatever stress or emotion I was trying to escape), and a temporary rush of pleasure."

6. Look at the positive aspects, your reasons for the habit every time you engage it.

As I sat in contemplation of this practice, I began to think about how it might work better for some habits, like cigarettes and sugar, than others, like alcohol and speedballs, but even so, it's powerful to see why we literally love our habits. That's my two cents, at least.

One of the positives or payoffs for Anne when she did this exercise in regards to her smoking habit was that she realized it connected her to her father, who had passed away. "We had a very conflicted relationship, and one of the few ways that we could have loving contact was that we shared the habit of smoking. Not that he smoked with me or that he supported my habit, but he smoked, and therefore I smoked. There was an unconscious agreement that I could be tethered to my father through this habit. We were from that village of smokers.

"I decided to partner with my addiction in a new way, which was to bring gratitude to it. I didn't try to stop. I didn't try to change it. Every time I smoked, my first inhale was dedicated to my father. I would say, 'This one's for you.' I was saying that a lot throughout the day. Gradually it began to change my behavior toward smoking, until I didn't smoke anymore.

"That approach worked in that instance and that context for me because I was working on the relational part of how I was associating to smoking. There was a physiological addiction that was going on as well, and it would draw on things that happened subtly over a period of time, but the hook for me was that relationship. Now, that can be true across many habits, whether it's drinking, drugging, overspending, sexcapades."

This ultimately puts us back in control. "By accepting that the addiction is what it is—not good, bad, or neutral, it just is—there's a level of approval that begins to permeate the situation. You're not trying to run away from it. You're not trying to stop it. You're not trying to do anything. It's more like a curiosity, like 'Whoa, I'm addicted to cigarettes. That's fascinating. What's up with that? God, that's brilliant. It's providing this connection to my father. My unconscious is genius!'"

I too found this to be a fascinating exploration of why I engage in this certain behavior, what its "payoffs" are as opposed to the harm it causes, and have since used it to be increasingly mindful of the reasons when I act out like this. Sure, it hasn't cured me of my sugar "appreciation" (let's call it), but it has helped me look at the behavior in real time as it's happening (incidents of which have become increasingly fewer) and be honest with myself about what I'm doing in those moments and why.

There is something to be said for that level of honesty in one's life. Real shit.

5

I DON'T BELIEVE IN ANYTHING

CONVERSATION WITH RAM DASS

Ram Dass is a revered spiritual teacher of bhakti, or devotional, yoga. He was one of the first teachers I resonated with when I stepped onto the spiritual path. I came across his classic *Be Here Now* at Russell Library in Middletown, Connecticut, while browsing the religion/spirituality section. For those unfamiliar with *Be Here Now*, it's like a divine cookbook, divided into three parts. The first covers ex-Harvard professor Richard Alpert's 1967 voyage to India, where, through a series of incredible events, he met Bhagavan Das, a fellow seeker who introduced him to his guru, Neem Karoli Baba (Maharajji). Alpert then became Ram Dass. The third section is a series of practices from meditation to yoga (and much more) to help readers as they begin their spiritual adventures. It was the middle section that spoke my language—108 pages of trippy, countercultural art, accompanied by some of the sagest advice and insight you'll find anywhere. The short version is "Love everyone. Serve everyone. Remember God. And tell the truth"—something so important to my own path that I have it tattooed on my arm. Good for a constant reminder, right?

My account was in good standing (an unusual state for me at Russell Library, since I was always overdue on something or other), so I took *Be Here Now* home. Since that day, I've considered Ram Dass an inadvertent punk-rock spiritual guide, so when I began working on this book, he was one of the first people I reached out to for his insights on how difficult times in our lives can become vehicles for awakening the courage and love that reside within each of us.

Ram Dass helped me see that sometimes, even if we have all the spiritual tools we need, we don't use them, because we distract ourselves. We get caught up in our thoughts, but our positive and negative habits are all in the mind. Ram Dass believes we've become captivated by our drama or by things in the outside world, and we get stuck. "We're too identified with the thoughts that are going around the situation, whatever it may be. We need to bring the identification from the thoughts to the *watcher* of the thoughts, and that takes us away from the thoughts. Then we should watch these thoughts as our perspective shifts around them."

That made sense. If we take a step back from thinking and look at thoughts, they lose their hold over us. A powerful first step to help in this is to take a slow, deep, intentional breath that begins to break the chatter of what the Buddhists refer to as our "monkey mind." When we recognize that we're caught up in our judgments and feelings, we can use this realization about our minds to connect with what Ram Dass calls our "witness" and work with any sort of difficulty. This can apply to drug addiction, grief, or abuse, or even bad habits like smoking cigarettes or an overindulgence in Snapchat. You see, observing our thoughts can become a vehicle for awakening the courage and love inside us. Please, try this yourself the next time you're tangled in opinions and emotion.

Ram Dass explains that "your thoughts of addiction or other hard times happen in your mind, your head. It feels thick there, but you start in the head with the understanding that you're aiming for the soul." He says that when it comes to addiction, we need to pull back or zoom out like a movie camera. "Pulling back to the witness and recognizing that the witness is part of the soul identifies you with your soul, and that's freedom. With addiction, you pull back and you witness the addiction, and then you're identified with the witness *watching* the addiction."

Now, I know some of you reading this may have a difficult time with the word "soul." I get that. Really, I do. Recently, when I was on a retreat in Maui, I thoroughly enjoyed watching Ram Dass and Sharon Salzberg (you'll meet her later) banter about soul or a lack thereof as they gave dharma talks together. No matter what side of this belief line you fall on, when it comes to soul, I believe you'll appreciate Ram Dass's take on the concept: When we're identified with the part of ourselves that is greater than our small, finite limited self (spiritually speaking, this refers to our bodies, thoughts, and egos), we're able to connect with an awareness or witness. This is the part of ourselves that is always available, underlying every second of every day, behind whatever life situation we find ourselves in. It's there impartially observing, as if it's merely a curious onlooker.

R am Dass teaches a mantra practice that can help with this. He suggested repeating, "I am loving awareness . . . I am loving awareness . . . I am loving awareness." As you do this, move your consciousness down from your thinking mind into your heart center, the place in the middle of your chest. In other words, don't stay stuck in your head, but breathe from your heart. Now add to the mantra: "I breathe in love and breathe out love . . . I watch all the thoughts that create the stuff of my mind, and I love everything, I love everything I can be aware of. I just love, just love, just love. I love from my heart-mind."

Try it, please, and see for yourself.

I am loving awareness . . . I am loving awareness . . . I am loving
   awareness.
I breathe in love and breathe out love.
I watch all the thoughts that create the stuff of my mind.

I love everything, love everything I can be aware of.
I just love, just love, just love.
I love from my heart-mind.

Ram Dass taught me that when you can accept love, you can give that love. And that includes love to and from ourselves. "You can give love to all you perceive, all the time. You can be aware of your eyes seeing, your ears hearing, your skin feeling, and your mind producing thought after thought after thought. Thoughts are seductive, but you don't have to identify with them." That's the tricky part—getting unstuck. "You identify not with the thoughts, but with the *awareness* of the thoughts. To bring loving awareness to everything you turn your awareness to is to be love. This moment is love.

"From that perspective, you can look back at your stuckness and you can love your stuckness, because if you don't love your stuckness, you bruise your heart, you bruise your soul." In other words, anything that enters our field of awareness at that point is loved, because it's experienced from the place of loving awareness.

Back in India, when Ram Dass's teacher, Neem Karoli Baba, told him to "Love everybody," Ram Dass replied, "I can't do it." Maharajji persisted, saying, "Love everybody," until Ram Dass grasped that love had to do with the soul and not the ego. This is because "the ego judges, but the soul loves everybody—because everybody is a soul, and a soul loves another soul. It's not that the small, limited ego 'I' loves you, but it's an unconditional love, because it comes from the ocean of infinite love."

I wish I could share how it felt to hear these small yet enormous words, how it opened my heart. Honestly, it was almost too much to bear. I'm not over-romanticizing this; I wanted to cry—not tears of sadness, but of joy. What the fuck was going on? I asked Ram Dass if he had any ideas.

He told me I wasn't the first one to be moved by this practice. He was passing on to me, like he does with all his students and devotees, the experience of love he received from Maharajji. "That love, that feeling of love is something you have wanted and wanted and wanted, and here it is, and you cry and say, 'I'm crying. I'm feeling at home.' When you contact your soul from your heart, the emotional heart is activated and it becomes unbearable, the emotion, and you leave the emotion behind and then you go into the soul, and it's so much. 'I'm home.' You feel like you just have to cry. The crying is not sad or happy, it's just crying. *I'm home*."

I think some of that experience for me also comes from the deep-rooted pain I have stored within, because I recognize that a part of me, somewhere deep within my unconscious, doesn't feel worthy of love, especially after a relapse. How do we learn to realistically change so we can begin to feel worthy of this love?

Ram Dass reminded me that we must love ourselves. The foundation of all healing, of all recovery, of all spiritual work is loving ourselves as *souls*. The voice in your head that says, "I've failed again. I'll never get it right. I've done evil things"—that's the mind talking. Ram Dass assured me that when you "step back from that and go to the heart, to the soul, you find love, because the soul loves itself, and the soul is what you really are. Not your ego. Your ego is a dream."

I was digging this, but here was that word again: soul. I know a lot of people have a problem with it—not to mention God. Some people are just cynical, while others have had bad experiences based on their religious upbringing. Ram Dass shined a light on this for me by explaining that the word "soul" has so many meanings because we have so many paths to choose from—Buddhism, Hinduism, Christianity, Judaism, agnosticism, and so on. "These paths have different methods. I am an atheist in the sense that I don't believe in anything, because belief is all in the mind. Belief is not faith. Belief is in the mind; faith is in the heart. I would say, go into your imagination and you can imagine a God, or soul, and feel that love, because everyone wants love—it's the conceptual mind that keeps us from this love."

This made me think of an excerpt of a talk from Ram Dass's website:

> *There are many stages of the process of transformation.*
>   *There is a stage where you feel something in you that is behind your social facade and your social relationships to people. You feel a somebody-ness which we call a soul. You feel yourself as an entity. Then, as you get deeper into the transformative work, that thing starts to dissolve. Then there is no self, there is nobody, there is only one.*[1]

When we spoke, he illuminated this further by saying that "life is one level of consciousness and the soul is one level of consciousness, and the One is another level of consciousness." By "the One," he means all of it—the whole shebang. "If you decide to make the journey from your soul to the One, you're starting the vehicle of your soul. It's like diving into the ocean. You're on the shore and you leave your shoes behind and your 'self' behind and go diving into the water and become a part of the ocean, yet are still a separate wave. This is a subtle understanding . . . you've got to shift perspective."

Speaking of shifts in perspective, I'd seen a picture of Ram Dass's puja table—his personal altar—and noticed that along with lots of pictures of Maharajji was one of Donald Trump. It was a great reminder to me to cultivate compassion for everyone—not just the people I feel "deserve" it.

Ram Dass said that Trump is an excellent example. "The only thing we have to work with is his present incarnation, but he's a soul who has a terrible incarnation this time around. Having compassion in our hearts for that soul, for that incarnation, is another way of looking at it. I have compassion for the soul that has karma that has led to his current incarnation. Poor soul. Poor, poor, poor soul. He's going to have his comeuppance."

I wish I shared his equanimity. Fortunately, "The stepping-stones are within each of us. Don't look outside for gratification, look inside. Inside is your guru, your God, whatever name you'd like to use. Your strength is all your intuition, your voice from within. And if you can't trust that, where are you? Your strength is not in your thinking mind but rather in your spirit. That has immeasurable strength. You might find yourself in a predicament in your life, and all you have to do is go within, go inside. I had a stroke, which affected my brain. I just went inside to save myself. I have a guru. You have a guru, too. Not in India. It's a guide, a companion in your life, and he'll remind you what you are and guide you back inside. You can only find this being within. He comes into your imagination, which is where he'll meet you. Your imagination is healthy; just go into it."

There was so much to percolate, to think through. It's no secret that I've struggled with drugs and alcohol in my life, and much of the work I do is with people who've suffered in similar ways, with substances, depression, self-harm, and other self-destructive behaviors. I know so many people—myself included—who change their lives for the better for a while, but who then return to these self-destructive patterns, knowing full well that they will not result in anything good.

Ram Dass had a powerful suggestion for how we can protect ourselves from returning to self-defeating behaviors. It was simple and yet perfect:

Stay in the present moment.

In the present moment, we're not an addict or an alcoholic—that's our past, even if it was one minute ago, one second ago. That's why the motto "one day at a time" works. That's why when I'm asked, "How long have you been clean for?" I respond, "Today." Relapsing is getting stuck in our past habits and behaviors. Ram Dass cautioned against getting stuck there or even thinking about them too much. "The past is the past. I know that there are traumatic things in the past, but you are a new person every moment. Just now. Just now. Just now. Just now. *Ah* . . . Addictions are a manifestation from karma. But now, in this moment, you're a new person. The soul has no addictions except the one addiction to go to God. If you've gotten into your soul, you are free of addictions. Go into your soul and be free."

Wow! This utterly fucking resonated and gave me a whole new meaning to "Be here now."

PRACTICE

Be Here Now

Okay, this isn't an officially licensed or sanctioned meditation, but it will indeed help you to be here now, so in keeping with the spirit of this chapter, I figured why not. This is a two-part, go-to practice I often use when I find myself feeling stressed, anxious, or (insert any other unpleasant human experience here). The beauty is that the practice can be done in as little as one to two minutes (although it certainly can be used for longer if need be).

This practice is a four/seven/eight-breath count that I learned about from Dr. Andrew Weil. It is recommended that you do four rounds twice daily, once upon awakening and once before going to bed. According to Dr. Weil, the practice takes time to have a deep and lasting effect, but "the theory is that by imposing certain rhythms on the breath with your voluntary system, gradually these are induced in the involuntary system. And that comes with time, so it's the regularity of doing it that counts."[2]

That's not to say that you won't experience some initial benefits from this practice right away! It's great for immediate help with stress, anxiety, and panic. It's also a wonderful way for those who struggle with insomnia to fall (and stay) asleep at night. I speak from experience. The practice is as follows:

- You can do this in any position. Standing, seated, lying down—all are fine.

- Since this is a form of yogic breathing, you're asked to keep the tip of your tongue touching the ridge of tissue in front of your upper front teeth. It's said that this completes an energy circuit, but what do I know? I'm just trying to share this as accurately as possible.
- Begin by inhaling through your nose quietly to a count of four (using a count of "one one-thousand, two one-thousand").
- Next, hold your breath for a count of seven (again using a count of "one one-thousand").
- Then exhale through your mouth, pursing your lips, for eight counts, making a *swoosh* noise while doing so.
- After you've finished your exhalation, immediately begin the next inhalation, and repeat the cycle four times.

The most important part of this practice is doing it in cycles of four rounds, twice per day (or more throughout the day, if you'd like), while keeping the breath ratio of four/seven/eight as consistent as possible. I believe that's what Michael Scott would call a "win-win-win." (If you don't know who Michael Scott is, please, please, please do yourself a favor and watch season one of *The Office* right now. Seriously, forget about reading this book and go. It's streaming on Netflix for your convenience.)

6

THE PLACE WHERE THE SWEETNESS HURTS

CONVERSATION WITH MICHAEL TAFT

I first encountered Michael Taft through his website Deconstructing Yourself. As I began reading his articles, they resonated for me—especially his down-to-earth and accessible manner. Next I devoured his books—*The Mindful Geek* and *Nondualism*—and I was hooked. I couldn't wait to speak with him!

Because mindfulness is used in so many contexts, from a way to sell overpriced athleisure wear to a lifelong study of the Satipatthana Sutta, I thought it would be good to start with Michael's definition. He told me, "Technically, mindfulness is a skill that one has when doing Vipassana Buddhist practice, but for the basic definition, we can say it's a meditation in which you're having a moment-by-moment awareness of sensory phenomena, or sensory experience. For example, you're feeling your feet right now in the present moment, but feeling the sensory experience of having feet—that's mindfulness meditation. It can apply to any sensory experience, including internal experiences like thinking.

"I'd add that it's nonjudgmental awareness, because you're allowing whatever arises to arise without trying to control or change it. Let's say you're feeling your feet in the present moment, which is mindfulness meditation, but one foot feels good and the other one hurts. You're treating those both equally; you're not trying to ignore the painful one and move toward the pleasurable one or vice versa, necessarily. That's the basic idea of mindfulness."

He cautioned me: "We have some misconceptions about mindfulness that come from other forms of meditation. There are two I constantly hear from my students. One is that when you're mindful, you're not supposed to have any thoughts, which is not true. The other is that you are supposed to feel only joy, bliss, or peace, or at least total relaxation. That may be true for some forms of concentration meditations, but it's not true for mindfulness. What's great about that is that it means you can be mindful even when you're having an incredibly shitty day, when nothing is pleasant, when nothing is relaxed, when everything is chaotic and intense. You can still pay moment-by-moment attention to that experience nonjudgmentally, and have quite an intense and powerful and fruitful mindfulness meditation."

This was such an important point. A common misperception is that it's all love and light—meditation is supposed to be a blissed-out experience. When I was first looking for ways out of drug and alcohol addiction and stumbled onto the meditation path (literally), I was terrible at it. I'd sit there for twenty or thirty minutes of nonstop monkey-mind chatter, barely catching myself to come back to the moment. Gradually I accrued some actual presence, but instead of its becoming nirvana, the floodgates opened and the wreckage of my past started to surface, and I was, like, "Whoa, whoa, what is this bullshit? Where's the good stuff?" I learned, however, that this is a cathartic and healing part of the practice, even though it feels terrible when it's happening. Telling it like it is—the raw and ragged truth instead of watered-down and fluffy clouds of promise—doesn't sell a lot of books, because that's not what most people want to hear, but they should. Seriously. Especially if they're looking for genuine healing, not just the five-quick-steps-to-make-everything-perfect, cotton-candy meditation bullshit that's sold at alarming rates to people when they first start looking.

Michael agreed. "It's not what we want to hear, but it is often what we need, especially when challenging material comes up that we need to work on. Peace and bliss meditations are best when you're alone in a silent cave, but if you want to have a practice that changes your life, a practice that you can take into the real world, it must include both positive and negative, pleasant and unpleasant experiences. The peace-and-bliss type of meditation (which I love) is a hothouse flower—you spend months on long, silent retreats to get there. Mindfulness is more industrial, more rubber meets the road, kind of 'Let's go take the stuff into the shit, into the trenches,' and it can be powerful in those situations. I love it for that robust quality it has."

I liked how he opened mindfulness up. I've found that reminding people in workshops I give that when you're not meditating on Buddha or Christ (not that there's anything wrong with that), but rather approaching meditation in this way, mindfully with the body, it can be more accessible, especially to the skeptics, which I'm happy to say there's no shortage of. I mean, think about it—there's nothing inherently Buddhist or Christian about our bodies or our breath. When we were born, we were born as human beings, and when we practice mindfulness in this way, it becomes a human practice, nothing more and nothing less. This led to another question I had about meditation. In the first chapter of *The Mindful Geek*, Michael writes: "Can mindfulness meditation truly deliver, or is all this some New Age marketing scam?"[1] The New Age marketing scam is something I've spent a good deal of time thinking (and writing) about. *Does* mindfulness meditation work? What's the deal?

Michael spoke to my concerns. "When we look online, we find many claims made for mindfulness and for meditation. Even when we study some of the research, it sounds like nothing could be *that* good, right? There are promises that mindfulness can do everything, and although that probably isn't the case, what's fascinating is that, with some caveats, mindfulness *can* do amazing stuff. That's because it's such a fundamental skill. Mindfulness works on such a basic level of our minds, such a basic level of our psychologies, that it can affect a lot of different areas of behavior or systems of the brain, leading to a variety of positive effects across the board—things like increased concentration, increased creativity, better connection with other humans, more calm, and the like."

I know my way around a meditation cushion, and this was all cool and true, but here's where I found his words getting particularly interesting: "For the most part, especially in the psychological or corporate levels of mindfulness teaching, mindfulness is undersold in a way that's fascinating. We go out of our way to show that it will calm us down and make us more creative and productive and a better team member and have more emotional empathy and intelligence, but we're not saying much about how it can fundamentally restructure our understanding of the world and our own lives. We talk a lot about how mindfulness will help people attain their goals, but then we're not talking a lot about how it will make us *reconsider* our goals and even *who's having goals* in the first place."

Cool, right? People can see how the practice can help them meet deadlines and reach their goals, but miss how it can help them in their own humanity. Michael likes the idea of change from within the system—and you can't get more *within* than corporate America. "That's a meditation viewpoint: 'Let's go in and help transform these corporate cultures, which are such a big part of our lives. Let's help to change them into something that's maybe a little more compassionate and thoughtful as well as productive.'"

Pairing "meditation" with "corporate" wasn't Michael's only unusual juxtaposition. In *The Mindful Geek*, he focused on meditation *as*

technology. "If we think of technology as a systematized understanding of a subject or area, meditation—and even mindfulness—qualifies as a type of technology. It's a case of knowing that if you try X and Y, you'll often get a specific result: Z. That's the most basic understanding of technology, and meditation fulfills that idea." Michael was taking a page out of the books of Timothy Leary, Robert Anton Wilson, and the cyberpunks by looking at these as technologies. "Things like mindfulness and meditation are ancient brain-hacking technologies that can be used to do some cool, useful, and helpful things. That's why, in writing a book called *The Mindful Geek* that's geared toward people in the STEM—science, technological, engineering, and math—communities, I thought it would be great to use that word 'technology' because it gives a different flavor, a different feel for what we're doing when we're meditating."

It makes sense to meet people where they are, and even though I don't work in the corporate world, his use of terminology didn't throw me at all. Maybe it's generational? Everyone on the planet can benefit from this stuff.

Michael kept me from getting too carried away. "I would qualify that and say there are certainly people who might need a specialized form of practice. If someone is undergoing a psychotic experience or has a serious mental illness, it might take a while to have the effect that we're looking for, but yes, most people could use a nice dose of mindfulness."

To take that thought further, I asked about another passage from *The Mindful Geek,* in which he presented the three elements, a meditation theory called CCA: concentration, clarity, and acceptance. Could he tell me more about it?

It turns out that it's an adaptation of a theory from Michael's teacher, Shinzen Young, who refers to the third element as equanimity instead of acceptance. Michael opted for acceptance over equanimity—which may be perceived by some as a "weird" Buddhist word—making the thought more accessible. "The two qualities—concentration and acceptance—are interesting. They go together in almost every form of meditation, whether it's Buddhist or Hindu, whether it's a concentration practice or Vipassana practice. You want to have a modicum of concentration, of being able to bring your attention to what you want to bring it to, when you want to bring it, for as much time as you want to bring it. In other words, concentration is paying attention to what you want to pay attention to.

"Then there's acceptance, or equanimity, and that is the nonjudgmental part. You are accepting whatever is happening in a very matter-of-fact way. If your foot hurts, your foot hurts right now; it doesn't have to be a big deal. If a weird, fucked-up, difficult, unpleasant thought is arising—well, that thought is arising, and you say okay. That's the acceptance. When you put concentration and acceptance together, you can get some very powerful meditation going.

"However, the combination of concentration and acceptance is still a little broad. There are many different forms of meditation that fall under or employ these two features. What makes mindfulness special is the aspect of sensory clarity, wherein we try to deconstruct the sensory elements of experience in a very fine-grained way. Let's go back to the foot. When people meditate on their foot, it's not 'Hey, there's my foot, check, done'; it's a matter of getting into the details of the feelings, and then the details of the details of the feeling, to the nth degree. That's sensory clarity. If you have concentration and acceptance going, that's good, but when you get into that sensory clarity element, that is when the meditation starts to go deep, deep, deep, deep.

"It's simply taking the thread of sensory experience and following it. It's like unraveling a sweater—you keep following that strand of wool all the way to the end, and at the end, the sweater isn't there anymore and you have a skein of yarn. In the same way, if you take the thread of sensory experience of the feeling of your foot all the way to the end, it will unravel into emptiness."

Michael had succeeded in expanding my understanding of mindfulness, so now I wanted to apply it to recovery. We're all recovering from something, so how can mindfulness help us to truly heal? How can it lead to recovery from whatever dis-ease we're suffering in our lives?

"This is a question I could go on about for a long time. The fundamental point is that mindfulness asks us to confront reality. This is the beginning and the end of how it helps us recover—from drugs or alcohol, emotional abuse, physical trauma or disease, or even the suffering of the everyday vagaries of existence. I've worked with mindfulness in this capacity with thousands of people and seen truly beautiful and inspiring results. We tend to want to think about anything but the main issue, because we know it hurts and has caused us a lot of pain. At the core of all of this is whatever behavior or whatever difficulty was there in the first place."

To counteract this, we use drugs or Netflix or sex to numb ourselves. "These short-term coping mechanisms are things we absorbed by osmosis along the way. We absorbed them because they work a little bit, but the problem is that they all have downsides, and some downsides are bigger than others. An example of a large downside with almost no upside would be sniffing glue. It doesn't do that much and it doesn't do it for very long, but it will destroy your brain—yet there are people who use this as a coping mechanism." But it's not just drugs. "People can live their whole lives narcissistically self-absorbed in their own wonderfulness while ignoring their own pain and shortcomings and the real needs of others. A lot of people get a long way on that coping strategy, and yet it also has major downsides. The beautiful thing about mindfulness is that it says we're not going to pretend that it didn't happen, we're not going to ignore the pain you're in. We're going to look at that clearly, and at the same time, we're going to look at your strategy and how it does and doesn't work, and think about other ways that might work better."

Let's say we're doing what Michael suggested: We're addressing the core of the problem—the pain and whatever else is coming up for us. What then? How do we engage and work with that?

"The first thing I want to come back to is that mindfulness allows you to see the core issue clearly. It's not enough to say 'Yes, that exists.' You've got to get in there and notice the details. Once you do that, it gives you the means to move forward, because you're no longer resisting it. A big part of people's coping mechanisms is the desire not to engage pain—we want to move away from it—but mindfulness, from the beginning, is giving us the skill to engage it with at least a little bit of acceptance, and later with a lot of acceptance. If you're already touching your pain and not resisting it and in fact meeting it with acceptance, you might already be past your addiction or bad behavior. It's that move of first acknowledging pain and then accepting it—deeply and in detail—that is the essence of the practice.

"The short version is that you should approach the pain one tiny baby step at a time, taking on as much as you can handle, but not too much. That's where kindness and compassion for yourself come in. Often people call this loving-kindness, but I don't like that term. To me, that's not the right translation or even the right mood for what works. What works is kindness. What happens is people, particularly people who have a long history of trauma and perhaps addiction, have a lot of material to beat themselves up about. If you're going to add 'I can't accept my pain' to the list, it's not going to help.

"We must be extremely gentle with ourselves in this process and make sure that we're not overwhelmed. Make sure that we're not re-traumatizing ourselves or beating ourselves up. All it takes is sitting with kindness—that's the whole thing. Sitting with it with kindness and caring, and the minute it's too much, the minute it feels like it's doing damage, then you back off. The thing is, it's going to hurt. I don't mean that you should back off the minute it hurts. You've got to be willing to sit with some pain, but it's when the pain is being mean to yourself or overwhelming, or somehow too much."

In other words, directly acknowledge the pain or suffering in an experiential way. "It's not enough to say 'Yes, I'm in pain.' You must acknowledge and experience it. Then, little by little, accept it. To me, that's the entirety of the path. Simple, but not necessarily easy at all."

I couldn't get enough of *The Mindful Geek*. I had one more excerpt I loved and had to share:

> *When I first began teaching meditation, I thought that nothing could be easier than asking students to relax. Who wouldn't like that? Boy, did my students teach me differently. Asking them to relax elicited a variety of negative responses. Some people got upset, anxious, or angry in feeling that they were doing it wrong. Others noticed that they were not relaxed, and got freaked out by how stressed they felt. Still others felt that they couldn't relax, no matter how hard they tried. Sometimes the response I got was basically, "You want me to relax?! Fuck You!"[2]*

Why do so many people have this reaction when they first come to meditation?

Michael said, "It's that we live in a stressed-out society, and the triggers—fear, oversaturation, overwhelm, and things like that—are driving the stress. If people are working through a lot of issues with something like substance addiction or some psychological material, there's a strong need to not go there and be distracted from it. Simply being asked to relax is like saying, 'Um, hey, get well.' On top of it, we don't live in a very relaxing society, and it's hard for people. You'd think it would be easy, but this is the same reason many people have difficulty falling asleep at night—all the bed wants from you is for you to relax."

This brought up something that I still deal with quite often—coping with *too much* feeling, that experience of being emotionally overwhelmed that can occur while meditating (or, honestly, at any given moment of the day). Could Michael talk about that and what meditators can do when it happens?

The initial prognosis wasn't great: "It will continue to happen. I don't believe there's a healthy state of a human being where you don't have emotions, including negative emotions, and there will always be the possibility of overwhelm that's called life." Fortunately, it gets better: "There's nothing wrong with that. If overwhelm happens, whether it's on the cushion or walking around, we need to be able to work with that. The number-one thing is acceptance. 'Okay, I'm having an overwhelming emotional experience right now. I'm freaking out.' That's not bad, and that doesn't make me a shitty meditator—that makes me a person. That's fine.

"Beyond that, you should realize that we spend our days trying to suppress emotions, especially negative emotions. We're trying to hold them in. You can feel it because emotions are bodily sensations. We try to contain them, squeeze them down, and then distract, distract, distract. That's the social method. 'Let's watch a movie instead of feeling those feelings.' When you're meditating and you're more open, you start to feel it more, or sometimes stuff gets to be too big to ignore. You may start to freak out, but the main thing to understand is the difference between the physical part of the emotion and the ideas about it. Most of the overwhelm and freak-out part is from the ideas about the emotions, because the actual body sensations, no matter how uncomfortable they get, aren't that bad. They're not as bad as hitting your thumb with a hammer.

"It's the reaction to the emotion and the ideas about the emotion that start to turn it into something that's difficult. Number one is noticing the difference between the body sensation of the emotion and the thoughts about it. Once you start tracking those separately, it cuts the feedback loop between 'I'm having a feeling in my body' and 'Oh my God! I'm having a feeling; I'm thinking about it and freaking out,' which causes more feeling to happen, which causes more freaking out to happen. They're tied together, so when you start tracking body sensations, emotion, and thoughts separately—*detangling* those, to use Shinzen's term—you stop the feedback and they're easier to handle."

This talk of detangling brought me to thoughts of nondual awareness versus nondualism, something else I wanted to discuss. In his book *Nondualism*, Michael wrote:

Nondual awareness is an experience.

Nondualism is a philosophy that talks about that experience and its meaning.

These two things are very different, and confusing them can lead to all sorts of problems.[3]

How would he elaborate on that point so we could avoid confusion and subsequent problems?

"Twenty years ago, I noticed a giant resurgence of interest in nondualism in America, particularly with Neo-Advaita derived from the teachings of Ramana Maharshi, but also in the Buddhist world. What was interesting, especially in the Neo-Advaita community but also in general, was that people were giving instructions and talking about their nondual experience, which was cool and a powerful teaching, but I noticed that there seemed to be a fundamental lack of any understanding about the history of people doing this and the philosophy behind it. There was also an active aggression toward talking about the history or the philosophy. I understand that we want to get people out of their conceptual bubbles and heads and into their nondual experience, but I felt that was happening at the expense of thousands of years of experience and knowledge. It doesn't somehow ding my nondual experience to talk about nondual philosophy. I got fed up with this anti-intellectual strain of nondual teaching in America."

I always found this fascinating. Could he talk about the ways in which these seemingly contradictory statements were pointing to the same thing?

Michael explained that the teachings of nondualism come from various Upanishads, the sacred Indian texts that emerged before Buddhism and modern Hinduism, around 800 BCE to 500 BCE. One of the best-known mantras from the Upanishads is Tat Tvam Asi, which means "thou art that" or "you are it." Michael told me, "What that basically means—and this is a fundamental statement of nondualism—is, if you're looking at a chair, you're a chair. If you're feeling a breeze, you're the breeze. If you see the sun, you're the sun.

Thou art that. You are it. There's no difference between you and that thing.

"We could contrast this with neti neti, which means 'not it' or 'not this, not that,' and is another way of teaching nondualism. It says no matter what you see, hear, feel, you are not that—you are not the chair, you are not the breeze or the sun or whatever. Tat Tvam Asi and neti neti sound like diametric opposites. Which is it? This is where the teachings point to the essence of the matter:

"*It's simple, honestly.* Your brain is a bunch of meat inside a bone cage. It's sealed in a box, and it's got peripheral devices telling it about the outside world—our eyes and ears, etc. The brain is receiving those signals from the peripheral devices and decoding them and assembling them into a picture of a self and a world. If you understand that, you'll get everything you need to know about nondualism.

"Because if that's the case, then the brain's experience of the outside world, its sights and sounds, and the inside worlds, the feelings of your body and thoughts, all arise in the same generated model of the exterior and interior world all at once. I'll put it another way: It's a virtual world you build in your head. It's like being in a first-person shooter game—the avatar, the weapon, the battlefield, and the guy's head that you're blowing off are all on a screen, it's all the same thing. What these two sayings from the Upanishads are trying to tell us is, you can think of yourself as being everything on that screen equally, or nothing on the screen completely. It means the same thing, because everything that's arising in sensory experience is activity or signals in sensory experience. Every thought or feeling of being *you* is equivalent to every external experience of the sun rising or a tree in the wind, because it's all sensory signals. From a nondual perspective, you're either identified with all the sensory signals equally or noticing that you are simply the awareness of those sensory signals and are none of the content—not your thoughts, not your feelings, not any of it."

That was pretty much the best description of Vedic nondualism I'd ever heard. How would that look in the Western traditions?

Michael helped me see how it's the same thing. "Nobody owns human experience." I'm just going to repeat that because it's so fucking great: *Nobody owns human experience.* Okay, back to Michael, who said, "People everywhere at all times have the capacity to notice nondual experience. In Western tradition, Judaism, Christianity, Islam, there are certainly plenty of people having nondual experience and talking about nondual experience, particularly like some of the well-known Christian saints, the Hasidic or cabalistic masters in Judaism, and the Sufis in Islam. They describe this experience, and one of the interesting things about nondual experience is that it doesn't have any problem talking about God. You can have a theistic nondualism as easily as you can have a nontheistic dualism, but in certain ways Western religion is friendly toward nondualism."

Okay, then—so what can nondualism teach us about healing and potentially avoiding relapse altogether or returning to self-destructive behaviors? Is it even possible?

Before he could give me a full answer, Michael wanted to define relapse. "My view on any bad behavior or addiction is simple. *It's not a problem unless it's a problem.* Everything we do in life is in one way or another a habit, and habits themselves are not the problem. It's not bad to have the habit of brushing your teeth. It's not bad to have the habit of checking the rearview mirror while you're driving on the highway. Why don't people call those addictions? Because they're not a problem, they're a benefit. To me, relapse indicates returning to a behavior that is destructive, that is causing issues in your life. You know it, you know it's bad, you know that it's going to cause trouble, and yet, for whatever reason, you decide to go back in and engage that behavior again. It's that simple."

I needed to unpack that! I've experienced several relapses, the last one almost killing me. I know many other people who've struggled with relapse for years—not just with drugs and alcohol, but with food, shopping, and relationships as well. From Michael's point of view, what's happening when we decide to go back to those behaviors? To stay in the bad habits?

"It's when the pain gets to be too much. The coping mechanisms for working with the pain are not enough. Instead of reaching out for help, the person hits a critical moment of self-pity. At this point we should distinguish between self-compassion—which is extremely helpful, useful, and important—and self-pity. Self-pity is when you can't take the pain anymore; you need it to stop immediately, regardless of what it does to you or others. That's the difference. If it was *self-compassion*, you would take an action that would be good for you, good for the future you, and good for others. It's being nice to you as a person. In self-pity, the pain becomes too much and there's a part of you that feels, like, 'Fuck it.' Self-pity is the moment where you sell yourself out and don't care what happens to you. It's that selling yourself out that is crucial to pay attention to, because there's good stuff available in that moment when you're fully acknowledging the pain, when you're fully truthful and real about how much it hurts. That's when you're also understanding that you want to be nice to yourself.

"That's the whole point—to be nice to yourself. For example, in a twelve-step program, you might call your sponsor; that's a self-compassionate act, and you know your future self is going to be happy about that. Plus, you know that person will sit with you in that pain and not try to pretend it doesn't hurt. That's an act of self-compassion. The self-pity will say, 'Fuck it, I don't care,' and what's weird about self-pity is that it's a form of self-hatred. The compound includes the word 'pity,' but it's not giving a fuck about yourself and believing the story that you suck, that you don't deserve to feel better, that everything that's happened to you is your fault and responsibility, and that you're an unlovable piece of shit. That's what self-pity is—the opposite of compassion.

"You've got to get real when that's happening. Notice that the minute it comes up, you start thinking about bad behaviors. You're going to want to drink or go to a whorehouse or do something that's probably not that good for your life, because you're feeling bad *right now* and you're a piece of shit anyway. When that comes up, even in its most background, ephemeral, barely there way, you want to look at that and start to deconstruct it in the mindfulness manner. What images is it made of? What mental talk is it made of? What emotions is it made of? How do those emotions feel in the body? Then get a little psychological with it. Is any of what you're saying to yourself objectively true? How many of those things happened when you were a little kid that you had no control over? Stuff like that."

As Michael was talking about becoming honest with yourself in these different ways, a quote from the Big Book of Alcoholics Anonymous came to mind. It's one that I've often feared was applicable to me:

> *Rarely have we seen a person fail who has thoroughly followed our path. Those who do not recover are people who cannot or will not completely give themselves to this simple program, usually men and women who are constitutionally incapable of being honest with themselves. There are such unfortunates. They are not at fault; they seem to have been born that way. They are naturally incapable of grasping and developing a manner of living which demands rigorous honesty. Their chances are less than average.*[4]

That popped up because of what Michael said about how we need to be honest with ourselves. Did he believe that there are some people who are constitutionally incapable of doing that?

Michael pressed pause on the word "constitutionally." "Does that mean it's in their DNA? Does that mean it's in their upbringing? Unfortunately, what they mean is something about your soul or your essence. We know that dealing with things as essences is the way you get into trouble. Dealing with people as having essences is the way you cause conflict. I would reject any statement that's essentialist like that. More specifically, there are people who have a much, much harder time with that kind of honesty. Maybe because they're traumatized and triggered. If they work hard enough, they will make progress, but remember, progress means one minute at a time. It doesn't mean that they're going to rack up an impressive number of years instantly. It's that in this moment, they're not trying to kill themselves, either quickly or slowly, but in fact are doing something positive.

"I should also say, regarding addiction and relapse, if you're feeling like you've got to have a drink, that's the thing to look at and work with and not resist. Because resisting blows it up. My deepest, closest friends are twelve-step people, and the program has saved their lives, but it is one of 'You must resist at all costs,' and the thing is, *mindfulness is not about resistance*. Real healing is not about resistance. The whole resistance piece is crucial at the stage of harm reduction. When people are most vulnerable, the best thing to do is to tell them never to do it again, especially drug addicts, because they might die the very next time they shoot up. I appreciate that and accept it, yet if all you're doing is resisting, the urge is always going to be there. *Always.* I know people who were junkies thirty years ago and they've never shot up again, but the urge is there, and twelve-step programs tell them that's normal. It is when you don't go in and deal with the basis of the urge to begin with."

The difference is sobriety versus recovery. Sobriety is remaining abstinent from the substances—white-knuckling it and so on—whereas recovery is a life lived thriving and healing. "I'm all about recovery," Michael added. "The recovery part is going in and touching that urge. That might mean sitting with it in a very deep way, but only when you feel very solid."

This brought us back to nondualism and relapse. Michael hopped right on this. "The most powerful thing that nondualism can offer is that no matter what's going on with you, there's always a part of you that's completely sane, completely healed and healthy, completely uplifted and inspired. It might not be your whole experience. It might be only a teeny-tiny part of your experience. There's a part of you that is

in fact perfectly fine and never was anything but. From a nondual perspective, you have access to that at any moment. It's right there, right
now, completely open and radiant and accepting. Even though I say it's
inside you, it's also outside you. The entire world right now, the beauty
of nature, the depth and brilliance of the sky, the touch of the ground
under your feet—all of it is a radical sanity and openness and wholeness and is present and available. If you can begin to relate to that at all,
it will provide a resource unparalleled in its ability to help you stabilize,
heal, and then grow."

That sounded good to me. How would we implement that? Especially someone who's not that familiar with nonduality? Is there some
simple action we can take?

Michael brought us full circle back to mindfulness. "It's as simple as finding something beautiful in nature and sitting with it. Even
if it's a rock or a flower or a beautiful sound, or maybe your dog. The
thing that people run up against is that they're filled with pain and
negativity—and understandably so; there's no judgment about that,
it's the way of the world we're living in, and the way we're built. I often
hear people say, 'Well, I can't find any of that—there's nothing beautiful.' I want to challenge that and say, 'Really? There's not even one
thing in the whole world right now that you find beautiful or simply
peaceful or somehow sane? Not one thing?' If you investigate your experience, you'll find there is *something*. If there isn't anything in the real
world, then imagine something. I've done this with people who truly
believed there was nothing in their entire environment or life, but they
could feel beauty and love from a Pokémon character like Pikachu—
and they were serious. That's fine. There's a way that this can come
off sounding completely like bullshit or Pollyannaish, and I want to
emphasize that it's not like you're somehow ignoring the difficulties
of life. Instead, for the moment, you're refocusing your attention on
something that is true or beautiful or good or sane in some way. Then
you can sit with it and observe it in whatever way makes sense to you
and drink that in.

"It starts out as a simple contact with things and expands as you get better at it into a mindful exploration, almost an aesthetic sensory openness that becomes artistic. The beauty of the color and the richness and depth of the sound. If you get absorbed enough in that mood, as more and more of your attention is poured upon this object and as you open to it more and more, eventually it's not an object anymore, it's you. That's how we go from something that may sound Pollyanna-ish, like 'look at a pretty cloud,' to having a true nondual experience of cloudness that heals our spirit from the inside out . . . or from the outside in."

The "Pollyannaish" struck a chord with me. It's something I bring up a lot when I teach and write—you've got to try this shit! It may seem too good to be true, but give it a go with an open heart. If you do that and think it's still bullshit afterward, that's cool. I won't argue that with you, and if anything, I'd respect you for giving it a fair shot. Thing is, more times than not, when people *do* give it a shot, they see that it does work.

Michael had a well-tuned bullshit detector of his own. "I come from a very punk-rock, fuck-you-asshole background, and nobody is quicker than me to think this all sounds like a bunch of trash. To mistrust it, and to criticize it and make fun of it. But what I found was that when somebody challenged me to feel good or positive about something, it wasn't that I thought that this was stupid—I simply couldn't do it. I couldn't do it. That to me was a real wake-up call. Like, what the fuck is wrong with me? It's one thing to think it's not cool or that it's a scam, but it's another to not even be able to contact something in that open, fresh, innocent, beautiful way. I began working with it and had some strong experiences that opened me up to it, but I also did some stuff that I previously would have found unimaginable. I tried going to kirtan, and if you don't know what kirtan is, it's Hindu chanting to God, and it's about the most syrupy, sweet, relentlessly positive thing you can imagine. I found that the sweetness hurt. I was so cynical and ironic and mistrustful of that energy that it hurt. That place where that sweetness hurts, that's the place that needs healing. I couldn't take very much of it at first, but gradually I got into it more and more and noticed that a larger and larger part of me could take in something that was innocent and sweet. It didn't have a dark side."

It's funny that Michael said that. The first time I heard a kirtan album, it was one from Krishna Das, and I'd been turned on to him by Ram Dass through either a dharma talk or a book. I'll never forget sitting in my apartment and playing the CD I'd taken out of my local library. The reason I'll never forget it is because I had almost the same exact experience then as I did the first time I was at a friend's house and he put on a hardcore record—both punk rock and kirtan cut to the core of me. It hit me in the heart in a very deep and passionate way. Now, kirtan is different from punk, but depending on which punk or hardcore band you're talking about, there's often a lot of sincere heart stuff going on there, too. Much passion and raw truth. It was amazing to me that I had the same experience with both of those genres of music; I'll never forget it. Then, lo and behold, who did I run into a few months ago during a Krishna Das kirtan in Maui but none other than Rick *fucking* Rubin, the legendary producer who's worked with everyone from Slayer to Metallica to the Beastie Boys and Johnny Cash, and Krishna Das, too.

Michael had his punk-rock adventures to share as well. "I would go to shows in the eighties with, like, the Cro-Mags, and after the show they were chanting Hare Krishna at everyone, and they meant it. There's always been a strong connection between punk and kirtan. One of the ways we got involved was going to get free food, because the Krishnas would feed you. If they fed you, they made you sing kirtan, so it was fascinating how many gutter punks went for some rice and dal and ended up loving Krishna core or Krishna music."

Absolutely. I covered the first Warped Tour for an indie zine I was doing at the time called *Speak Only When Spoken To* (it was so bad), and one of my old favorite bands, Shelter, was on the tour, and I was backstage. Sure enough, there they were, cooking food and giving it away to everyone for free. Behind them was a basketball hoop, where Chino Moreno from Deftones was playing with Anthony Civarelli (CIV), Chaka Malik from Orange 9mm, and some of the guys from Quicksand and Sick of It All. It was a pretty surreal scene, especially since I was only fifteen at the time. It's also fair to say that I'll never forget the smell (and taste) of that delicious rice and dal.

We both agreed there were lots of different avenues to meditation. Another big one for Michael was drawing and painting. "There's a way when you're looking at something to draw it, it loses its 'object-ness' and instead becomes a collection of qualities—like shape, light, space, texture, things like that. This is what you're doing with mindfulness, with everything. That way of seeing, for me, drawing things and getting into that way of seeing, allowed me to contact a beautiful truth of the thusness in everyday things. It's possible to become absorbed in that if you work with it long enough, but even on the simplest level, where it's almost a distraction from your pain, if you continue to work with it, you'll notice that that beauty and that truth and even thusness and openness coming from that object you're drawing will begin to work on you inside and begin to heal you."

In my experience, it's not just the making of art but the magnificence of life that can creep up on you at any moment—the beauty and truth and thusness that is all that there is and simply waits patiently for our gaze to fall upon it, whether we're rocking the fuck out to 1980s hardcore classics or looking over the Grand Canyon in all its glory. It's all real and beautiful and sometimes too much to bear (in the best possible way), so who can blame you for looking away for a while? Just don't forget to allow your heart to be set ablaze from time to time. Everything in moderation, I suppose.

PRACTICE

Mindfulness 101

Michael took me through the basic steps of mindfulness practice, and by basic, I mean *basic* (in the best sense of the word). Of all the meditation practices, it's the one I find myself returning to most frequently when I need a grounding and reorientation into the present moment. Give it a go and see for yourself. The beauty is that it can be done pretty much anytime and anywhere—for example, sitting at your desk at work, on a long-ass plane ride cross-country, or waiting for that friend who's habitually late when you meet for dinner (you know, *that* friend). The instructions are super-simple, but the one caveat I'd add is that if it is possible to close your eyes, I find that helps you to eliminate unnecessary external distraction and go deeper into the practice. Let's go.

- Assume the position. Get into a comfortable posture. It helps if you keep your back straight.
- Turn your attention to your feet, the sensation of first one foot and then the other. Think the word "body" or "body sensation."
- Feel your left foot. Just that. Don't think about it, don't imagine it, and don't visualize it. Feel it and then label the feeling ("body") and let it go.
- Move on to the right foot and do the same thing. Connect, don't reject.

- Keep doing this, moving up your body—your ankles, calves, knees, hips, belly, lower back, chest, spine, one arm and then the other, one hand and then the other, shoulders, neck, face, head. Contact the sensation there nonjudgmentally in the present moment, label it, and keep going.
- Pause and experience the sensation of your entire body.
- If you're digging this and want to keep at it, begin with the top of your head and work your way back down to your feet.

7

THE LOVE THAT ROLLS UP ITS SLEEVES AND GETS MUDDY

CONVERSATION WITH SERA BEAK

I was first turned on to the work of Sera Beak by the editor we shared while I was working on my second book, *Everything Mind*. Within five minutes of our first Skype conversation I knew she was a soul sister. We connected at the level of raw vulnerability in sharing ourselves as well as our passion for our life's calling, which could be summed up as showing up and helping others to heal in whatever way we can.

In Sera's books and talks, she often refers to the soul or inner wisdom, especially in regard to recovering from any self-destructive behavior. The first thing I wanted to know was how we connect with our soul or inner wisdom. Sera reminded me that this paradox is almost a spiritual cliché. "It's simple to connect to our soul, our inner wisdom, but so many of us throw a bunch of things in front of that—things that have happened to us or that we've done to others. Or life has made us doubt our inner wisdom and our ability to receive it and accurately translate it into our daily lives." She went on to say that this understanding is always with us. We can reach it by closing our eyes, grounding into our body, and feeling our heart, and asking ourselves a simple question. Or allowing ourselves to feel something, thus creating an environment where the inner wisdom can show up. When we do that, "we begin to feel more or sense more. Some of us might even hear something or have a little bit of a vision of some kind." There's a huge range of ways we can allow our soul, our wise inner self, to show up, but the first step, which is easy, is also incredibly difficult: *Shut up, be still, and listen.*

There are as many ways to get to this place as there are spiritual traditions. Sera seeks it out every day, but it wasn't always easy. "Each one of us has our own individual process for how we reconnect with our soul or inner wisdom and how we allow it more freedom in our life. Reaching the point of beginning to trust my own intuition, my own experience, my own inner knowing was a long process for me, because I'm a bit stubborn and thickheaded, too much of a mental case, perhaps because I was academically trained."

I found it fascinating that education and training could be an obstacle to self-understanding instead of an asset. I'm not an academic, not Harvard-trained, as Sera is, but for so much of my life I favored intellect over feeling. I'm the kind of person who wants to understand: I need to figure things out, I need to know. Intellect impeded my spiritual work and kept me stuck in a place where I couldn't grow beyond addictions. I had such a hard time breaking down the wall between head and heart and finding my way to be my true self—the self that didn't want, need, or have to take drugs or overeat—rather than trying to rationally understand it. There's something to be said for the intellect, but at the end of the day, the soul or inner wisdom or whatever you want to call it needs to be directly experienced in a way that has nothing to do with intellectualization.

Paul Brunton, a student of Ramana Maharishi (whom Michael Taft mentioned in the previous chapter regarding nondualism), wrote an amazing book called *The Short Path to Enlightenment*. When I read that title, I was turned off because I thought he meant he had a shortcut to enlightenment, but that isn't what the book is about at all. Brunton distinguishes between the long path and the short path to enlightenment.

The long path is what most "spiritual seekers" take, doing the same practices day in and day out and risking getting stuck. The time spent on the long path is not for nothing, though. It does its work of grinding away whatever it is that we need ground away, like sifting through the root causes of our depression or feelings of low self-esteem. Brunton maintains, however, that these practices are still ego practices, and one cannot see through the illusion of being a separate self from the place of an ego. As Brunton wrote:

> *The end of all his efforts on the Long Path will be the discovery that although the ego can be refined, thinned, and disciplined, it will still remain highly rarefied and extremely subtle. The disciplining of the self can go on and on and on. There will be no end to it. For the ego will always be able to find ways to keep the aspirant busy in self-improvement, thus blinding him to the fact that the self is still there behind all his improvements. For why should the ego kill itself? Yet the enlightenment which is the goal he strives to reach can never be obtained unless the ego ceases to bar the way to it. At this discovery he will have no alternative to, and will be quite ready for, the Short Path.*[1]

Hence, the short path to enlightenment, which Brunton says is self-inquiry. For my own purposes, I describe this as the practice of direct looking, where I see beyond a shadow of a doubt that everything I'm looking for is right here, right now, and all that is left is the direct seeing of this wisdom, soul, or whatever you want to call it. It's not even "me" seeing at this point. It's the see-er, the seeing, and the seen experienced as one, because at that point, ladies and gentlemen, "Chris" has left the building. When I allow my mind to get in the way, I lose the connection. Especially in times when we're repeating destructive behavior, it's important to scrape away all the stuff—the self-loathing, anger, fear—and see our true selves. When we can, we see a glimmer of light on the path out of whatever our situation happens to be.

Sera calls that place the "soul realm," and then she said something that I found to be so fucking beautiful: "The soul realms don't make a lot of sense, but they make a lot of love." Imagine having that understanding, that truth in your heart, when you're beating yourself up for falling off the wagon or perhaps yelling at a loved one?

Sera took it deeper. "I've had so many experiences with my soul when I'm in that space, when nothing feels more honest or natural or true for me, but when I come out of it in some way—a car might honk at me, or I've gotten into an argument or stepped into the collective consciousness of this planet—and suddenly I doubt what I experienced, because it doesn't make sense. Or it doesn't fit into the spiritual status quo or the social mores or whatever we want to call it. Self-doubt has been a big part of my path." Man, I loved that: *Self-doubt has been a big part of my path.* It's the not-knowing as much as—if not more than—the knowing that gets us to the truth we seek.

As she broke it down, Sera said, "Being able to look at how I feel instead of what I think about my experience brings me more into my skin, my body, and my humanity. It opens my heart, even if it's excruciating and painful. I trust what I see in the soul realms. No matter how crazy it might sound to my external ears, my inner ears know when they're hearing the truth. Sifting through and coming up against everything else is a part of the practice."

That's a fundamental belief Sera and I have in common: You've got to find the answer for yourself. Spiritual teachers, friends, mentors, therapists, or experts can be wonderful guides, but at the end of the day, they can give you only *their* answers, not your own. Ruthlessly test and question everything in your experience and find out directly what is and what is not true. Do this unapologetically, which is not easy— it's something I still struggle with. If you step onto this path of direct experience and are sincerely walking it, you're going to experience some crazy shit, but also some miraculous shit. These truths, these direct experiences are undeniable, and being apologetic when talking about them is such a disservice. This, again, has been one of my struggles—I don't intentionally want to offend anyone, and I don't like confrontation. On top of that, when I'm giving a talk or a workshop, particularly with younger people, I picture my younger self listening and reacting to what I'm saying: "This fucking guy is nuts, talking about compassion and loving-kindness. *And* nonduality? How is he not institutionalized right now?" Maybe I wouldn't have been that harsh, but I also wouldn't have been very receptive, either. Yet I appreciate the skeptical attitude many people have toward the whole "spirituality" thing, because there is so much bullshit that comes along with it. It's a fine line to walk.

Sera helped me see another side of this. "I spent much of my life embarrassed by my spiritual passion and my own experiences. Those times when we walk around feeling, sensing what's happening beneath the layers. Or when something opens our heart in a way that makes us feel God or the universe or life coursing through everything. And then looking around and seeing everyone in that moment, buried in their cell phone, or jaded and angry. There can be a sense of embarrassment and apologies." Something shifted for Sera when leadership coach Robert Rabbin, who teaches the Speaking Truthfully workshops, heard one of Sera's talks. She suffers terribly from stage fright, and she shared this with her audience. Afterward, Rabbin called Sera and said, "You need to stop apologizing for who you are." Even though she didn't use those exact words in her talk, he picked up on her message of "sorry I'm like this" as she spoke. "It was a good wake-up call for me. I can't say I'm completely over the stage fright, but it was something that shook me enough to look at why I'm so apologetic and ask myself why I'm embarrassed about my own truth."

Being comfortable in our truth, not to mention our own skin, is something I consider to be a huge act of bravery. In my own experience, I've found so many spiritual teachings and practices to help with this, from loving-kindness meditation to mantra repetition to basic, bare-bones mindfulness breathing. I'll say it again: There is so much bullshit out there that's labeled "spiritual." I understand that there is no right or wrong way, but I wanted Sera's perspective. If there's no right or wrong, what is authentic spirituality and how do we connect with a true spiritual practice?

"Authentic spirituality," according to Sera, "often has an organic quality to it. It feels simple and natural, even if some of the practices can seem a little complex. I often say—because this is my own experience—when I am connected to my soul or when I feel connected to the souls of others or the soul of this planet or the soul of this universe, it predates religion or any techniques or methods or teachers. It predates that shit. It's life living itself. It's a beautiful combination of very wild and natural. It sounds so simple, but the way the human and the Divine crash and crunch into each other—the awkwardness and the grace of that—to me looks and feels authentic. It's not someone trying to be spiritual. And it's not someone who thinks he is only a meat robot. It's someone who understands and is wrestling with and inviting that crazy experience of being both human and Divine.

"That's why authentic spirituality is without pretense. It's not trying to cover anything; it's trying to reveal. It's not trying to be something it's not, whether that means trying to be better than it is or even worse than it is. I can gauge this by the way it makes my body feel. If something opens me and grounds me and allows my feminine body to be what it needs to be and do what it needs to do, that's an indicator to me. Humor is also a good indicator to me. But most of it is something I can't express in words. It's a pinpoint that comes from our heart that we all know when we've hit it, when we see it outside of us, when we're experiencing it as ourselves. We know when it's real—Real with a capital R. It's a huge relief."

That's something I love about Sera's work—that she's not afraid to go into the messiness of this human experience. Many people step onto the spiritual path because they want to avoid those experiences—the pain and heartbreak—but little do they know that if they're being real about their practice, in many cases it will serve to intensify the messiness of being human, at least for a little while. The grace and the grit are two sides of the same coin. Life can fucking suck sometimes. Take, for example, that right now people we love are perhaps sick or dying, or just lost a job or had their heart broken. On the other side of that, perhaps people we love just beat cancer or gave birth to a healthy baby or got a promotion at work or got married to their soul mate. There are two sides of the same coin called life.

Sera showed me that that's why we need to create our own spiritual space. It can be meditation or singing or anything that returns us to our own bodies, calms down our nervous system, and allows us to stand in the world and embrace it. "Not float above it, not try to deny it, not turn away or cloud it with spiritual incense, but walk right into it. Any practice that helps us do that would fall into the category of authentic spirituality. What I love about my own experience and my own soul is that she shoves me back down into my body. She's doesn't allow me to escape or close my eyes. She allows me to rest, relax, and recharge, but she's not interested in my avoiding things. She's interested in my learning how to feel again. That's one of the trickiest parts of becoming human. It's been a huge part of my path, learning how to be okay with being human while also being Divine at the same time. For many of us, it's almost an innate embarrassment that we're both. It's a challenge to bring those together in a way that keeps us fully here—really, really here—while also remembering we have constant, twenty-four-hour access to Divine love, to universal support, to life itself. Anything that tips the scale to one side or the other for too long doesn't feel healthy."

That made me think of a saying I love: "We are spiritual beings having a human experience, but we are also human beings having a spiritual experience. They are indistinguishable." In response to that saying, what did Sera think it meant to accept ourselves fully in all our perfect human imperfections; to take an honest, fearless look at our naked selves and stay there, acknowledging both the frailty and the glory in the same glance?

"Quite honestly, that's the reason I'm here—to do that. It's something I've wrestled with—how to fully accept every aspect of me, or at least the aspects that I'm aware of, and even the ones that I'm not as aware of but can still feel banging around. I don't want to overspiritualize it, but acceptance—total self-acceptance—means we're accepting the parts of us that are very difficult—our shadows, wounds, addictions, pains, jealousies—while simultaneously accepting that we are Divine. How to accept both of those is the biggest revolution we can create, both in our own lives and on this planet. It's something we hear everywhere in the spiritual world and the self-help world: Accept yourself. It's repeated all the time, and as is true with any spiritual platitudes or clichés, we can ignore it or even have some practice around it, but the real profound belly of that feels much bigger. The very reason I came here, the very reason I incarnated as a soul, was to experience both—the Divine and the human. Once we experience it, we can accept, and once we can accept, we can love."

I dug that. It made me think about how I had no problem accepting the shitty aspects of who I was for so many years—the worthless addict or the fat loser—but how it was almost impossible to accept and embrace anything good. Noah Levine (whom I'll introduce you to later in this book) once said something very interesting to me: "People don't always relapse because their lives are shitty, but sometimes because they're going well and a part of them doesn't feel worthy or know how to live with goodness." That fundamental human struggle was something I could relate to. It's underneath almost everything we do. How could we use those times of unworthiness, our difficult life experiences, and the struggles we face as catalysts toward spiritual awakening?

Sera affirmed what many spiritual teachers and traditions have taught—that it's about changing perspectives on that experience—but she put her own spin on it. "I don't think it means that you have to stay in only one perspective, like a spiritual perspective on every single shitty experience. I do think it means developing the flexibility to look through several different lenses at what is happening or has happened to us, to someone else, to the world in general, that feels difficult to deal with.

"What I call soul work, which for me is equivalent to organic spirituality, is about feeling the difficulty of the situation that I am in or that I was in or that someone else was in—*fully* feel it. That can take some time. If I allow myself to go into the difficulty and the pain, and I'm in a safe enough space to do that—and sometimes that might require having outside help to hold the space for me—it's a natural portal or pathway to the bigger perspective. The bigger perspective overlaps with my human perspective, it doesn't override it; it expands it and says, 'Yeah, this is shitty as fuck and hurts like hell, and is there some deeper reason—not reasoning from the mind, but from the heart—for why this is happening?' I'm looking for an answer that comes from a place that knows only love. I'm not talking about 'love and light.' I'm talking about the love that gets in the dark mud and rolls up its sleeves and embraces bloody bodies. This is the love that can hold a difficulty I'm experiencing and match it in a way that my mind and human perspective can't.

"Sometimes, depending on the work I do with my soul, it's an exchange between me and my soul, and that can be powerful, too. I can get a dialogue going about how this has happened and what I as a soul might be attempting to learn through this experience. I must always be careful with that when I'm talking about it, because again, I'm not trying to turn it into some New Age thing. I do know that when I'm hearing from my Soul (with a capital S) why she might want to experience some of the most horrific things you can think of experiencing, it doesn't float me above them, it sinks me into the heart of them in a way that allows me to be there and allows all of it to briefly be okay. It doesn't mean I don't still have to get active and change things and do my best to help things outside of me and any injustice in the world, but it helps me know that there is also something behind this that is much bigger than what I can imagine or what I can project onto it."

She was talking about holding space, or having others hold space for us when we can't, which is important. When I went through my relapse, one of the big problems was that I was horrible at reaching out to others for help. I learned through that experience that it was truly something I needed to change. In the twelve-step programs, participants say *we* recover, and I dig that because it's implied we don't do it alone. Unfortunately I was really bad at connecting with any support networks, let alone with friends in general. It goes back to the introvert thing. I realized I needed to get the fuck over myself, because had I been in regular communication with some support system, there was a significantly better chance that I wouldn't have ended up relapsing. But I did, and I've used that experience to light a fire under my ass in many different areas of my life, but especially when it comes to talking with others and sharing my pain. Sometimes we don't have access to friends, family, or support networks, and we are on our own. During those times, how do we learn to create an open space for healing ourselves?

Sera saw this as a case-by-case situation. She suggested asking ourselves questions like " 'What makes me feel safe?' 'What makes me feel held?' 'What do I need in this moment to feel like I can feel this feeling and have this experience as it is?' It might be something like needing to be around flowers. Or the ocean. Or on the beach or in the neighborhood park or next to that tree. I can feel it when I lean up against a tree—it's enough of a presence, a sense of support that I can grieve or feel the anger or begin to process whatever I'm going through. What it is for each of us is a question we need to ask, and the answer might change depending on the circumstances.

"Cultivating that awareness of what holds us is huge. So is trusting. I know I'm a little bit rebellious. I've never had a formal teacher. I've never been a part of a recognized tradition or lineage. I've never even had a so-called traditional practice in some ways. In other ways, I probably have a very traditional practice. I firmly believe, based on my own experience, and based on working with people and looking out at life, that we can hold ourselves and create an environment that can help hold us. We have everything that it takes to cultivate and explore our inner terrain. When we can be honest about that, then we can say,

'Yeah, I've created the right space, there are candles, there are flowers, maybe I took a bath, but I'm still feeling uneasy, so I'm going to call my dear friend.' Or 'I'm going to wait and try to find somebody on Skype who I can talk to who will sit there and hold the space for me.' All of that, to me, is part of it. I will always go back to how I know that the soul is the 'us' of us, and we are here for ourselves. We know how to move through this, but a lot of the time it's about reestablishing that trust, remembering how to do that, and allowing it to happen naturally instead of in a forced or prescribed way."

This is one of the ways I identify with Sera. She doesn't come from a specific background or tradition, and I don't, either. I've had guides, and I'm very grateful for that, but I've never been formally initiated in a specific path, and that's worked for me. I guess you could say the pathless path has been my path. It comes down to direct, undeniable experience.

Any great teacher will point their student in that direction regardless of the tradition. We each find our own way there, while being brutally honest with ourselves in the process. Like Sera said, the soul will nudge us toward where we need to go, whether it's to a specific teacher or through a specific life experience. In all fairness, sometimes those life experiences can seem like they're too much and more than we can handle, like life is shitting on us. That's certainly what I felt when I found myself time and again back on another fucking detox unit.

This relates to something I've been exploring for a long time, especially in the context of relapse. Why is it so many of us who have the tools, who've been in recovery, who've been on a spiritual path and worked with mantras, meditation, prayer, yoga, and so forth, don't use what we know will help us and maybe even save us during difficult times?

Sera bluntly answered: "Because we're human!" She acknowledged that an answer to that depends on one's orientation, be it psychological, behavioral, or spiritual, but essentially it comes down to just being human. "We're going to be clear and own our shit, and we're going to get unclear and get fucked by our shit. I don't feel like that's supposed to end. We can grow in our ways of handling stuff and being with ourselves through that if we can expand our own love around how our fuckups are part of being human. It doesn't excuse us. It doesn't mean that we're not supposed to do the work around it. But it means that we can let ourselves off the holy hook a little bit."

So then is belief in God or considering oneself "spiritual" even necessary to living a spiritual life?

"No, no, no!" Sera was adamant about this. "I know it's cliché, but it's so fucking true that each of us has people in our lives who don't practice meditation or yoga or read the books or go to church or believe in God, and they are by far the most alive and loving humans some of us have ever met. In fact, having been publicly in America's spiritual arena for over a decade, I have to say that I am more naturally drawn to the people who don't necessarily consider themselves to be spiritual. That might be my own shit; it might also be that I'm burned out by some of the spiritual ideals that feel like they chip away at our humanity. What I find myself craving, because this is something that I'm reawakening to, is the human-human.

"Here's what I mean by the human-human. Several years ago, in Dharamsala, India, I had the opportunity to meet the Dalai Lama. Now, granted, it's the Dalai freakin' Lama, so you already get everything that's packed in that package, but at the same time when I got to meet him in person, my experience wasn't 'He is so spiritual. I want to ask him all these profound questions because he's emanating this glowing gloriousness.' Instead, what I was struck by was his humanity. After the encounter, I ran out of there and went and called my mom from one of those funny and unreliable pay phones. Everyone is in the street shouting and rickshaws are going by and it was madness. My mom picked up her phone in Chicago, where it was some ridiculous time in the morning. 'What? What? Who's calling?'

"I said, 'Mom, I just met my first human!'

" 'What? Are you on drugs? What's happening over there?' my mom asked. It was such a revelation, because it wasn't his spirituality that was impressing me, it was his humanity. He was so alive, and that's what I go by. Who is living? Even if it's just that they're living by screaming in pain, or maybe they're depressed that day and are the furthest fucking thing from manifesting their positive intentions, but the ones among us who are human-human have a quality and a pulse that's unmistakable.

"It's a pulse that we all crave, both inside and outside ourselves. I don't think this has anything to do with spirituality. Sometimes spirituality can get in the way of what's most truly alive in us. The soul realm brings us back to life—it's the part of us all that I try to keep my eyes and my heart open to."

PRACTICE

Perfectly Imperfect

I think Sera and I agree we're both aware that each of us is still a highly flawed and fucked-up being. It comes with the territory of this whole human experience, and to pretend otherwise is a disservice to cultivating a relationship with our lives and how we can use them to help tap into the Divine nature (or source, life, God, Buddha mind, Christ consciousness, Brahman, the One, or whatever you care to call it). I like the term "perfectly imperfect" because to me it sums up the dualistic nature we live our lives from. A lot of the time we're identified with our limited and finite self, our bodies. For the sake of clarity, let's explore this a little deeper before moving on to the practice itself.

We have five cognitive senses: hearing, touch, sight, taste, and smell. We have organs of speech, locomotion, grasping, excretion, and procreation. We also have a mind that thinks and brings awareness to this experience of our physical manifestation. When these things are removed from the equation, however, all that's left is pure, present, witnessing awareness, and that is our true *Self* (or again, whatever you care to call it).

The cool thing is that this witnessing awareness underlies every moment of every day, whether we're aware of it or not. It's always there. In his book *The Integral Vision*, Ken Wilber (whom you'll meet later in this book) gives some simple yet remarkably lucid instructions on how to engage this practice:

> *Notice your present awareness. Notice the objects arising in your awareness—the images and thoughts arising in your mind, the feelings and sensations arising in your body, the myriad objects arising around you in the room or environment. All of these objects arising in your awareness.*
>
> *Now think about what was in your awareness 5 minutes ago. Most of the thoughts have changed, most of the bodily sensations have changed, and probably most of the environment has changed. But something has not changed. Something in you is the same now as it was 5 minutes ago. What is present now that was present 5 minutes ago?*
>
> *I AMness. The feeling-awareness of I AMness is still present. I am that ever-present I AMness. That I AMness is present now, it was present a moment ago, it was present a minute ago, it was present 5 minutes ago.*[2]

What I love is that Ken goes on to ask us to consider that this witnessing, present awareness, or I AMness, was extant not only five minutes ago but also five hours ago, five years ago, five centuries ago, five millennia ago, and so forth. It always has been and always will be, especially right now in this very moment, because when you get right down to it, what else is there besides this very moment?

As I've worked with this practice over the years, it's helped me soften to the flawed human being that is Chris Grosso, because it's shown me in the most undeniable of terms (which is to say, direct experience) that this physical body, which is certainly a part of my experience, is just that—only a *part* of my experience, and a very temporary one at best. When I find I'm locked in a mental shit storm about how I fucked something up or why I'm such a terrible human being, on a good day, I'm able to catch myself, take a couple of slow, deep breaths, and anchor into the I AMness to impartially witness the mental parade of ridiculousness that's going on. In that place of impartial witnessing, it's A-okay that I'm imperfect, because as I AMness, *I'm also perfect*, and that's just the way this crazy fucking thing called life is. This practice helps us learn to relax into life's often-tumultuous currents instead of fighting them, to just take the ride. Like the Zen proverb says, "Let go or be dragged."

8

A LONELY CONSCIOUSNESS
IN A BAG OF FLESH

CONVERSATION WITH CHELSEA ROFF

I'd known about Chelsea Roff for years, and even though I'm sure we've given presentations at many of the same conferences, our paths never crossed, which bummed me out, because I was familiar with her story of overcoming a severe eating disorder that almost took her life but instead led to her becoming a well-respected and sought-after yoga teacher. Knowing of Chelsea's commitment to helping others who struggle with eating disorders and other afflictions heal, plus her ability to connect her understanding to neuroscience, I was excited to include her story and wisdom in this book.

I wanted to begin with an excerpt from an article she so beautifully and candidly wrote:

> *Fifteen-year-olds aren't supposed to have strokes. At least that's what I thought. I try not to think about it too much. Even now, I only have bits and pieces; shards of memories that somehow remained intact even through the trauma my brain endured that day.*

When I arrived at Children's Medical Center, I weighed just 58 pounds. After a five-year battle with Anorexia Nervosa, my body had reached its breaking point. Nearly every system in my body was shutting down. All four valves in my heart were leaking. My skin was yellow from liver failure. I hadn't taken a shit in over a month. I was dying.

The first emotion I remember is rage. It was a violent, fire-in-your-veins, so-angry-you-could-kill-someone kind of rage. I wanted out. I wanted the pain to be over. I wanted to die. I was mad at myself for not having the courage to just do it quickly, angry at the hospital staff for thwarting my masked attempt. I was convinced that I was "meant to" endure this, that my long-drawn-out starving to death would prove my willpower to God. In the days prior to my stroke, I'd had vivid hallucinations—of Jesus on a wooden cross outside my bedroom window and a satanic figure sneaking up under my bedroom covers to suffocate me at night. I thought I was meant to be a martyr.

I thought God wanted me to die.[1]

The details of Chelsea's and my stories are different circumstantially, but they intersect in many ways, particularly that at such a young age, we both believed God wanted us to die. I was sure it wasn't easy for her to talk about those experiences, but I hoped she'd discuss whatever she could about those times, to help readers truly understand that no matter how bad it gets, it's never too late to come back—there's always hope.

Chelsea was willing to share this dark period of her life, though she knew it wouldn't be easy. "That excerpt begins at the height of my experience. Up until that point, I'd endured a five-year battle with anorexia. It didn't develop out of nowhere. When I looked back at my family system, I realized I had a biological predisposition to mental health challenges: My mom dealt with an eating disorder in her youth, and throughout my mom's family there was anxiety, depression, and substance abuse. During my childhood, my mom was an active alcoholic and dealt with some drug issues as well. I was raised by a lesbian couple in the late eighties before marriage equality, and in some way that compounded that strife, because the political situation had an impact on my childhood. My other mom couldn't get custody of my sister and me as my mom sort of descended into her own mental health challenges. There were issues with violence and neglect, and it was a chaotic household. There was no safe place.

"The thing that they say about eating disorders and any mental health and substance abuse challenge is that genetics loads the gun and trauma pulls the trigger. I may have been biologically predisposed to undereating or to using food to cope with difficult emotions, but I think because I had a lot of adversity early in life, I was more likely to grab on to coping mechanisms that weren't healthy in the long run. I was nine or ten when my body started to change, and that was right around the time that things got the most difficult at home. I think going on a diet felt like the most logical response to not feeling okay in the world.

"I often say that eating disorders are socioculturally shaped illnesses. I had an experience when I was nine or ten years old of suffering, and I think we all have that experience of pain. It's like Buddhism 101—life is pain. One of the ways people respond to suffering is with food or substances, so I thought if I could change and fix my body, I'll finally feel okay again. Because of the genetic predisposition I had, it spiraled into more than a diet. It became addictive in the same way that alcohol or other substances can be addictive. I found that when I was thinking about what I was going to eat or not going to eat, or what I had just eaten or how long I was going to spend on the treadmill, there was no room for pain or fear or shame or any of the difficult emotions that had become hard to deal with. It was just the ultimate distraction. I felt a sense of power and control. That was compounded by sexual trauma in my adolescence. I found that as I lost weight, I became less attractive to men, and that was comforting, because it made me feel safe. There was a massive confluence of circumstances, and the stroke was at the very height of all of that."

What Chelsea said made me think about a workshop I held with some young adults at a rehab facility. We were talking about how some of them struggled with food issues. I told them how I too have issues with food, and how later in my life I looked back and saw how when I was a child and a preteen, I ate sugary treats in the same way I would later consume drugs and alcohol—consume, consume, consume for that high that's never quite high enough. That's part of why, when I'm asked about my clean time now, I'll tell people I'm sober today (if that). This is because I do at times still eat in ways that are addictive, or binge-watch TV shows as a means of diversion. It's significantly less than it used to be, but I'm still acting out in obsessive and compulsive ways; I'm just abusing different substances. I know better, so I don't feel comfortable saying, "I'm clean and sober for x years," because I'm not. The substances are the substances, and the real issue is my behavior and the way I handle myself and act out at times again, regardless of the substance.

Chelsea got where I was coming from. "I always say I consider myself in recovery or even *recovered* from an eating disorder—it's been about ten years—but I'm not recovered from life. That means I'm not superhuman, so there are days when I reach toward relationships and work addiction or whatever to numb my feelings. I think the difference is that I've got more compassion and awareness around it, so instead of beating myself up or punishing myself, I have a compassionate curiosity."

Beautifully said. That's something I talked about at a workshop I led. One of the participants asked me to name one thing I would have changed about myself during my process of recovery and learning to live a spiritual lifestyle. I told him I wished I'd learned to cultivate a greater expression of compassion and softness toward myself. Just as Chelsea said—bringing a compassionate curiosity to my pain, because again, we're all in some sort of pain.

That's how I try to present the material I talk about or write about.

Sure, the underlying theme is going to be drugs and alcohol, because that's where my own pain and suffering cropped up, but you can replace "drugs and alcohol" with whatever your struggle happens to be. In my case, part of the pain and suffering was relapses. Was this something that happened for Chelsea?

It was. "As I moved along the path from ten to seventeen, there were multiple relapses. I would go from this raging river of my home life— there was a lot of violence and a lot of addiction there—to a hospital, which was a safe place. And it would be, like, 'I don't need my life vest here anymore, because the waters are a lot calmer,' but then they'd send me home and none of the coping techniques I'd learned in the hospital worked. I was drowning."

I don't think I'd ever heard anyone talk about this like Chelsea did! Even though I hated that I had to be in rehab, I was so *comfortable* there. I don't mean comfortable in the sense that they were cushy rehabs, because they were anything but, but I mean comfortable in that I was safe within those walls. Even if contraband was being brought in, which it often was, I'd always be in such a broken place by the time I'd enter a rehab that the last thing I wanted to do was touch drugs or alcohol. My body had had enough.

"That was always my experience in psychiatric hospitals—it was miserable, but it was better than where I'd been before. There was order and predictability, if you think of first-chakra stuff in yoga." The first chakra is associated in the yogic tradition with safety, grounding, and support. "When my first-chakra needs were met, it was better than where I'd been before. At seventeen I was emancipated and left the hospital. The first two years of recovery were rocky, but I wasn't relapsing. It was just tough. It was like going through mud. I had an experience of having an eating disorder, and that was one version of suffering. There was also an experience of *being in recovery from having an eating disorder*, and that experience was choosing not to give in to urges to starve myself because I wanted to live again. Every single time I sat down at a meal, I would have to choose. After a couple of years, the urge to starve myself went away, and that was remarkable, because I hadn't lived like

that before. The experience of looking in the mirror and loathing myself started to go away.

"I've had an experience of having an eating disorder *and* I've had an
experience of being in recovery from an eating disorder. The experience
that I refer to as 'recovered' is distinctly different than being in recovery. I'm not saying that it's the end of the path, but there's a difference
between resisting urges and not having the urge to starve or restrict at
all. It's gone, and I don't know where it went."

I was impressed by the lens through which Chelsea saw the world.
I know in some of the formal twelve-step fellowships it's said that
over time the obsession to use will be lifted. You must do the work—
whether it's the formal steps or other practices—but once you do that
and continue to sweep your side of the street, so to speak, the obsession
lifts. What I learned through many relapses is that I wasn't willing to
go in and touch those raw and vulnerable places. I had crafted some
strong heart-armor, but with time and work the pieces began to fall
away. However, there were still some very strong pieces in place, and
this became clear to me within the context of my marriage as I began
recognizing that there were aspects of pain and fear I wasn't willing to
go to in connection to that relationship. I also wasn't talking to anyone
about it, and sure enough, with time—relapse. It was inspiring to hear
where Chelsea was in her life now, a place she considered herself to be
recovered.

She added a caveat. "I don't know what the future holds. So maybe
ten years down the line I'll feel differently about this. The only reason
I use that language around it and have the experience of feeling recovered is that the urge is gone, and that's distinctly different. That's not
to say ten or fifteen years from now I couldn't lose a family member or
go through a divorce and everything might change. If there's one thing
that's constant, it's change."

I appreciated that and could certainly relate. What support did

Chelsea receive in recovery and in her recovered state, especially in terms of yoga, community, and the service of others?

Chelsea described these as three distinct medicines that are all connected. "Community was the first dose of medicine I got, and that was in the hospital. Part of my treatment came through the support system of nurses, doctors, and other patients, which I'm sure is true of most recovery programs. Other people there were on a healing path as well. What I found was that I went in feeling worthless and not deserving to live, to eat, and community gave me a sense of having a place where I belonged—a place at the table. It began with that.

"I had a few nurses who were so kind to me, and on days when I'd wake up and say some mean words like 'Fuck you. Leave me alone. I hate you,' they'd reply, 'No, Chelsea, I know you're having a hard day, but come walk around the floor with me. I'd like to spend some time with you.' I'd question why they'd want to be with such a miserable human being, and they'd tell me I wasn't miserable. So part of what community gave me was a sense of my own worth and place among people and in life. Community also gave me an opportunity to give to others and have somebody else's back. It wasn't just about me anymore."

This was a natural segue for Chelsea into service, which started in the hospital but then permeated her yoga community. "It showed up in simple things like breath—being in a room and breathing and having a visceral sense that I was breathing with others, that I was not alone in my struggle, that I was not alone in my life experience. Like most mental illnesses, the eating disorder was isolating, and my experience is that I'm a lonely consciousness in a bag of flesh." Yoga classes got her through this because of her sense of connection, and it's branched out from there. "These days I have it all over the place. I've got it in my organization, my friend circles, in salsa-dancing circles—it's just a sense that you matter to someone else and someone else matters to you.

"I always come back to that wonderful poem by Mary Oliver, 'Wild Geese,' in which she writes about how, no matter how lonely we are, we all have a place 'in the family of things.' That's my sense of community.

You have a sense of a place, of family, of things, and the service piece emerges from that. I found that gave me a sense of meaning beyond myself. Getting involved in volunteer and service opportunities made it not about me anymore. My health and my well-being and my waking up are tied to others, to something bigger than me.

"When I was nineteen, I got involved with Big Brothers Big Sisters, and that was fantastic. I had a little brother named Andy who was eight years old, and I would take him out to eat once a week. His mom was disabled, and the only food they had available was Taco Bell. Right after my mom was diagnosed with dementia, I met up with Andy. I remember experiencing so many of feelings. I had a physical and visceral feeling of fullness and could hardly conceive of eating. I didn't know how I was going to put food into my body, but I took Andy out to IHOP because that was his favorite restaurant. He was going through this phase of if my favorite color was blue, his favorite color would also be blue. He looked at the menu and looked at me and said, 'Chelsea, what are you going to order?' I looked at him and realized that if I ordered what I wanted to order, which was a garden salad with no dressing, he'd order the same thing. How could I pass this thing that took me to such a dark place on to someone I loved? How could I share that with him? The service relationship I had with him was more important than my self-starvation as a coping mechanism. I ordered the ham-and-cheese omelet.

"I think that's what service is. It's a sort of medicine that, if used in the right way, creates a relationship or purpose that can be more important than self-sabotaging behaviors. Whether that's with a human being or a cat, or is just a sense of connection to the world in general, suddenly your well-being is tied up with something bigger than you— it's not just about you anymore. I've found that to be a massive catalyst to my growth."

I also connected to what Chelsea said about the embodiment piece of her recovery. "Yoga and meditation gave me an ability to sense what was happening inside my body. I didn't have a sense of when I was hungry or full. My heart would start beating out of my chest, and I would think I was dying. I call that 'interoception' or 'interoceptive awareness'—which is your ability to sense what's happening inside your body at any given time. I found you can't have a happy, healthy, free life if you aren't living inside your body with a sense of awareness and two-way communication. For me, yoga built up that ability to recognize what was happening inside my body and then eventually an ability to self-regulate, which is that two-way communication."

Yoga, community, and service led Chelsea to create Eat Breathe Thrive. It's a program that combines yoga, meditation, and psycho-education to help people fully overcome food and body-image issues. I appreciated on EBT's website that it said the program taught individuals critical skills for long-term recovery, including how to track hunger and fullness signals, cope with difficult emotions, and create a sense of being at home in one's own skin.

First, how can individuals who struggle with eating issues (which I do myself) learn how to track hunger and fullness signals? How can we learn to cope with difficult emotions? Did Chelsea have a specific practice or technique to share? And to create a sense of home in one's own skin—that is *huge*. Could she talk about this?

She tied it back into interoception or interoceptive awareness. "There are lots of different types of interoception—hunger, fullness, heart rate, muscle stretching, tension, body temperature, thirst, and more. During the past six years I've worked with clients with eating disorders, one thing that I've seen—and I would say this seems to be true of substance abuse, too—is that they tend to have very poor hunger and fullness signals, and they seem to be hypersensitive, along with other types of interoception. For example, they may not be good at saying they're hungry and need to eat. They don't have that hunger signal coming up and telling their brain to eat. They've trained themselves to ignore it. Same thing with fullness. They might be hypersensitive to heart rate, so when their heart starts to beat out of their chest, it comes as such an overwhelming experience of panic or rage."

In her work, Chelsea had observed something I was concerned about as well. "What I find with eating disorders and most mental illnesses is that people have a lot of tools in their toolbox, but they don't use them at appropriate times." *Right?* Why was that?

"For instance, if we're dealing with anxiety and panic, in a moment of anxiety, we may want to go for a run. That's probably the worst thing you can do for your body in the middle of anxiety. If you go for a run, you're going to kick your sympathetic nervous system higher into gear. A practice to move it down might be something like restorative yoga, or yoga nidra, or diaphragmatic breathing. These have all been shown to activate the parasympathetic branch, and vice versa. If I'm in the middle of depression and I'm feeling lethargic and I can't get myself out of bed in the morning, then I *need* something to activate my sympathetic branch, like breath of fire or a Vinyasa yoga class, or a run around the block, or a bike ride, or a loud social situation, or a cold shower. Part of what we're doing with Eat Breathe Thrive is teaching people how their bodies work, how their nervous system works, and helping them identify tools that are already in their toolbox that they can use more effectively."

This brought me to a third component I wanted to explore, one I think is big for many people: How we can learn to feel a sense of home in our own skin in a way that we can accept and that we're comfortable with?

This is probably the emergent process of Chelsea's entire program, but there's no single tool or method. "I think part of that process of creating a sense of home in your own skin is dropping into the knowledge, the realization, that you are in no way separate from yourself, from your physicality. You are a conscious being, a sentient being having a human, physical, embodied experience. Your body is the substrate that allows you to have a conscious experience in this form. My words, my thoughts, my feelings, my sense of connection with others all live and emerge from my body. There's nowhere to be but at home. This is your home because you cannot leave it. You're beautifully and magnificently and phenomenally tied up with this thing called your body.

"I think the other part of that realization is recognizing that often the judgments we have about our bodies are nothing more than the judgments we have about ourselves. We talk about our relationship with our body, but what we're talking about is our relationship with ourselves. When we say we're not worthy or that our body is too much or too fat, that's often a reflection of 'I'm too much' or 'I'm too greedy' or 'I'm not enough' or whatever. We're talking about how we feel about ourselves."

Chelsea gave me so much to think about. Another thing I found fascinating was how she combined her yoga training with a study of neuroscience. What light could she shine on the neuroscience underlying disorders and addictions—from anorexia and bulimia to drug and alcohol addiction, to sex addiction and workaholism? What's going on with our physical chemistry, and how can we then take this knowledge and begin to make lasting changes in our behavior?

This was something Chelsea was passionate about! There was one thing she especially wanted to delve into. "We can talk a lot about the autonomic nervous system, but I can't point to an area of the brain solely responsible for causing eating disorders. We can say that most addictive disorders tend to have similar effects in the brain, but the research is so new. We know that dopamine is involved in addictive disorders, but dopamine is also involved in movement and in brushing your teeth. I would say that when it comes to neuroscience, so far, as of 2017, our instruments are very blunt. For the past decade, fMRI [functional magnetic resonance imaging, a type of brain scan] has been one of the most popular tools in neuroscience. What it allows us to see is where blood is going in the brain. This means we can put somebody in a scanner and tell him or her to think about drinking alcohol or food and look at where blood goes in the brain. We're not looking at the *cause* of addiction or anorexia, but instead at what parts of the brain appear active when we're *thinking* about food or alcohol. Neuroscience is starting to give us a picture of what might be involved, but I would say the big takeaways are not simplistic. I'm very excited for the day when we'll have an instrument that allows us to look at the entire body and the entire nervous system. I'd love to be able to do the yoga asana downward dog in an fMRI scanner, but you can't do that right now."

Chelsea turned me on to the work of Marc Lewis, author of *Memoirs of an Addicted Brain*. "He says that addiction isn't a disease in the same way that cancer is a disease. It's not something you get infected with. Humans have evolved to have reward pathways in the brain, so, for example, you might initially find that alcohol or dieting or cookies are rewarding. What your brain does is get hyperfocused on that reward, and the neural pathways to that reward deepen. Think of it like a path through the woods: If you walked on that path repeatedly for ten years, the plants and trees around it would grow thick and hard to navigate. You've got a nice path, but it takes you to a swamp that's horrible—like addiction, dieting. But you've walked down that path many times because the brain created reward pathways, and it's nearly impossible to walk down another pathway that might also be rewarding—like community or connection. Part of the process of recovery is like wandering through the woods seeking a different reward. Eventually trees will start to grow over that old pathway."

Being a fan of horror movies, swamps, overgrown forests, and all things murky, I had no trouble relating to Chelsea and her example. It reminded me of so many times in my life when I'd had to venture out after returning to drugs and alcohol and begin clearing a new path (both metaphorically and literally). Let that be yet another testament to anyone who is struggling while reading these words—it absolutely is doable. *You can do this.* I swear.

had another question for Chelsea, one that was more neurobehavioral than neuroscientific, but I knew she'd have great insights. There have been many recent studies about genetics and epigenetics related to both eating disorders and substance addiction. What did she think about the connection? How can we undo what seems to be hardwired or rewired?

It turns out she's passionate about the genetics and epigenetics around eating disorders and substance abuse. "Mostly because I think there's a lot of misinformation out there. One thing we do know is that eating disorders and substance abuse issues are highly heritable. Studies suggest that the heritability for anorexia, bulimia, and binge eating disorder is 54 to 83 percent,[2] which tells us that if we're looking at the causes that lead to conditions like full-blown eating disorders, 54 to 83 percent of the causes are due to genetics or epigenetics. That's fascinating. Another one that blew my mind is that individuals are 11.3 times more likely to develop anorexia nervosa if one of their parents has had the illness, and between 4.4 and 9.6 times more likely to develop bulimia if one of their parents has had the illness.[3] That's kind of mind-blowing. If one of your parents dealt with an eating disorder, you come into the world 5 to 12 times more likely to develop it. Talk about having the odds stacked against you.

"I don't know the research on substance abuse right now, but I'd imagine it's even higher than that. That said, genes alone don't cause eating disorders or substance abuse issues. There are biological causes, psychological causes, and social causes. I find that there's a lot of variation between individual cases. The other thing we've learned over the past couple of decades through genetic research is that almost no expression of genes is solely genetic—it's almost all epigenetic. Epigenetics is essentially the study of genetic and environmental interactions—how your genetics interact with your environment and how that affects what's expressed. For example, you may have inherited a gene that predisposes you to be six feet tall, but you must have certain environmental factors present to fully embody that genetic predisposition. If you're malnourished growing up, you're probably not going to reach the full potential of your height.

"The same is true with eating disorders and substance abuse. You might come into the world predisposed to develop substance abuse issues, but there are environmental variables that must be present for you to express that genetic predisposition. Many of those environmental things are psychological. We talk about big T traumas and little t traumas, and we define trauma as any experience that overwhelms our ability to cope. Kaiser Permanente conducted the Adverse Childhood Experiences Study (ACE Study) on 17,000 people in the 1990s.[4] It's one of the greatest studies on trauma out there. It found that adverse childhood events or experiences are essentially traumatic experiences. Eighty percent of individuals who experience adverse childhood events meet the criteria for at least one psychiatric illness by twenty-one years old."

Think about that: *80* percent!

"The other thing they found is that two out of three adults experience at least one adverse event in childhood, and that more than one in five report three or more. The powerful thing about this is that in addition to showing that adverse childhood events can kick those genes into gear and cause substance abuse issues and eating disorders and things like that, they found that they predispose one to heart disease, diabetes, every single variable you can think of physically, even early death. Trauma shortens life-spans. The study demonstrated that if you have those environmental factors present, you're more likely to turn on the genes that cause cancer, diabetes, substance abuse, and things of that nature. I think if there's one sort of misunderstanding out there, it's that genes alone cause substance abuse."

I was grateful for Chelsea's knowledge and empathy. It illuminated my life trajectory in a way I hadn't considered before. Perhaps if certain social conditions had been different, I wouldn't have ended up becoming addicted to alcohol. Perhaps if my family's economic situation had been different, I wouldn't have had such deep issues around money and feeling worthy of it in my life. There were a whole lot of maybes and what-ifs I watched come up, but as I did, I was able to say *fuck* that! We are who we are today, and that's a beautiful thing. I thank all the environmental, economic, social, and geographical components that laid the foundation for my life experience, culminating in this day. It really is all good. For sure.

PRACTICE

Tracking of Needs

Chelsea tuned me onto a practice to rebuild interoception and interoceptive awareness. It's a tool that's helpful in rebuilding hunger and fullness symbols, and it's easy! It's a simple belly-breathing meditation in four parts: sensation, need, reaction, and action.

- First, notice what sensations are arising in the belly—and by sensation, Chelsea didn't mean hunger, but rather things like rumbling or pain or tightness or tenderness or numbness.
- From those sensations, ask yourself what you need. Is there a need for rest? Is there a need for soothing? Is there a need for food?
- The third part of the meditation is to become aware of your reactions to the sensations.
- Finally, we reach a point of considering what action we can take to respond to the sensations with compassion. Ask yourself if there is anything you can do in the next few moments to address the needs showing up in your body. If you noticed a need for food, it might be to eat a meal. If you noticed a need for rest, you may need to take a nap. If you noticed a need for presence or acknowledgment, it might be to sit quietly with yourself and just check in.

9

A HAPPINESS THAT ISN'T GOING TO SHATTER

CONVERSATION WITH SHARON SALZBERG

esides being one of the most respected and celebrated Buddhist teachers in America, Sharon Salzberg has influenced my spiritual development and that of many others, particularly in regard to finding what she calls "true" happiness. I spoke with Sharon to dig into what it means to be truly happy—an elusive thing, since few of us are typically taught that we're capable of happiness or that we even deserve it. Sharon flips the script, demonstrating how happiness—*true* happiness—is attainable for all beings. It's something we can achieve beginning right this minute, no matter whether we've led a life of perfection or we've fucked up so many times that we've lost count.

I wanted to start with a definition of happiness. Often it's something we seek in misguided ways when we engage in any sort of addictive behavior. Sharon took the meaning beyond a superficial pursuit of pleasure or conflict avoidance. "When I talk about happiness, I mean a sense of inner resource or wherewithal that allows us to be resilient, allows us to face adversity. And when I talk about *real* happiness, the 'real' refers to something we can access that's not dependent on conditions." In other words, we can access it even if the weather isn't good, we don't have money in the bank, or *Stranger Things* gets canceled. (God, please don't let that happen for a very, very long time, though, okay?) "We can access it, but we're not usually trained to look within. We're usually very experience-oriented, and we also tend to be intensity focused. Many of us need a sense of intensity to feel alive, so we're endlessly seeking."

That made sense to me. In my own case, seeking intense experiences like mystical union with God—or simply just not waking up going through withdrawals (talk about *intense*)—had led me in many different directions, and not necessarily good ones. Although there have been times when my quest brought me toward the spiritual, there have been others when it's led me to drugs and alcohol for instant gratification and escape from painful emotions. Real happiness sounded like something more than that, but it has been very elusive for me and for so many people I talk to—those new to recovery, those who've been on a healing path for some time, and, of course, those who have struggled with relapse. I wanted to know more about the way happiness does or does not manifest in people's lives.

For Sharon, it all comes down to conditioning. "We're not taught that we're capable of happiness, that we deserve happiness, or that we can find it outside of particular channels of experience." For me, that meant an endless pursuit of booze and empty sexual encounters and snorting shit up my nose. "We tend not to look at the quality of our presence as playing any role in our dissatisfaction, because mostly we're looking at our experiences. 'Was it intense enough?' So we're caught in a spiral."

I knew that spiral all too well. Drink cheap vodka. Snort cocaine (or Ritalin if I was broke) to keep it going. Drink more cheap vodka. Possibly throw up. Possibly find a female to come over. Possibly both. Wake up and do it all over again (and then some). Add a shitload of guilt and shame into the mix, and that was my existence off and on for many years. We get caught, we spin around, and either we find our way out or we don't, through means such as meditation, mantra, yoga, service work, and myriad other ways. So often, though, even after we've experienced life out of that spiral, we still return to self-defeating behaviors. Even those of us who have self-care tools, who've been in recovery, who've been on a spiritual path or in fellowship, forget or refuse to use their resources during difficult times. I was still trying to wrap my mind around that.

Sharon thinks returning to the spiral is probably inevitable, because nothing in life is a straight shot. "We don't have a great breakthrough and then it's smooth sailing from then on. We're always needing resilience and starting over and making an adjustment after making a mistake, which may not be that big, but we're still making mistakes and must begin again. Or maybe we do make a big mistake and must begin again. That's the rhythm of life."

Then she said something that reverberated with me. "There are certain kinds of pain that are hard for us to sit and be with. The impulse is to be anywhere but in the face of that." Once I returned home after the hospitalization I wrote about in the introduction, the reality of everything that had happened began to set in. My marriage was over. I'd gone back to drinking. I'd nearly died again. I experienced a sincerely significant trauma waking up in that hospital bed, strapped down and unable to breathe past the tubes in my throat. I felt like I was supposed to turn toward the pain and sit with it. That's what we're taught on this spiritual path, right? To lean into the pain? But it was just too much. I would sit for a moment or two in meditation or work with a compassion practice, but I just couldn't do it.

That's when I remembered something I'd spoken about in a workshop I'd given the year before. I told someone who had just lost a loved one and was having an incredibly difficult time with it that it was okay to create space between the pain and her. What I meant by that was that it was okay to not lean into it, to not face it down in that moment. It was okay to distract herself with television or music or whatever felt right to her, because sometimes *not* leaning into overwhelming pain *is* the most compassionate thing we can do for ourselves, regardless of what many spiritual teachers say. As I remembered this, I allowed myself to shift away from the utterly terrible fucking feeling of everything crashing down on me at once. I watched some episodes of *Curb Your Enthusiasm*, and it helped more than meditation would have in those moments. Of course we should be steadfast in watching our emotions, and when some time and space has allowed for softening the blow, go back and tend to the wounds. We must always remember to go back. Always.

After a couple of days, as I began to feel better, I turned to friends and community to help me get through what I was experiencing. That's not the case for everybody. Although, as Sharon pointed out, "Even if they do, there's still a chance that a relapse might happen anyway. Sometimes a contributing factor is a sense of going it alone, and there are also certain behavioral patterns that we may not have the mindfulness to see on our own, but when we are with a therapist or friends, they may see what we can't."

Let's say we get through the difficult time, we put down the bourbon, toss out the razor blades, stop eating processed foods. There are still bound to be feelings of shame or guilt or remorse and all sorts of negative thoughts and emotions regarding what we've gone through, as well as what we've done to others. How can we forgive ourselves after we've fucked up?

Sharon had the best answer: *common humanity.* "It has a lot to do with our sense of common humanity, that even though we're bearing the burden of what we've done or said, we're not the exception—people make mistakes. It's interesting, because people don't tend to come together around vulnerability because they think that's a weakness, but when we do, we can help each other more and care for one another more because it's what we share." What an amazing concept—to reframe vulnerability so that it's no longer perceived as a weakness, but instead as an opportunity for strength. "We can have a real awakening as we come to see these things."

This made me think of the time I spoke with my friend and colleague Deron Drumm (someone else you'll meet later in the book). He'd just gone through a difficult experience at work. He lost his cool with a coworker and raised his voice in a way that he hadn't in many years. As we spoke on the phone after it happened, I could hear how upset he was with himself, so I met up with him for lunch later that day. As he described what happened, he expressed how it oddly left him feeling like he'd relapsed, even though he didn't pick up a bottle or return to gambling (his addiction of choice). I hadn't spoken to Deron about my hospitalization the previous year. I had opened up to a few other close friends and a therapist I saw after it happened, but I was still harboring shame, embarrassment, and guilt about the whole thing. As I drove to meet Deron for lunch, I vacillated about whether I should tell him or not. I knew I should, but the embarrassed and ashamed part of me was saying, "No way, don't do it!" As we sat there eating our salads, Deron allowed himself to be vulnerable and confided everything he felt after that experience. I knew I absolutely had to tell him, and not spare any of the details. That interaction was one of the most open, intimate, and meaningful ones I've ever had. It showed me the power of vulnerability firsthand. I mean, I try to be as open as possible in my writing and workshops, but there was just something about the two of us—two grown men revealing their hearts and baring their souls to each other—that truly showed me the power of vulnerability. (It was as if a Brené Brown book had come to life!)

I loved the idea of vulnerability being a source of strength instead of weakness, but what about shame and remorse? Even after I'd gotten clean and made amends, I still felt remorse. Sharon believes that shame is inevitable. She quoted a beautiful line from the Buddha: "If you truly loved yourself, you would never harm another." She explained that it

had two meanings. "One is that harming another is like harming ourselves, because we'll live with the residue. The other is that if we're truly
capable of a Buddhist vision of life, of tremendous compassion and wisdom, then to behave in a negative way would take us in a different direction. We need to be able to distinguish between those two kinds of
pain, the one that is onward-leading and the one that isn't."

A lot of the people I work with or who have read my books are incarcerated or in rehab or just out. They have limited access (if any) to
learning about meditation or other self-care practices, or sitting with a
sangha or satsang or any sort of spiritual community. Sharon recommended that people in these raw and often fragile situations, especially
those with very limited emotional and spiritual-care resources, start
simple—with a basic meditation practice of sitting still and following the breath and paying attention when our mind wanders. "With
this letting go and starting over, what we're learning, even if we've
never used the words, is a forgiveness for ourselves, a self-compassion."
She described it like weight training—you increase the weight as you
grow stronger. And just as is true in weight lifting, there are no short-
cuts: "I don't think you can successfully do the meditation without forgiveness, because you're going to issue a tirade against yourself when
your mind wanders. People freak out on themselves. To be able to let
go and start over, which is inevitable anyway, means you're deepening
self-compassion and forgiveness. In Buddhist psychology, we would say
there is a difference between remorse and guilt, which is a new notion
for most people, but the moral grid is not good and bad or right and
wrong—it's what's skillful or unskillful. What's going to help us, and
what's going to bring us down? The notion of guilt just brings us down
because it drains us of energy. We feel stuck when we're identified only
with that negativity, and we need to realize that it's true, it happened,
maybe we have to make amends for it or feel the pain, but that's not
all we are."

Man, I loved that. It reminded me of something I'd heard Sharon talk about before: those magic moments of realizing that we're lost in thought, and how these recognitions are in and of themselves little moments of enlightenment. If every time we fall or return to a self-defeating behavior we catch ourselves and make the course correction that gets us back on track, we can look at what led us off the path in the first place and remember that as we begin again on our voyage of healing, that's a moment of enlightenment for us. It doesn't have to be just the big things, either. Little, everyday stuff absolutely counts, too—the way we treat ourselves or treat others. I find it helps at the end of the day to recap what has happened since I woke up, looking to see if I've mistreated myself or mistreated others, and if I have, I do my best to forgive myself for whatever unskillful ways I acted, and then, if it's pertinent, seek forgiveness when the time is right from someone else I may have treated poorly.

That made me think of another of Sharon's great insights:

The mind thinks thoughts that we don't plan. It's not as if we say, "At 9:10 I'm going to be filled with self-hatred."[1]

This seems like such a clear way into understanding our minds and how they work, and honestly, who reading these words right now can't relate? Our day will be going fine, perhaps even great, and then *Bam!* Completely out of the blue, something, perhaps a song or a smell, triggers a memory—sometimes good, more often bad—and off to the races our minds go.

Sharon told me that this understanding came from one of her spiritual teachers, who'd say, " 'Everything arises due to causes and conditions, and we might be able to affect those conditions, but we can't ever control them.' We can't say something like 'I'm never going to fall asleep meditating again.' We can maybe not eat a huge meal and then meditate, or we can try to affect the conditions, but we can't swear that we'll never fall asleep meditating again. We can't say that anger or fear will never come up in our mind again, because we don't know. I like to ask, 'What are we blaming ourselves for unfairly? What do we think we should be in control of that we can't control?' Once we've looked at that, we can recognize how we come down on ourselves because we're not in control. Then imagine recapturing all that energy we usually spend blaming ourselves and utilizing it on what we *can* do, which is to relate differently to what's come up in our mind. Just because we've had a thought or a feeling doesn't mean we have to take it to heart or let it define us." I'd say the same about any kind of relapse or negative behavior—it's what we did, not who we are.

Speaking of who we are, I think our not feeling at home in our own skin is such a big condition for the experience of unsatisfactoriness in our lives. It can lead to various means of aversion—including drugs, alcohol, food, sex, and shopping—to mask the painful emotions. I was curious what Sharon thought about being born into this human form and how we can learn to feel at home in our lives.

She told me she usually talks about this in the context of the Buddha having been a human being. Because of this, he'd had to face some "very human questions, like what does it mean to be so vulnerable as an infant, so subject to the actions of those around us, and then to grow older and get sick and die whether we want that or not. Could there be a quality of happiness that isn't going to shatter as the body does its thing? And what does it mean to have a human mind with a cascade of emotions? Maybe we wake up in the morning and we're frightened, and then we're glad and then we're sorry and then we're full of faith and full of doubt. There's a constantly changing torrent of thoughts and feelings, and we can't always stop it and say, 'Only happy thoughts from now on.' They say the Buddha as a human being had those kinds of questions. Anything he discovered, he discovered through the power of his own awareness, and so can we. Whatever our questions are, we have that same capacity for awareness and can come to the resolution of our deepest questions about life: 'What does it mean? How do I belong?'"

That made me think of a quote I've always loved from Sharon's book *Lovingkindness*:

> *No matter how wonderful or terrible our lives have been, no matter how many traumas and scars we may carry from the past, no matter what we have gone through or what we are suffering now, our intrinsic wholeness is always present, and we can recognize it.*[2]

I always wondered exactly what she meant by "intrinsic wholeness." How is it always present, and how we can recognize it?

"That's a belief that as human beings we all have a capacity for understanding our lives, for wisdom, for generosity, for connection, for love, even if somehow it's been covered over or obscured, or it's hard to find or hard to trust, but it's there. Nothing can ever destroy it. Even if we don't touch it in this life, it's there—no matter what we may have gone through, no matter what we are yet to go through. It's the bottom line of who we are underneath all the things we've done or the fears we have, or whatever it might be—that's who we are. When we do something like loving-kindness meditation—instead of, for example, going down the list of our faults, *again*—we wish ourselves well. Giving a little airtime to caring and compassion, which we don't necessarily spend much time doing."

I still struggle with this, because some beliefs become so ingrained—in my case, the recurring belief that I'm not worthy of good things. I think everyone can relate to struggling with entrenched beliefs—no matter how little truth is contained within them. One thing that brought me closer to forgiving myself and wishing myself well was the Buddhist teaching of interconnectedness. I mean, if we're all connected, then to some degree, the mental shit storms we all weather must have some effect beyond just this weirdo named Chris Grosso. How could truly understanding interconnection and practicing it help us to cultivate greater compassion for all beings and ourselves?

Sharon showed me the answer by taking it beyond the spiritual realm and out into the world at large—things like economic and environmental consciousness. She shared a story about how she grew up in a time when the world was much more compartmentalized—what happened to someone in the Amazon had nothing to do with a person in the United States. "To think something in the rain forest might affect the rainfall on my head in New York was ludicrous. Now we live in a time where the interconnectedness of things is much more apparent, but we don't often stop and pay attention to what that means. We get into this thing of sink or swim alone, but we're truly more together than that. That's just the reality of things.

"Sometimes if I go into an office or some workplace to teach, I say, 'Here's a thought. How many other people have to be doing their job well for you to be doing your job well?' And most people don't stop and think about that, but if you're a surgeon in a hospital and have a lousy housekeeper, you're in trouble. We're counting on each other, all of us. Sometimes I'm in a car coming up to one of those mechanical arms at a tollbooth that's reading my E-ZPass, and I wonder, what if the mechanic who checks on these things didn't do a good job and it doesn't work, and then there will be fifty cars behind me and the whole system falls apart?

"We live in an interdependent universe—that's just how it is. We don't often take that in. We often don't give others enough credit or think about their lives. We don't often look at our own actions and how they're going to ripple out and affect other people. There are some odd connections between restorative justice and interconnection. Imagine if somebody shoplifted from my store and thought it was nothing, but because of it I couldn't help my sister with her rent and she got evicted, and a chain of events was set off by that one action. That's not something we often think about, but when it's brought to consciousness, that's often a big wake-up call. That action rippled out to all those people."

We truly are all interconnected and dependent upon one another in ways many of us overlook daily. There is a saying that "Hurt people hurt people," but on the flip side of that, healed (or healing) people help people, and for true healing to occur, we must begin within; and from there, we can let it ripple out into this crazy interconnected world of which each of us is an integral part.

PRACTICE

Loving-Kindness Meditation

One of the most profound ways I've experienced inner healing is through a meditative practice called loving-kindness. With her life-changing book aptly titled *Lovingkindness*, Sharon was one of the first people to make this practice accessible and popularize it in the West. I especially like to use it when I'm experiencing feelings of self-doubt and worthlessness, or when I feel disconnected from others—family, friends, or the whole goddamn world. It's a way to cultivate a deeper sense of joy, compassion, equanimity, and friendliness toward others and yourself. Here are some basic instructions to help get you started.

- Begin by closing your eyes and taking two or three long, slow, deep breaths into your belly. Breathe in through the nose, out through the mouth. Take a moment to relax and bring your awareness to what's right here and now.
- Loving-kindness originates with you and then spreads out into the cosmos. I'm good with the "sending love out into the universe" part, but beginning with myself can be tricky, and it might be for you as well if you've struggled with self-love and self-worth issues. Stick with it!
- Begin by bringing awareness into your heart center, located in the middle of your chest. Don't think about this area, but rather, be attentive. You may feel it begin to grow warm or tin-

gle or both, or nothing (and that's fine). Just hold your awareness there for a moment. I like to place both my hands over my
heart center, as I find it helps me go deeper as an added act of
self-care and compassion.

- Next comes the aspiration or intention, like a mantra: "May
  I be safe. May I be happy. May I be healthy. May I live with
  ease." If this language doesn't work for you, make up your own.

- After you've had a taste of loving-kindness toward yourself,
  move on to someone you love. This can be your partner, a
  child, a spiritual teacher, an artist who inspires you, or even
  your dog—any being you can love easily. With eyes closed,
  send this person loving-kindness from your heart to theirs.
  Again, state the aspiration or intention: "May you be safe. May
  you be happy. May you be healthy. May you live with ease." Or
  whatever words you feel most comfortable using.

- Move on to sending loving-kindness to a positive person, someone you feel goodwill toward—perhaps a friend or relative. I
  usually picture one of my friends who has seen me through
  some difficult times or someone whom I may not know personally but who has inspired me to be better in one way or another
  in my life. And from your heart to theirs, mentally send them
  loving aspiration.

- Then think of someone neutral. This can be a barista at your
  local coffee shop or maybe the person next to you on the sub-
  way. Perhaps it's the person you pass from time to time in your
  apartment building but have never spoken with, or anyone else
  you're impartial toward. And again, from your heart to theirs,
  send them loving-kindness.

- From the neutral person, move on to a difficult person. This is
  where it can get fucking hard. For example, this can be a boss
  or coworker, an in-law, the president, a neighbor who leaves his
  dog in the backyard all day, or generally anyone who is a source
  of irritation in our lives. Because this can be such a challenging part of the meditation, I like to suggest taking a moment

to contemplate how this person, just like you—in fact, just like every single person who's ever been here on Earth—has experienced some form of pain and suffering. I have a friend who likes to remind herself that we were all once someone's precious infant. Then take a moment to remember a time when you've experienced pain or suffering. It doesn't have to be the worst experience of your life—just something to help you soften your heart toward this difficult person. From there, as best you can in the moment, send loving aspiration.

- After you've sent loving-kindness to yourself, a loved one, a positive person, a neutral person, and a difficult person, picture all of them standing together in a room with you. Say their names and your own, and then state: "May we all be safe. May we all be happy. May we all be healthy. May we all live with ease."

- Now picture your love as a glowing white light extending out from your heart center, gradually engulfing all the people in the imaginary room. Marvel at the light as it spreads out to include the entire Earth, the moon, and the stars, and continues on to the farthest reaches of space, until all that is left is a radiance of loving-kindness and compassion. From this place that is no place, state your final aspiration or intention: "May all beings be safe. May all beings be happy. May all beings be healthy. May all beings live with ease."

10

WRITING AND FIGHTING FOR FORGIVENESS

CONVERSATION WITH J. IVY

I met J. Ivy at the 2016 Sun Valley Wellness Festival, where we were both presenters. We connected over our shared admiration for conscious hip-hop like A Tribe Called Quest, De La Soul, and Black Star, and immediately became friends. I was interested in talking to J. about relapse, because his life was impacted by addiction—he grew up with an alcoholic father who became his greatest life lesson in forgiveness. I wanted to explore living with addiction from the other side (the effect on a family member), and to learn how to recognize and release the wounds it creates, as well as how to forgive ourselves and others. I knew J. was the man to go to for guidance, because his book *Dear Father: Breaking the Cycle of Pain* had resonated for me. In it, he described his dad like this:

> *I don't remember him saying "I love you" when I was young, but he showed it by cooking us Malt-O-Meal or pork and beans. He showed it thru his smile when he would take us to fly kites, and*

when he would sing me happy birthday. Or when he would surprise me and pop up at my school to see how I was doing in class. I felt the love when I would drive around the city with him and be proudly introduced as his son Jimmy.[1]

Things changed for J. when he was around twelve or thirteen and his father lost his job as a DJ. Alcohol and drugs became a factor. I wondered what kind of effect that had on him: seeing a loving parent turn into someone unrecognizable.

It made sense that there was a radical change in J.'s world. His home life got crazy. J. told me that as he reflected on that time, "The word that kept popping up in my head was 'confusing'—it was so very confusing. There were lots of laughs and jokes and good times, and then the shift happened, and being a child, you don't know what to make of it. You don't know what's happening. I heard things like 'Stay out of grown folks' business,' and it was exactly that—it was grown folks' business. I remember being confused, scared, and wishing that I was bigger and able to stop the fights and the arguing. I also remember becoming very shut off. I became the true definition of an introvert. I was so closed and quiet, and I lacked confidence. I wasn't aware of it. I was going through the motions. I'd go to school, come home, a fight would break out or my mother would wake us up in the middle of the night and we'd pack things up and leave for my grandmother's or my auntie's house, where we would spend Christmas or Thanksgiving, and it was an awkward adventure." J.'s mom had finally had enough and filed for divorce. They moved to the suburbs south of Chicago.

Many of my friends and I are introverts (surprise, surprise—we tend to stick together—separately—at home), and I have experienced bouts of deep depression in my life, so I knew where he was coming from. My first real memories of this were during high school after giving up sports to focus on skateboarding and learning to play guitar, bass, and drums. I lived in a small town, and being a punk-rock skate-boarder made me an outcast. I did my best to live up to the anarchist creed of not giving a fuck, but inside, a part of me did. It wasn't easy often being mocked or blamed for things you didn't do (though, sure, sometimes I did do them), but I remember feeling "other than" so much of the time, as well as empty inside, which I later understood was what depression felt like. This is where the self-cutting came in, and later, the drugs and alcohol. Isolation can be debilitating and a risk for any-one who engages in self-destructive behavior, because depression—like fear—is often at the root of it. J. had some great insights into how to pull out of it. Like so many of us, he turned to his art, to self-expression.

"A big help was knowing that things get better with time, but that was centered around hope. I could have all the time in the world, but if I didn't have any hope, I would continue down a dark road. One of the things that allowed me to get through was writing poetry, which I was introduced to in high school when I was dealing with depression and anger and sadness. I had a teacher named Ms. Argue, and I always joke that what I learned is that I can't argue with somebody named Ms. Argue. She introduced me to the stage. She introduced me to writ-ing. Later, that became the vehicle, the tool I used to get to know my-self. In some ways, writing is what opened the door for the depression to heal, because writing was my way of getting to know myself. I would tap into my creativity, and thoughts would flow onto the page. I was always amazed by them, and the more amazed I was by the writing, the more I became inspired to write. I kept writing and writing and writ-ing. The more I looked at my life, the more I got to know the things that I *did* like, the things that I *didn't* like, the things that I loved and hated. I saw that the huge gap, the huge hole in my life, was that my father wasn't there. But high school had a lot of positive distractions. I had my friends, my family, and schoolwork. I was doing shows and chasing girls. I had sports and was playing football and running track. I was hooping with my boys."

In *Dear Father*, J. writes candidly about a deep depression he expe-rienced later in his life, which led him to isolate—to stop going to class and work. "By the time I was in college, I hadn't seen or heard from my father for close to ten years. I'd wake up in the middle of the night punching the walls, and it had a lot to do with him not being there. During college, it was as if I was on an island surrounded by people, but I felt alone. My pen and paper became my companions. I stopped going to work and classes. The only thing I found joy in was writing. And maybe with girls, smoking a little weed, or playing a video game, but they were only temporary help. When I got home from college, I opened up to my cousin and told her how I was feeling. She said, 'You need to learn how to forgive. If you don't learn how to forgive, you're going to carry that pain around with you for the rest of your life.'"

All of the wisdom around relapse, recovery, and almost every kind of human suffering is contained in J.'s cousin's words, so let's repeat them:

You need to learn how to forgive. If you don't learn how to forgive, you're going to carry that pain around with you for the rest of your life.

"That was the first time I was ever introduced to the idea of forgiveness. It never crossed my mind that I needed to forgive somebody who wasn't even around to forgive. Through writing and through exercises in creativity and forgiveness, that's how I eventually became able to write my way through this pain."

I was feeling inspired by this talk of forgiveness, because it's something I've worked so hard on in my own healing. I wanted to hear J. speak about this, and he did.

"Forgiveness frees you from whatever negative power has been holding you down and has shackled you in the depths of the ocean—that heaviness on you. I was taught that when you're able to forgive someone, you take the power back. People confuse forgiveness with forgetting—some small details may fade from your memory, but you don't forget. A television show will come on or you'll drive through a certain intersection; the wind will blow a smell from a restaurant; there are so many things that can trigger the past." This was something I could certainly relate to in my own experience with drugs and alcohol. A certain song would come on or I would drive through an old neighborhood—almost anything could trigger memories. For those who've struggled with depression, anxiety, and various kinds of addiction, those memories often aren't for the better.

J. explained that he got through those flashback moments by *remembering*, not forgetting. "You remember the lesson instead of the pain. You remember what the pain felt like, but you allow yourself to not go through it again. I like to say, 'If you don't deal with your emotions, one day your emotions will deal with you.'"

After J. had that talk with his cousin about forgiveness, he was performing at a youth revival at a church on the South Side of Chicago. "There was a buddy of mine giving testimony about how his sister had passed. Seeing his void, that hurt, that pain, that loss that couldn't be filled by anything reminded me of *my* void. I broke down, and it was in that moment that I prayed to God and said, 'God, I forgive my father. I want to see him and tell him I love him and I miss him.' It was overwhelming. Two weeks later God answered my prayers, and my father, after over ten years, called me up out of the blue! I was overwhelmed. Again. Some time went by and we reconnected, and then some more time went by and he passed away.

"When he did pass, I found myself going through it all over again. I'd forgiven him before. I got a chance to see him, love him, hug him, talk with him, sit down with him and watch football games, but then I was back in it. It was even worse than it was before. I was depressed. I was living in Nashville with my girl, Tarrey. We broke up, and I moved back to Chicago with plans of going to New York. Then I fell into the deepest depression. I was at my mama's house and I didn't leave my room for the whole summer. I was just in this room. I came out to eat, but then I'd go right back into the room. I was reliving it all over again. Those voices and those feelings were all taking over.

"When I finally got to the point of truly forgiving my father was when I had a conversation with my mother. She asked me what was going on. She mentioned how I hadn't been talking to her or Tarrey. I talked to my mother about my father for the first time. She listened, and after a few minutes she lit into me, saying, 'Look! Your father was a good man. Let him rest in peace.' This was my *mother* telling me this. One, I was going to listen because I love my mama. And two, she'd been through the most with him; if anyone had the right to say anything negative about him, it was her, but she never spoke negatively about him, and I did know he was a good man.

"At the end of it, I know he was a good man who had been hurt as a child. He grew up with his pain, and he didn't know how to cope with it or deal with it . . . and then he passed on. The compassion I could find in that moment, the understanding, and even the wisdom of my own life experiences and knowing what it is to be an adult with real-life issues, real feelings—all those things came together, and I heard her. I could hear Tarrey telling me that I needed to break the cycle. I could hear my cousin telling me I needed to learn to forgive, and it was in that moment I decided to finally, truly, truly forgive.

"That's when I wrote the poem 'Dear Father.' I was able to get down those feelings, thoughts, ideas, pain, and years of heaviness and feelings of being lost and devalued. I put it all on the page. There were tears on the page when I wrote the poem. I wrote it, and immediately I felt this weight lift. I put everything into that, as many of my memories and thoughts as I could think of. It was ultimately forgiveness that let me see the lessons from that. I took the lessons from those moments, but I left the pain. I took the lessons and was willing to learn from the pain, but I want to be happy. At the end of the day, I want to be happy. Forgiveness to me is, again, finding that freedom."

I too had found freedom in writing. It has been a very cathartic experience for me, one I've often suggested that others try. But after hearing multiple times that people felt intimidated by the idea because "I'm not a writer," it made me wonder what advice J. had for people who shared that concern. Or even for those who *were* open to the idea but just didn't know how to get started.

J.'s advice was not to think about it, to do it. "It sounds simple, but I know over the years when I've found myself flowing, I was writing, writing, writing, but then I hit what's called writer's block, and that's when I found I was overthinking it, telling myself: 'It has to be this. It has to be good.' When I take myself out of that space and write down whatever comes to mind, I'm not thinking about if it's good or not good. I'm just putting it onto the page.

"I tell people it's like meditation. It's a matter of being still and listening. Writing is the next step in. 'Okay, I'm still. I'm listening. Whatever I hear I'm going to write down. I'm not going to think about what I'm hearing. I'm going to write it down, and then from there, I'll structure and rewrite and go back through it.' Be free with it. Don't have any expectations. Don't have any reservations. Don't give in to fear. A lot of people harbor fear, and that's huge. It will get in the way. Often people are worried about what other people will think, but don't worry about that. What do *you* think? Don't worry about it being good or bad. Feel it. Whatever you feel, write that down.

"I've found that if I feel it, other people feel it. If I like it, other people love it. It's a matter of being confident and knowing that you have a gift. You have an amazing ability to put thoughts together. Be still. Listen. And write."

I loved that. One important piece of advice J. gave was not to worry what other people think. Many people, including me, will stop in the middle of writing because they begin to compare themselves to other writers. Learning to let go of that is huge. The other thing that works well for me is to write like today is my last day on Earth, my last day of being alive. Write with that kind of passion and abandonment. Pretend this is your last chance to sit down and write, so let it all out. Fuck what anyone else thinks.

J. connected with what I was saying, too, when he worked on his verse for the song "Never Let Me Down" on Kanye West's *College Dropout*. He asked himself, "What if I never get another opportunity like this one?" Writing out of desperation pulls something out of you, and it makes listening even easier. Another important piece of advice is not to let your ego get in the way, because your ego is the part of you that makes you think about what everybody will say. As J. put it, "If you can get the ego out, that's another factor. Be free with it. That experience was a huge lesson for me when it came to writing, because after the record came out I went through a long period of overthinking, and the overthinking came from me having the idea, 'Okay, now that this record is out, and now that it's been heard by millions of people and I'm on a record with Kanye and Jay-Z, I have to do that again, or better.' I found myself struggling with trying to emulate that, and my thoughts got in the way. After a long period of struggling, one day I woke up and asked, 'What am I doing? I wrote that piece one day freely, having fun. That's cool. But write something else now. The gift hasn't gone anywhere.' So yeah, overthinking will kill it."

Appreciating our gifts segued nicely into something else I wanted to explore with J.: gratitude. It was something he described as being very important in his own life. In the chapter "Fear Is a Hell of a Drug," he wrote:

> *In that moment I forgot to be grateful for what I did have in my life. I forgot to live in gratitude. I was spoiled by the success I had been experiencing, and falling off of that high made me feel so low. Not doing led to no money. No money led to isolation. Isolation led me back to feeling depressed.*
>
> *Depression led to not writing and doing what I naturally loved. With each step not being taken, I felt lower and lower. The negative spirits of old were haunting me again. Those negative voices were telling me that I wouldn't amount to anything, telling me that I would fail like my father did. Those voices were whispering to me that my dad left 'cause I was worthless, 'cause I was nothing, 'cause*

I didn't deserve to be loved. Those same voices were telling me that the world would follow suit and abandon me. Those voices were telling me to shut up, to stop writing, to stop performing, they were telling me that no one wanted to hear what I had to say.[2]

That rang true for me because to this day, those voices still creep into my head—the ones that tell me, as they did J., that indeed I am worthless and don't deserve to be loved. Sometimes they go a step further and become darker, saying the world would be a better place without me in it, and things to that effect. It's during those times (on a good day) that I pull myself back into the moment and remember that I have so much to be grateful for, the least of which certainly not being that after all the shit I've been through I'm still alive and can be of service to others. Thinking about that, I asked J. to elaborate a bit more on gratitude and how that impacted him.

J. told me that "gratitude is major. With gratitude, one of the things it does is keep you in the moment. If you're grateful for what you have right now, then you're in the moment. You're not in the past harping on what did or didn't happen, or who did what, or why life is a certain way or not. You don't harp on it. Instead, you're grateful in the moment. I'm grateful that I'm breathing, that I have life, that I have a beautiful wife, that I have opportunities and blessings coming my way. I have a roof over my head and I have food. I'm grateful that I have another day to create a world, to build on the steps from the past. I have lessons and knowledge and different experiences, and I won't, hopefully, make the same mistakes going forward.

"Gratitude is huge. I remember when I was writing my book, I was on a plane flying from Chicago to New York and I had the final version from the editor—when they send you the actual pages and you have to write on them and mark them up. I was on the plane and flipping through and taking notes, making sure everything was in order, and I reread the 'Dear Father' poem.

"I became overwhelmed with gratitude. I started thinking about how I went through a lot and how I was grateful that I could *come through it.* I was grateful that my father and I did have a relationship when I was younger. He brought me here. He taught me a lot, even when he wasn't here. He taught me things, and I learned from him; I knew he was walking with me on this path of *Dear Father.* I knew he was opening doors. I was grateful for having the ability to write this story and the gift of being able to get out and perform it and meet people and speak. I became overwhelmed as I thought about how if I hadn't have gone through any of this and my life had been perfect, maybe I would have been grateful for other things, but I wouldn't have been in this moment. I wouldn't have had this story to tell. I wouldn't have these experiences to share with people so they might help someone else. Gratitude is huge for me."

Like J., gratitude and forgiveness have been huge for me as well. When it comes to forgiveness, however, what is different in my case is that I've been on the receiving end of a lot more forgiveness than I've had to give; I suppose that's what happens when your life is overwhelmed by drugs and alcohol. Fortunately for me, I've been blessed with the most incredibly compassionate and supportive family a person could ask for, something I know others aren't so fortunate to have. I've also had some pretty incredible friends who've had my back through it all. The chorus from the song "Dead at Birth" by Connecticut hardcore band Death Threat sums up what I've felt for so much of my life: "I've got nothin' but I've still got friends. / I'm fuckin' broke but I still make ends. / I love my family / and all the friends who stood by me."

J. closed our conversation with some of the best advice I've gotten in a long time. "Stay lifted, stay positive. A new day is coming. Live in gratitude and be grateful for what you have. A long time ago, a buddy of mine said, 'Pain is a temporary inconvenience,' and the key word is 'temporary.' It isn't eternal. No storm ever lasted forever, and it's important that we remind ourselves of that. Better times are coming. Keep fighting for it. It can be a beautiful and fun fight. Just keep fighting for it."

PRACTICE

Write Because Your Heart Demands It

Journaling has been a hugely cathartic practice for J., me, and so many other people I know, so I'd like to share some thoughts (rather than instructions) that will hopefully help get you started if words are your thing.

- Write like today is your last day on Earth, your last day of being alive. Write with that kind of passion and abandonment. If this was your last chance, what would you say?
- Fuck what anyone else thinks.
- Get out of your head. Sit in stillness and write what you feel. Write for release, for healing . . . maybe even for sanity.
- Don't force yourself to write every day if you're not feeling it. I know this would be considered blasphemy by many writers, but this is my truth, so I'm going to share it how it is. This is something I learned very early on while writing songs. If you're forcing it, it's going to be ugly, *if* it happens at all. If that's the case, leave it alone and come back to it when you feel inspired. One of the worst things I think a writer can do is force it.
- If you feel you *must* write every day, I'll be the last one to tell you not to, but if that is the case, you're bound to run into times when the well is dry and nothing is coming out. When this happens, Google is your friend. Simply type in something

like "writing prompts" or "journaling prompts," and you're sure to get a ton of websites that will provide you with enough writing ideas to last a lifetime.

- Don't write for money or fame. Please, just don't. It's almost guaranteed to come off as empty, soulless, contrived, and just fucking gross. Instead, write because you want to be heard, even if it's only by yourself.

- Write because your heart fucking demands it of you.

- Write because it's the only thing in that moment that will help you find any semblance of understanding in this screwed-up world . . . or don't. What the fuck do I know, anyway?

11

RISING FROM THE WOUNDEDNESS

CONVERSATION WITH JP SEARS

esides being the funniest man on the spirituality and wellness circuit, JP Sears is a dear friend and an incredible guide when it comes to working through difficult emotional experiences, particularly childhood pain. He's known for his *Awaken with JP* video series, which is a YouTube sensation, and is the author of *How to Be Ultra Spiritual*. I went to him for help figuring out how the wounds of childhood affect our adult lives and how we can begin to uncover and release them, freeing years of pent-up suffering and negative emotional energy and preventing future relapse into destructive behavior.

JP defines relapse as "when we slide backward into a recurring pattern of dysfunction from our past that we've been distanced from for a while. In other words, experiencing the shadow of the past in the present." It's that shadow I wanted to delve into and its connection to our inner child. Hold up: When I talk about "inner child," I mean the part of our psyches we still carry from childhood—bumps, bruises, scrapes, traumas, delights, and all. For me, that might look like the kid who from his earliest memories never felt like he fit in and struggled to find his place in the world. For someone else it might be the child who witnessed his or her alcoholic parents fighting on a regular basis or endured physical abuse at the hands of a sibling.

Our inner child can be wounded in so many ways. Physical, emotional, or sexual abuse come to mind first, but there are more subtle means of inflicting harm, like traumatizing religious teachings of fire, brimstone, and eternal damnation; cultural and toxic shame, such as having to be a "Perfect 10" or the smartest, fastest, or best; not to mention institutionalized racism and sexism, which scientific studies have shown begin damaging us from a very early age.[1] Many of these wounds of childhood manifest in addictive behavior when we're adults as we take the wrong path toward self-healing.

JP had an interesting take on the whole concept of childhood wounds. "Because we're infinitely creative beings, as children we create many ways to be wounded. I use the word 'creation' because all wounding is a matter of our perception. It has very little to do with what happened but everything to do with our experience."

Then he took it further, saying: "It's *essential* that we become wounded." That struck me as strange until he elaborated. "I know that sounds a bit Jeffrey Dahmer–ish, but I want to pay great respect to the sacredness of being wounded. If as children we didn't unconsciously invest in creating wounding perspectives for ourselves, how the hell could we ever grow and get strong? One of the paradoxes of life is if you want to grow strong, you must be wounded. In other words, wounding is where we feel weak. Weakness is what gives rise to strength. Just like if you go to the weight room and want to build stronger biceps, you physically wound your biceps when you're lifting weights. You're wounding your muscle, breaking it down. As children, we make a sacred agreement at some level: 'Yes, I will go through this experience so that I can perceive trauma, pain, suffering from it.' That is a gift that the child gives its future self, because its strength arises out of its wounded-ness."

He added a caveat: "I don't think any of us need to go out and intentionally or consciously create wounding experiences. From the innocence and naiveté of our child self, we take on the appropriate level of woundedness in our formative years. It takes a long damn time to process it, to recover from it. And this is probably one of the reasons that life takes so long, because we pack in a lot of density of experience that we might call our wounds—it takes a while to sort through. Our wounds can occur in the vertical dimension of time, so someone might inappropriately touch us and the act might take five seconds, but to a significant degree, it impacts us based on our perception of the experience. So much so that we're not going to heal it in five seconds; it might take five months, five years, or five decades."

JP paraphrased Carl Jung as saying: "There are two principal wounds, two principal perceptions that create a wound: As a child I perceive that I am either overwhelmed or underwhelmed, which is the same thing as abandonment." JP added to that: "When we're overwhelmed, we're perceiving our boundaries, our sense of self as being violated, and if we can't process what's happening in the moment, then the emotions get stuck and create psychological scar tissue—that's the wound." I'd never heard of this overwhelm/underwhelm concept before and found it fascinating.

It works in the other direction as well. We may be underwhelmed, "which is not feeling close enough. We may not have our sense of self validated when we need it. There's too much distance between self and others, so typically what happens is we walk away when we're underwhelmed, abandoned, with a sense that we don't matter, that we're not enough. Part of how the wound is created is we typically assign a sense of 'it's my fault.'

"Whatever happened, whether we were overwhelmed—physically, emotionally, mentally, sexually—or underwhelmed, we harbor a sense of 'this is my fault.' We internalize it. It's a way for us to feel control over that which we perceive to be uncontrollable. If wacky stuff is happening and it's overwhelming, it's painful, and we can't control it, we look for what can give us a sense of safety, because being out of control is fear. Often what gives us a sense of safety is to anesthetize that fear."

I knew where JP was coming from. There were so many times when the only way I could cope with my self-loathing was to drown it in a bottle of cheap vodka or overindulge in sugary and processed foods. Anything that gave me even the slightest sense of relief from having to be me for a little while could become a remedy.

JP explained how to move that blame in a new direction. "If I can say, 'It's my fault,' and I get to feel a sense of control within the context of that which I cannot control, the degree to which I need to have a sense of control out of making this my fault is the degree that I internalize my felt experience, my perceived experience, and my thoughts about what's happening. I internalize it to a deep degree, so it's buried inside. It's hard to access, hard to process, and that's part of what makes a wound a wound, rather than a painful challenge that's overcome in the moment." He made the distinction between a challenge—"this was tough to go through, but I got through it"—and a wound—"this is tough to go through, but I haven't gone through it yet." It may take weeks, months, years, or lifetimes to turn challenges into wounds.

JP's insights into challenges and wounds made me think about how when it comes to kids, they're going to get wounded, even if they're growing up in what would typically be considered a healthy household with loving parents, positive reinforcement, and all that. What can those of us who are parents do to potentially lessen this wounding? I was curious, because for so many people I've worked with, particularly those dealing with drug and alcohol addiction, the issues are predominantly rooted in childhood, and aren't just big things like molestation but can be seemingly minor or innocent—such as being ignored by your parents or spanked as a punishment—and yet weren't experienced that way by the child. When I spoke with Gabor Maté (chapter 2), he shared his belief that all addiction stems from childhood traumas, noting that a trauma is not always a big event like most people consider it to be. How can a parent take a preventive approach to these wounds?

JP had a great suggestion: Don't try to avoid the issue. "Avoiding it means we flip-flop. For example, a parent might say, 'When I was a kid, my parents lived through me, and boy, that was painful. I'm not going to do that with my kid. I want to avoid wounding my kid like that.' In defiance of how they were raised, parents reverse polarities. They think they're not going to wound their child with overwhelm, but their child will likely perceive a wound of abandonment. Trying to avoid wounds just inflicts more wounds. Make space for wounding and know that even if you are a perfect parent, that too will wound your child *because they need to be wounded*" to grow both mentally and spiritually. Think about it like removing the dead foliage from a plant—if you don't "wound" the plant by pruning it, the plant can't grow.

JP suggested we make space for pain and make space for emotions. That space is one of the "greatest gifts a parent can give a child. If the child is angry, that's some heavy stuff they are processing, and it's a great gift when the child is given space. 'It's okay that you're angry, let it out.' Or, 'It's okay that you're sad. You don't need to convince me why you're sad or have a valid or logical reason as to why you have this emotion. You're simply allowed to have the emotion and let me make space for you. I'll be here with you so it can be safe for you. It will feel safe for you to feel this unsafe feeling.' That support is so important to give a child."

The other way JP suggested we could transform wounding in a way that would be beneficial to a child is for parents to work on their own emotional wellness. As is often said, "The greatest burden that a child must bear is the unlived life of a parent."

"I believe that our emotional DNA, our emotional residues are passed on to our children. They are way more brilliant than we can comprehend. They are incredibly intuitive. If we have heavy emotional energy blockages in our systems, even if we're numb to them and we don't know they're there, children feel them. They absolutely feel them, and they'll want to bring balance to not only you but the overall dynamic of the family. Whatever you ride around with constipated in your emotional energy system, if you don't take care of you, your child will try and compensate for you. And aside from that, just being a burden, as Carl Jung points out, it will ultimately leave the child with another wound that says, 'I'm not enough. No matter how much I become the good little boy or girl, or no matter how much I overachieve, or no matter how much I am defiant, or no matter how much I try to do what seems like needs to be done to compensate for this heavy, subtle energy Mom or Dad is carrying, I'm not enough to do it.' There's a great wound of shame, of 'I'm not enough' that comes when a child naturally unconsciously tries to carry the burden of the unlived life of the parent."

"I'm not enough" is something I could relate to, as it's a belief I've carried for the better part of my life. I know it's played a role in many, if not all, of the relapses I've experienced throughout the years. And even after all the time I've spent working with the various mind, body, and spirit practices I use, it still rears its ugly head from time to time. Fortunately, I've gotten better at smiling at those thoughts when they arise rather than buying into them and believing them as gospel, as I would have done in the past.

As JP points out, when parents work on their own emotional health and allow their passions and dreams to flourish, it will impact their children and allow them to live out their own dreams, not their parents' expectations. "It's said so often, but honestly I don't think it's said enough, because I know I haven't learned the lesson, I still need to hear it probably ten thousand more times: We need to fill our own cup up before we can help fill other cups." That's true of all relationships but especially the parent-child relationship.

This is so incredibly important. I know it's part of what happened during my last relapse. I was feeling spread so thin in all areas of my life. Much of the stress was a result of my cup being virtually empty, yet I kept trying to fill up others whenever and wherever I could. That's how I've always been. Finding balance is one of the most difficult things to manage in life, especially when you're in a line of work where you're trying to help others.

Assuming we make it through childhood, I was curious what impact JP thought the wounded inner child had on our lives as adults. He answered with one word: "significant." And then elaborated, saying, "Childhood is called the 'formative' years for a damn good reason. We are being formed during those years. We may be coherent in our formation or we're twisted and scarred by wounds to our psyche. Either way, it's formation. When we drop a pebble in a still lake, the ripples keep going long and far past the time the pebble hit the water, but that pebble, the shape and speed of its impact, that's the formative experience that creates ripples." He had another great analogy: "If we're aiming to live a good life, just as if we're aiming to get to the moon, when we launch our rocket, if our aim is even half a degree off, we'll miss the mark unless we compensate. Otherwise we'll miss the moon and end up lost in outer space. As adults, when we realize we're living in a way that's significantly incongruent with what our heart wants, this is often because we're still on a trajectory that was misdirected by the wounds of our formative years. It's like when we're physically wounded."

JP didn't leave us drifting in space with bleeding wounds. He had some concrete ideas for reclaiming our inner child and healing those wounds. "It's a journey with a lot of layers, but essentially we need to find the buried feelings, connect with them, make space for them, and feel them. Then we can allow memories to come into our conscious experience to help reshape our wounded or *mal*formation. Look at what happened, both the good and the bad, through the eyes of our inner child—not our adult mind. We're just going to over-rationalize things if we look at them only through our adult eyes. We can ask ourselves, 'Okay, Dad left when I was seven years old. What did that mean?' Our adult eyes will typically see the situation and report something like, 'Well, I understand my parents' marriage just didn't work out. It's good, because it might have just been worse if they had stayed together.' There's no heart in that, no emotion in that. We serve ourselves better when we ask, 'What was this like *for my seven-year-old self*?' For me, when my parents separated, from the perspective of my seven-year-old inner child, my world shattered. That's a little bit hard to process. It's not that my parents divorced—that's the literal explanation that my adult mind can accept. But from my inner child perspective, my world shattered. Your inner child needs to have a voice, and it won't have a voice until there are ears there to hear it. That's one of the reasons why we need to go back and revisit our childhood experiences, to listen and hear. For me, honoring the inner child's perspective, not trying to change it, not trying to talk the inner child into optimistically putting a positive spin on things—all this helps that inner child move out of being stuck and live more fully.

"Acceptance of what is, or acceptance of what was, for the inner child through the feelings and perceptions is important. Inner children are funny. They're just like adults. Their perceptions are completely delusional, but these perceptions are their own and need to be honored. Our job when we're looking at our childhood experiences isn't to shame our inner child and say, 'Oh, that's not how it was.' Screw that. If that's how my inner child saw it, then that's the perception that the inner child reacted to, which is what created the pain, so that perception needs to be honored. It needs to be voiced before it can possibly be moved beyond."

I loved the permission and acceptance aspect of what JP had to say. *Just allow this to be there. Honor it for what it is.* What about people who are completely cut off from their childhood self? Perhaps they've suppressed it to the point where it's completely in their unconscious. They've dissociated from it. I think this can often lead to suppressing feelings and returning to self-harming behaviors like numbing ourselves with drugs and alcohol because there's an underlying discomfort in our mental and emotional (and sometimes even physical) lives that we can't quite place our fingers on—hence its unconscious nature. Is there something proactive we can do to get back in touch with our repressed childhood self aside from therapy, which isn't always an accessible or a realistic option?

JP's suggestion was so pure and brilliant: *play!* "Just find a way to play. Not compete. Not compare yourself. Not seek approval. Not avoid disapproval. Those are all words that don't mean playfulness. I'm talking about finding a way to truly play. I won't accept the limited beliefs of people who say 'I'm not playful' or 'I don't have time to play.' Playfulness doesn't take linear time—it's a state of mind. A lot of us need an activity to facilitate that, whether it's getting together with friends or going hiking or painting. Finding and making space for playfulness—whether it's through a deliberate activity or a state of mind—are so important. It soothes the inner child. Taking a direct approach, saying, 'Dear inner child, tell me about your pain!' doesn't always work. Your inner child might need to be soothed a bit with playfulness to create a safe space to express the other aspects of childhood that are seemingly more threatening than playfulness."

I'd never associated playfulness and threat, but JP made a great point. "Playfulness is another term for releasing control. If you're in control, you're not being playful, and how many of us have been shamed or threatened for losing control? Say we knocked over a lamp when we were a child because we were careless, so when we're punished for that, our perception probably writes the script that says, 'Yeah, it's not good to be playful. Playfulness equals getting yelled at. Getting yelled at equals feeling ashamed. Feeling ashamed equals feeling unworthy. Feeling unworthy makes it feel like we don't belong in the family, and that can be inherently scary as hell.'"

As JP talked about this, he helped me realize I had an association between playfulness and using, as it was a way to experience being out of control. As sick as I would get and as much as I hated being caught in addiction, there was also a part of me that was attracted to chaos and getting as close to the edge as humanly possible without quite falling off. It's fucked-up, but then again, there's not much about addiction that isn't.

Another way to get in touch with residual childhood wounds is to work with our bodily sensations in the present moment. "Our sensations are the corridors, or they lead down the corridors to sensations that are much deeper. As in the martial arts—you're not going to be a black belt without becoming a white belt first. When it comes to knowing your child self, the white belt is getting in touch with simple body sensations. Learning to feel feelings. Tingling in the arm. Tightness in the chest. Lightness in the chest. Heaviness. Some might say, 'That's stupid. That's easy,' but we have to lift lighter weights to have the strength to lift heavier weights. Making the effort is where the therapy is. The effort creates connection. Accuracy does not necessarily create connection."

This made sense to me within the context of the relapses I'd suffered. It made me want to look at the larger picture. Why did JP think relapses happened? Why do we return to self-defeating behaviors we know from experience will harm us, especially once we've had some time in recovery or on the spiritual path?

First JP acknowledged the physical and chemical aspects of many addictions, and then he took it further. "Beyond any kind of chemical component, one of the reasons we all return to addictive substances or behaviors or patterns is because a part of us fears the unknown and becomes desperate to return to the familiar, even if the familiar is discomfort. The dominant comfort of the discomfort of the familiar—the dominant familiarity—has very little to do with the habit that we're dealing with and more to do with how we react to ourselves about the habit. In other words, if you fall off the wagon and the next day your inner critical voice may be red hot—you're kicking your own ass—I would say that critical voice is the familiarity that we're craving. It's very uncomfortable, but the discomfort of it is comfortable because it's familiar."

Again, this was something I could relate to in regard to addiction—the comfort in the discomfort because it was familiar. Change can be fucking terrifying. I have watched the television show *Intervention*, in which a camera crew follows around someone struggling with a kind of addiction (drugs, alcohol, binge/purge eating, hoarding, and so on). Toward the end of each episode, they stage an intervention, in which family and friends come together to speak about the way in which the individual's addiction has affected their lives. Then the addicted person is given the opportunity to go to a detox or rehab facility free of charge, and almost every time, you can see the internal battle going on—it's written so clearly on the person's face. In most cases, people agree to go to treatment, and in that moment, you can see a visible shift in their facial demeanor. They made it through the dialogue and the thoughts about why they shouldn't or couldn't go, and said yes. In that moment of agreeing to treatment, whether they're conscious of it or not, they've experienced some semblance of hope and peace. Sure, many of them are terrified, but I have to say from my own personal experience that they are also excited by the prospect of freedom from a life like that. Unfortunately, many people leave treatment early and relapse, or complete the treatment and still relapse. Most of the people on *Intervention* and in real life who struggle with addiction and engage in some type of treatment program experience how change is exactly what they needed and what freedom from the hell of addiction tastes like.

"Part of our psyche speaks in the critical voice, and another part of our psyche receives it. The receiver is the familiarity with which we become self-identified. Who are we as we're being belittled and criticized by this voice? Typically, our answer to 'Who am I?' when we're doing this is 'I'm someone insignificant; I'm someone who basically feels worthless.' We can look at that and say, 'Wow! I was starting to go further into the unknowns, the mystery of my life, which is synonymous with stepping deeper toward my great gifts in life, which is our true source of significance.' Like Nelson Mandela said, 'I learned that courage was not the absence of fear, but the triumph over it. . . . The brave man is not he who does not feel afraid, but he who conquers that fear.'[2] We're far more afraid of our power than our weakness."

PRACTICE

Reshaping Our Wounds

When I was in Mexico teaching with JP a couple of years ago, he shared a practice that I found immensely beneficial. It was a way to move stuck energy and allowed me to get back in touch with little Chris and explore some of the hurt I was holding. It was a cathartic experience and a practice I've worked with many times since.

It's another journaling practice, but a little bit more structured this time. The idea is to get your inner child to put the words on paper. Our adult hand may be writing, but the information is coming from our child mind.

- Start with a memory.
- Then write a challenging memory, maybe a painful one. You might say, "I can't access my childhood memories. I'm so disconnected from that pain." But I know you can. What's a little thing you can access? Start there. Even if it was that you were picked last for the dodgeball game. Well, that's not a huge trauma, but it *was* a challenge, and if it's the most challenging memory that comes up, then great. It gives you traction.
- Then ask your child self how that felt. Write down your response.
- Now ask yourself what it meant to you. Feel free to approach this from a child's perspective, not an adult's. I'm right-handed,

so sometimes I do this with my left hand to return to the sensation of a child's uncertainty when holding a pencil and forming words.

- Now read what you wrote aloud and appreciate the release you've given your inner child, the freedom to voice its suffering. As you say the words, think of it as a ritual for moving stuck energy and emotions. It's a way of putting the emotional energy into words and then back into energy rather than letting it stay stuck in our energy system, in our psyche.

12

A TINY BIT MORE

CONVERSATION WITH MONA HAYDAR

I was introduced to Mona Haydar and her work by my dear friend Mirabai Starr. Mona is a poet, an activist, a practitioner of permaculture, a meditator, and a tireless God enthusiast who leads a life of sacred activism. Mona and her husband, Sebastian, set up a table in Cambridge, Massachusetts, with a sign that read TALK TO A MUSLIM. They gave out free coffee and donuts to encourage questions and open dialogue. This garnered the attention of NPR, Al Jazeera, and other media outlets. I sought to explore Mona's thoughts about relapse and forgiveness, especially within the context of the teachings of Islam, but first I wanted to know a little bit more about her.

What was her childhood like, and what was her relationship to spirituality? It turns out that, like me, Mona was a bit of a wild child. "I spent almost all my time outside. I feel like most of my childhood was spent in an apple tree in my parents' backyard. That was my introduction to the essence of the creator—I found God in nature. I connect the deepest even now to the sense that there's something greater than myself. Nothing else in my life has brought me such solace or contentment as that sense of depth and interconnectedness and still-ness."

After nature, Mona discovered poetry. She wrote her first poem in kindergarten: *I am dude. I am mood. I am Mona.* "It just kind of took off from there, and I've been writing ever since. It's one of the ways I connect to God and spirit, and one of the ways I ground myself. I can get lost in the world of form and in the world of busyness, and the God of busyness and the God of business, too. Writing helps bring me back into my spirit, myself, and my heart-centeredness.

"Along with nature and writing and reading to others, a huge part of my spirituality is giving thanks for those things, living in gratitude for those things, because they are what helped me to get connected." Mona knows about connection—she grew up with seven siblings. "I was number seven of eight, so ours was this huge Syrian family, but be-cause they were mostly older, I felt like I had to grow up a little faster, like I was playing catch-up. Perhaps I was a little more serious as a kid than my friends were because I was interested in what my siblings were doing when they were in university talking about lofty ideas. Because I grew up fast, I now hunger for fun and for that childlike playfulness, so I seek it out in my life."

That resonated as something that's always been important to me—staying in touch with my youthful spirit. I often joke that I'm an eleven-year-old and that I don't ever want to lose touch with that playful side. I also appreciated how Mona talked about finding and ex-periencing God in nature. There are people who get so caught up in the transcendental and mystic experiences, which can be very important and valuable, but they miss the experience of God in nature or nature in general because they believe it's all an illusion, so what's the point? I'm with Mona—I see God in all things. Like Buddhism teaches, form is emptiness, emptiness is form. Or, in the context of God, while God on the ultimate level has no ascertainable qualities, (s)he animates and imbues all things that take form. So form and emptiness, God and life, are one and the same.

Mona heard where I was coming from. "Nothing is devoid of God. Even if you want to just look at it in terms of God as the creator or imaginer of all. Any time we say that something is devoid of God, that's a separation, and it's breaking the magic, it's breaking the sacredness of the world as a whole—this whole universe, the seen and the unseen."

What Mona said is exactly why I titled my second book *Everything Mind*. It's all a part of it, so I appreciated what she was saying. Obviously, God can be a very loaded word for some people, and I wanted to talk to her about this through the perspective of Islam. I'm not going to pretend I'm any kind of expert on Islam, and the little bit I know is that in Arabic the root word for Islam means surrender, and from this root word you can also derive the word "peace." So Islam means the peace that is experienced when one's life is surrendered to God. It seemed like a good place to start.

Mona told me that was the Sunday-school definition of Islam. When she leads retreats with kids, she teaches them that Islam means peace. "It's a nice sound bite: *Islam means peace.* The word Islam comes from the root word for peace, which is *salaam*. It's how we greet each other: 'Peace be upon you.' The root word for salaam is safety, because when you're at peace, you're in safety. When you surrender, you're also in safety. One of my dear teachers says, and I believe it is a quote from the prophet Muhammad himself, that when a human being surrenders themselves to the Earth, to the universe, and to God, then the universe will surrender itself for that person, but when that person is working toward something and doing and toiling and has not submitted themselves, then the universe will go out of its way to trip that person up and create roadblocks. If you've surrendered, the universe will be in service to you."

I've experienced this firsthand on a number of occasions, especially when coming back from a relapse. When I've finally been beaten down into submission and have no more fight left in me, all that's left is surrender, and it's from this place of letting go and allowing guidance from that which is greater than me (whether one calls it a higher power or simply the help of friends or a support group) that things do begin to come into alignment and fall into place. Piece by piece, I regain mental clarity, and then the physical healing occurs, all while the spiritual elements are being reconciled in their own ways (sometimes it's prayer, sometimes it's mantra, sometimes it's meditation, sometimes it's silence in nature, and so on). But the common denominator in all of this is letting go, surrendering—basically just getting the fuck out of my own way.

"I find that huge for my theology—to say that Islam is about surrender—but it's also about being at peace. It is the way of Jesus in that it is the way of love, because love is the way of surrender. There's a saying, 'To the one who loves, you have surrendered.' This is because when you're in love, your beloved can wish you anything and can say or do anything. Especially in the very pure and innocent early love stages, that person can do no wrong; they can say nothing that will move your heart away from them. So one of the prominent Muslim prayers is to say, 'Oh, changer of hearts. Oh, turner of hearts. Make me steadfast. Make my heart steadfast upon this path.' Our hearts turn and turn and turn, so let us turn toward the One and be steadfast in that, because we often take long detours when we haven't submitted, when we haven't surrendered, and the universe wants to catch us and say, 'Hey! Give up, give in.' So when we do, it's a straight shot."

As I've said before, in my own life the universe has had to step in quite a few times and trip me up. The most recent and extreme example that comes to mind is, again, awakening in that hospital bed with the tubes in my throat while my wrists were strapped down. What an utterly horrific experience, but one that I've come to accept as a part of making mistakes and learning and growing. It's helped me in a very deep way to continue softening my heart toward myself and being gentle with my process—with being this awkward and determined human being.

I wanted to talk more about God. When it came to Islam, I'd heard the term "the One God," and I wondered how it differed from other religions' interpretations of God.

According to Mona, not much! "The One God does not differ in any way from any other god or gods. God is the overarching Oneness, the total inter-being and total interconnectedness that is everything. It's abstract because that God, that creator, created time and space, and because our minds are bound by that time and space, how can we understand that which is beyond time and space? In Muslim theology, it's quite simple, because God gave himself.

"We say 'him' because that's how God is referred to in the Quran, but it doesn't necessarily connote that God is male. This came from a patriarchal society, also a pagan society, but within the Muslim tradition. God often refers to himself as 'we,' and for me that ties back to interconnectedness. We learn about it as the 'royal we' because that's how the monarchs refer to themselves in their decrees, but I like to see it as the we that ties us all together, and we essentially are the we, and God discusses himself in the Quran as the beginning and the end. How can you be both the beginning and the end? He discusses himself as the seen and the unseen. If you're beyond time and space, you can do whatever you want. God is the most merciful and he is a punisher. He is the creator of all things and the destroyer, the giver of life and the taker. In all the polarities and extremes, there is God, so what about everything in between? Is God there, too? I would say yes. If God wanted us to believe that he is the beginning and the end, well then, isn't he the perfect now?"

I loved what Mona had to say! I drew so many connections to different wisdom traditions—Kali the creator and the destroyer came to mind. And when she spoke of the interconnectedness of all things, I thought about Thich Nhat Hanh and the Buddhist teachings, which I especially appreciated because some Buddhist practitioners take issue with the word God, but I think that's a beautiful way of showing some relation, some common ground that can be shared with Buddhists, and perhaps even some atheists. And there's common ground with the other Abrahamic religions, Judaism and Christianity. What's important to me is finding what we share. Rumi's garden beyond right and wrong. Where's the place we can meet upon and build on together?

It turns out that Mona has lived at the Lama Foundation in New Mexico, an interspiritual community and retreat center with strong ties to the Hanuman Temple in Taos and to Ram Dass. So she had a deep understanding of what it means to be interspiritual. "If the spirit of that place is anything, it is the weaving of the cosmic tapestry of all traditions and all spiritualities. I learned to use words that were less dogmatic. I grew up in a Judeo-Christian society, and the common language didn't necessarily sit with my brain, with my heart language. I loved the things I learned there, like inter-being from Thich Nhat Hanh and a lot of the other Buddhist teachings that resonated within me as a Muslim. People often ask if my Islam is lessened or threatened by my acceptance of other explanations of things like karma and reincarnation, but you know what? Hogwash! That's a bunch of bull. It's another one of these things that ties back to the use of language. It can separate us, but in the same way, it can also bring us together. I can use the language of the Buddhists and the descriptions of the Hindus and remain solidly and devotedly Muslim, because I believe in the God of everything. I believe in the god of the Hindus—in Kali, in Hanuman—and the Buddha, and everything in between."

Mona spoke to my heart! She was articulating exactly how I felt. I love that when I read Meister Eckhart's description of the godhead, it sounded just like the explanation of Dharmakaya from Buddhism and Brahman from Hinduism. It makes me feel grateful and connected to learn and grow from these other faiths and teachings. I struggle with labeling myself as *this* or *that*, and I probably resonate most loosely with the teachings of Buddhism. However, I have a deep love for God, and that's very important for me. Maharajji has been and is very important in my life, as are the teachings of Ram Dass. Finding that place beyond reconciliation—where they fit together, but it's okay when they don't—is a place we can all grow from. It's a beautiful conversation and dance we can have with one another.

This was a great insight. Maybe those places where they don't fit aren't real. Maybe that's ego. "We don't want it to fit because it messes with our historical understanding and explanations of things. That all stems from a human desire for grandeur or exclusivity: 'Mine is different and therefore better.' I just don't feel that way. I think we're all the same. We're all in the same shit. We're all doing the same things. At the end of the day, we're all made of the same earth stuff and we'll all return to the same earth, and in between, let's be kind to each other. I don't care what religion you practice or ideology you live under. Even if you're an atheist, if you're kind to humans and animals and creatures of all sorts and the Earth, I think that's what religion is—call it God or not. I think ego gets in the way; it's our funny little twisted sense of self that wants to be special, different, and better than."

The amazing things Mona was saying and how she included atheism in her explanation reminded me of my friend who's the humanist chaplain at Yale. He's an atheist and wrote a great book called *Faithiest*. His name is Chris Stedman, and he is one of the most spiritual, good-hearted guys I've ever met. He wouldn't call himself spiritual, but his whole thing is about working with people from all religions, finding where they can come together, meet, and be of service to humanity, to the betterment of us as a species. I think that's tremendous. That's such a beautiful thing. What he explained to me, and as he wrote in his book *Faithiest*, is that "faithiest" is a derogatory term that atheists use for other atheists who don't believe in God but are willing to talk with religious people and work with them. How crazy is that? It's ego, it's dogma. I think it's beautiful that there are faithiests in the world who just want to help and be of service.

I was digging the insights via Islam that Mona was giving me, and it made me hungry for more. What could she tell me about Muhammad?

It didn't take much prompting to get her started. "The invitation to speak about my beloved and the beloved of God warms my heart. Sure, he was the mouthpiece of God, but through the angel Gabriel. Muslims believe in the seen and the unseen, so we believe in all prophets who manifested in this world as humans. We're sent the same message. Muhammad is among his brothers in a long line of prophets. It's important to note that the Quran stipulates that although it mentions specific examples of who these prophets were, there are innumerable ones who are not mentioned. So I believe Krishna was a prophet of God. I believe that the Buddha was. I believe that there are countless other ones who came with the same message the Prophet Muhammad did: the message that we are one; that this whole universe with the beautiful Earth we were amazingly given, and that we honor and love, is here as a Quran for us, as a spiritual guidebook. It's like when you go into nature and experience biodiversity, you know that everything exists in the light of another. You know the different creatures and plants feed each other, and it all works together to produce a magnificent, glorious thing. The Prophet Muhammad said we are just one part of that. Humans are ambassadors on this earth, are caretakers of the Earth, and that is our vital role. Yes, our vital role is to know God, but it is specifically to know God through care of the Earth.

"One of the things that makes me both happy and sad is to see Muslims on the forefront of the global warming and climate change activism and movement. I just love seeing Muslims who are active, because to me, that is an integral part of our faith, our tradition, but it makes me sad to see so-called Muslim countries deplete the earth of its natural resources like oil and call themselves Muslim, because that's counter to what we believe. A huge part of what the prophet Muhammad taught was that we're not separate from each other, we're not separate from nature, and only when we see ourselves as separate can we lay so much destruction upon the Earth. We must work together to perpetuate the beauty in the world."

That took me right back to what we'd been discussing about so many of the wisdom traditions saying the exact same thing, each in their own language.

"One of the things Prophet Muhammad, peace be upon him, God says about him in the Quran, we did not send you except as a mercy, or as unconditional love to the world. And this message of unconditional love, which is wrapped in mercy, that's just not a message that I think is getting out there enough: that Mohammed was about love. Anything else is secondary. People want to talk a lot about jihad, and they want to talk a lot about sharia—well, I'll tell you right now what sharia is, sharia is all the things I just said. Sharia is the path and trajectory to attain gnosis of God, to attain a direct relationship with the creator. And how do we do that? By being stewards of the Earth. That is the way. By wrapping ourselves in the cloak and in the blanket of that unconditional love and mercy and saying that we're not separate from nature or one another, so how could we then harm one another? That's the integral message, and also to see God in the other, because if you see God in the other, you could never harm the other. And you see that there is *no* other. That it's just you and you and you and you and more and more and more, and it's all love."

With all this amazing talk about love, I knew it was time to ask Mona a question I'd been holding on to. What was her definition of relapse?

"My definition of relapse is to be attached to old patterns we know no longer serve us. Old patterns we've decided are in fact harmful and painful, but like muscle memory, we come back to them out of habit. Creating new habits is the key to ridding ourselves of the old ones. In Islam, it is said to take forty days to create a habit, and that the best of good actions is the one that is done consistently. So after forty days of doing something, we should set up plans of action that will help us tap into a consistency. The way to remove the possibility of relapse is to put something else in its place, something bigger and more beautiful, and commit it to memory and habit."

Once we begin to undo relapse, we need to address the damage we've done. It's often been said that "hurt people hurt people," as well as that true healing begins within—this is especially true in the context of relapse and repeating self- or relationship-destructive behaviors. I wanted to hear Mona's thoughts on this. How we can extend our personal healing work into the world to make a positive impact?

"Healing begins and ends with love. Many of us carry around our wounds and our pain like battle scars that we glorify and allow to re-open and fester when we become triggered or rehurt. There is a better option: In our daily lives and care, in our tenderness, we must apply salves and balms of love and healing to the places we know we have wounds by actively helping to remediate the harm done." She broke it down into steps:

- The first step is the recognition of the hurt.
- The second is identifying what needs to be healed. Sometimes our pain needs acknowledgment before it can transform into beauty and restoration.
- Third, we must actively apply the healing to the hurt.

"Affirmations are great, sometimes bodywork is necessary, sometimes meditation and ritual, but generally if we ask the hurt what it needs, it will tell us. We will want to do the thing that will lead to the healing whether we know to connect it or not. I know this sounds abstract and perhaps out in some outer-space la-la land, but it's real. I've seen it done, and I've done it myself. It works. Often those same wounds and the places where the wounds live become some of our greatest sources for building and working toward a more beautiful world. It's sort of magical."

This made me think of a note I wrote to readers in my second book, *Everything Mind*:

> *I want to give you my insides—unfiltered and undiluted. Along with this raw offering come—and in complete clarity, I might add—my imperfections. I write from this place of vulnerability because I want you to see me in all my humanity—all of it. I am a real person who would never pretend I have all the answers or this life thing entirely figured out. I don't. On top of that, I have no shortage of flaws, though I do try my best to be a little better each day, and I think there's something to be said for that. It's important for me to be real with you about this because I hope it encourages you to be real with yourself while doing whatever you need to in order to be a little better each day as well.*[1]

For me, those words were an homage to the beautiful wounds we all have and will continue to experience as life goes on being life. I believe wholeheartedly, just as Mona said, that these wounds—these painful, wretched, life-affirming, beautiful wounds—can "become some of our greatest sources for building and working toward a more beautiful world."

After healing comes forgiveness. I've talked about it a lot in this book because it's so important—without forgiveness, we're fucked.

Mona agreed: *Forgiveness is a key to the alleviation of so much suffering.* She went on to share, "My mother always encouraged me as a child never to hold on to hurt inflicted on me by others. She always reminded me that my holding on to that hurt, that pain, was more than just toxic to me, it was in fact toxic to the people I love, and yet it would never hurt who or whatever hurt *me*." And then she brought me back to love—self-love, to be precise. "We must choose to love ourselves enough to be free from the shackles of grudges and pain, and forgiveness unlocks those shackles. It's not so much a process of rationalizing anything, but instead of examining our feeling hearts and actively releasing the pain and hurt. It doesn't always work right away. Sometimes it takes a concerted and consistent effort to make it happen, but it's so possible. Once you've done it one time, that liberation is exhilarating. It's a real spiritual high that doesn't have a crash. We can all become masters of forgiveness, and when we do, we become lighter, more agile, more awakened."

Her words struck a chord with me. My practice of self-forgiveness since my relapse has certainly deepened. The self-negating thoughts still arise, and perhaps that will never change (or perhaps it will, who knows?), but no matter how often my mind tries to convince me I'm not worthy of forgiveness, that's complete and utter bullshit. Fuck it if this sounds cliché, but I am worthy of forgiveness and love and good things in life as much as anyone else, even when every cell in my brain is trying to convince me otherwise. I do my best to remember my truth. It's not always perfect, and sometimes, yes, I can still stay too long at the pity party, but it's diminishing. Yet, I wondered, is forgiveness always appropriate? What did Mona think?

"Always. Always. Always. To not forgive is to allow toxicity to dwell within us. Forgiveness doesn't mean returning to the source of the hurt and allowing it to continue to abuse us or cause pain. Forgiveness is a personal inward journey we all deserve—it's a love for our own sacredness, our own mystical spirits, that is always appropriate. Nothing should get in our way when it comes to this love."

I have to say that one more time: *Forgiveness is a love for our own sacredness.*

Wow.

And just a little more love . . . Mona ended our conversation by saying, "Reach out to your neighbors—whether you have Muslim neighbors or Hindu neighbors or anything neighbors. Reach out and give love and be love in the world, because there's not enough of it and we all have an infinite amount. One of my dear friends said to me, 'Mona, just work a little bit harder, just do a little bit more, and when you think you can't do a little bit more, just do a tiny bit more.' I think we can all do a tiny bit more to love more truly from our hearts. Maybe some of us can try a lot harder, but all of us can try at least a tiny bit harder to be more kind and friendly and smiley.

"In Islam, a smile is considered charity. Not like ho-hum charity in the metaphorical sense. It's considered charity as though you've given your money away. It's like what Ram Dass says about Maharajji telling him at the beginning of his journey to give it all—that's giving it all. A smile that's from your heart. So connect with people. Look them in the eye and be present with them. I think that's the only way out of our current state of affairs, and that's the only way out of our disconnectedness—to be there for one another, to see each other, and give a little bit more love, and then give a tiny bit more after that."

PRACTICE

You Could Be a Saint

A wise elder once told Mona, "If you try a little bit harder, you could be a saint." This led her to the most beautiful practice. It's simple yet profound.

Several times throughout your day, pause and ask yourself:

- Am I doing this excellently? Am I doing this beautifully? Am I giving it my full presence?
- Can I try a little harder?
- Listen for your answer.

That's it.

Mona told me, "I've seen what happens when I *do* try—my life becomes more full of love, more full of prayers and dreams manifesting themselves beautifully. It's almost a selfish act, because while it can be difficult at times to try harder or to take the moral high ground, it ultimately results in my own increase in contentment. This contentment is everything to me—it's gratitude wrapped up in a beautiful joy that makes me and mine shine—even if it's only in my own eyes."

13

THE INEVITABLE CATASTROPHE

CONVERSATION WITH DUNCAN TRUSSELL

I hit it off with Duncan during an event we did together in New York City hosted by Ram Dass's Love Serve Remember Foundation. Duncan is a comedian who speaks about how psychedelic drugs can help people heal conditions like depression and anxiety, as well as facilitate spiritual awakening (among a *wide* variety of other things, but this book has only so many pages). I wanted to find out where he saw psychedelics on the spectrum of addictive behavior, but Duncan had other plans. Before I could start asking a lot of questions, he told me he had something he wanted me to read. It was a passage from that seminal Hindu scripture, the Bhagavad Gita:

Arjuna said: What is the destination of the man of faith who does not persevere, who in the beginning takes to the process of self-realization but who later desists due to worldly-mindedness and thus does not attain perfection in mysticism?

"O mighty-armed Kṛṣṇa," Arjuna continues, "does not such a

*man, being deviated from the path of Transcendence, perish like a
riven cloud, with no position in any sphere?*

*"This is my doubt, O Kṛṣṇa, and I ask You to dispel it com-
pletely. But for Yourself, no one is to be found who can destroy this
doubt."*

*The Blessed Lord said: "Son of Pṛthā a transcendentalist en-
gaged in auspicious activities does not meet with destruction either in this world or in the spiritual world; one who does good, my
friend, is never overcome by evil."*[1]

Duncan explained that "as somebody who is constantly falling
away from the path," this passage was one of his favorites. "In fact, I
don't even know if I've gotten to the path yet. I'm falling away from
getting near the path." I loved that, and I loved the next line he read:

There is never any loss nor diminution on this path.

Duncan pointed out that "this is super cool, because in everything
else in the world, if you don't keep it up, if you don't keep your exercise
program up, you lose muscle. If you don't eat right, you're going to get
fat. But what the Bhagavad Gita is saying is that any kind of progression at all is an *eternal* progression, which is counterintuitive; it goes
against everything we understand." Duncan read some more:

*The unsuccessful yogi, after many, many years of enjoyment on the
planets of the pious living entities, is born into a family of righteous
people, or into a family of rich aristocracy. Or he takes his birth in a
family of transcendentalists who are surely great in wisdom. Verily,
such a birth is rare in this world.*

"The idea is, if you start this path and then you die, then in your
next incarnation—if you didn't finish or pick the path back up in this
one—little bread crumbs get dropped in your life." This creates opportunities for the things that feel predestined or meant to be. "That's the

'why do I feel this weird attraction to this book?' Of all the books on the shelf, suddenly you're pulling down whatever it may be, the Bhagavad Gita or some book on yoga or a Ram Dass book, and you feel more drawn to that, you feel a weird magnetic pull toward that rather than the hundreds or thousands of other books to choose from. This is a continuation of some momentum that you started days, weeks, months, years, or perhaps lifetimes ago, and it never stops."

That certainly resounded for me—especially what he was saying about the magnetic pull toward texts and teachers. Anyone who reads my books or listens to my podcasts knows I've had no shortage of those experiences. I also liked the idea of returning to the path across lifetimes, because we don't have to feel neurotic about losing what progress is made.

This made me think about my experiences of relapse. The first few times I felt like a complete failure—an utter fuckup and nothing more. As time went by and unfortunately more relapses happened, I began to see a pattern: They were growing shorter. While I would still bottom out, the bottoms were significantly less deep than in relapses gone by. What this taught me is that every day in recovery (not just sobriety, but actual recovery) has long-lasting ripple effects. With the continuing relapses, I also noticed a power greater than myself (however one chooses to label or define that) had not forsaken me; rather, I'd forsaken *myself*. That power was right there to help pick me (and the pieces) up when I was able and ready to surrender and begin again.

Most people who've been on a spiritual path a little while—hell, even those who haven't—have had glimpses of awakening, of truth, of nonduality, and sometimes coming out of that nondual experience can be terrifying to our ego selves because it shows us that there's nothing to hold on to, no past, no future; there's only now. Our ego hates this, because part of its function is grasping, regardless of what it's grasping for—just anything to keep it alive.

Duncan got where I was coming from and connected it to a story about a memorable teacher—Percy, who taught him how to swim when he was a kid. "I was terrified of swimming. I don't know if you remember, but when you're a kid, man, going out into the deep end is a big fucking deal. That's death for a kid. You will die in the deep end if you don't know how to swim. Kids who can make it to the deep end, you look at them like 'Holy shit! They're swimming in the deep end of the pool with no floaties!' Percy would take us out into the deep end of the pool, and the whole time he'd tell hilarious jokes. He knew we were terrified, so he'd have us laughing, and he would sing to us and do these ridiculous things, and before I knew it, I realized that he wasn't holding me anymore, that I was floating on my back in the deep end of the pool." This is what the best teachers do. "They come into the shallows where those of us are interested in going into that deep water hang out, and they start telling jokes. You don't realize it because they're so cool, but you start following them, and the next thing you know, you've become the thing they were talking about. And then, when you realize it, that's when you start sinking, like, 'Oh fuck, what?' And then the pattern repeats."

What a great analogy! It reminded me of an experience my brother Jay had in the deep end of the pool, which wasn't so enjoyable, and it's a pretty good metaphor for my own spiritual life. We were taking swimming lessons at a local YMCA, and my brother was terrified to go into the deep end. These two fucked-up swim instructors grabbed my brother by the ankles and the wrists and swung him back and forth, saying, "One, two, three—heave ho!" and threw him into the deep end. I was already in there myself and was an okay swimmer at that point, so I went over to help him back to the side of the pool, but that shit traumatized him. To this day, he won't swim. I think about that and how it was the hell of living in addiction that thrust me onto a spiritual path in a similar sink-or-swim sort of way. Fortunately,

I've also had teachers like Duncan's Percy (many of whom you're meeting in this book) who eased my transition with humor and compassion. There are so many people who don't learn to swim, who drown in the spiritual pool—which is to say, die in addiction.

Duncan got where I was coming from. He recognized that there are different levels from which we can experience "the inevitable catastrophe, and drug addiction is certainly one of the more popular ways to die these days." It reminded him of times in his life when he was addicted and suicidal, and likened addiction to a weird form of suicide.

"Even there in that place, and everyone has a different version of it, if your mind comes to you at all, and there isn't a wave of guilt or a wave of craving, then even down in that place you still experience this amazing sweetness, and that's always a shocking moment, because you're, like, 'I'm lying on a mattress kicking dope with roaches crawling on me and I was thinking about jumping out the window to commit suicide.' Even here, there's beauty in the world. On one level, it's catastrophe; on another level, it's more teaching.

"I get in trouble for this idea a lot. I might say, 'This is heaven. No matter what's going on. You're in heaven. There's no way out of it.'" Then someone will bring up something awful like a terminal illness or a hurricane or corrupt politicians and ask Duncan if *that* is heaven. Duncan says, "The answer is that we don't know the victims of the crisis, we don't know where they are. But people must ultimately decide which lens to look at the situation through. That lens can be 'This is an absurd and cruel universe with no meaning.' The best way I've heard it described is that there was a catastrophic accident that happened with matter—it became aware of itself. And it's tragic. There are no mistakes, and there are no non-mistakes, but basically we're the part of matter that became aware of itself. This was the very worst thing that could happen to matter, because if you're not aware of yourself, you get to non-exist, and to non-exist is to be truly in heaven, so we're fucked; that's the idea.

"That's one lens you get to decide to look through. The other lens you can decide to look through is the lens that people like Ram Dass point us toward, which is that even now, even now, whatever it is, even now, it's still perfect. Even amid the catastrophe that is inevitable, Krishna, God, realization is playing this game of hide-and-seek, and you can always find it in there."

I admire Duncan because he brings humor to dark situations and shakes up assumptions rooted in a dualistic experience of life. I'm not saying that any of us is better than any other, because (at least in regard to the ultimate reality, for which all the great wisdom traditions speak) there *is* no one else. However, the entire premise of this book—the relapses I've experienced and that we all endure in one form or another—arose because I was stuck in the belief of an isolated, lonely, fearful, separate self. From that place of dualism, it's natural to be outraged, because from the separate, egoic lens, it *is* outrageous. Then you encounter Ram Dass and many other teachers who speak from the place of ultimate reality, where there is *no more* separation. The see-er, the seeing, and the seen are all one, and that's why, even though horrible things happen, they can still be experienced as perfection, because they are unfolding as life unfolds. Yes, it's sad, oftentimes tragic, and as humans, even when we do start to awaken and the egoic stronghold of "me" and "them" begins to fall away, it's not as if our feelings vanish. We still experience pain. A loved one dies and we still grieve, but we can witness suffering from a place that sees the perfection in it. I know this sounds virtually impossible, borderline insanely absurd, but from my heart, I promise you I wouldn't write it if I hadn't experienced it myself, as well as heard many accounts of similar experiences from other people. It's important for me to relay the truth of this potential because I know how much it can hurt sometimes—overwhelmingly, painfully hurt—but as absolutely fucked as it sounds (and trust me, I know it sounds fucked), there is a sincere perfection in it.

An obvious example might be that of losing a parent or a pet, but seeing the perfection during times of sadness doesn't have to only be about life's big stuff. What comes to mind for me is the first day of November, the day after Halloween. I fucking *love* Halloween. Not only the holiday itself but the entire fall season. Hoodies, horror movies, pumpkin-flavored everything—yes, please! But sure enough, every year when November 1 hits, even though it's still fall, melancholy hits me right in the gut, basically to the same extent as when I was a kid, and that's saying a lot. As I awake to the first of November each year, I've begun to use it as a part of my practice, to see the perfection in each moment, to appreciate that, thanks to impermanence, not only will my feelings of sadness leave after some time but next year's Halloween will return after some time as well. Or maybe Christmas is your favorite holiday, and you can relate more specifically to that. Or maybe you think all holidays are a waste of time and can't relate at all, to which I'd say, "What happened to you as a child?" Jokingly, of course. (Well, half-jokingly, at least.)

Duncan sees the problem as being one of getting spiritually "stuck" on time. "I love conspiracy theories, but there's a great conspiracy theory that nobody wants to talk about. It's that we're all in a waiting room where we get called into oblivion at random times, generally unexpectedly. We're all hanging out in a terminal at an interdimensional airport, and people's flights are arriving all the time. Whenever a flight departs, we can either look at it as a tragedy, like the flight left early, or we can look at it like 'he lived a great life and now he is at peace.' The truth of the matter is that flights are always landing and taking off. Every person existing right now is for certain going to die."

Duncan turned me on to a great term he gleaned from C. S. Lewis: *spiritual amphibians.*

Humans are amphibians—half spirit and half animal. . . . As spirits they belong to the eternal world, but as animals they inhabit time. This means that while their spirit can be directed to an eternal object, their bodies, passions, and imaginations are in continual change, for to be in time means to change. Their nearest approach to constancy, therefore, is undulation—the repeated return to a level from which they repeatedly fall back, a series of troughs and peaks . . . a phenomenon which will do us no good unless you make a good use of it.[2]

Duncan believes "we emerge from whatever happened before we were born. We come into time and then we go back out of time again. This version of reality transforms the permanent notion of life. It's like when we're on a boat and we see dolphins show up and start doing flips in front of the boat. That's what a life is—a flip, a trick. It's our spirit coming to time. We can showboat. We can be famous. We can discover some incredible thing. We can do some awful thing. Often we're going to belly flop. We're going to come into the world, dive into time, look around, be completely perplexed, completely fuck up in every single way, and fall back into the nothingness with a weird look of, like, 'What the fuck happened?' on our face. That's the usual way to do it, and there's nothing wrong with it."

That reminded me of something Krishna Das (the kirtan artist) once told me during a conversation. I had asked him why, in his opinion, people turned to drugs. Why are we willing to compromise our best selves for a few moments (or hours) of relief when we know the potential consequences? He responded: "Well, on one hand, who the fuck are we? Where the fuck are we? What the fuck are we doing? How did we get here? We've been shot out of a cannon and we're hurtling through space and we're trying to get comfortable. It's almost impossible. We're trying to find a place to land. I think people are just so lost and so clueless and so hurt that they need to numb themselves. They need to anesthetize themselves and self-medicate, because how do you fucking deal with this? *What* is this? Even people who don't consciously ask that question are constantly running around trying to get money, trying to get jobs, trying to get pussy, trying to get cars, trying to get all kinds of stuff. They're compulsively doing all this shit, completely not present, and there's a part of you that just has to stop. But they have no tools for that. Their parents didn't know about that [various spiritual teachings and techniques]. The people they grew up with didn't know about that. Nobody in their life knows about that, so the only thing they know is chemicals. Sleeping pills, alcohol, drugs, dangerous sports—anything that pulls us out of our mind and out of our suffering, no matter how temporarily, is what we're going to go for. And the problem is that none of that stuff really works, except temporarily. Maharajji said, 'Go ahead into a room and smoke hash; the only problem is, it doesn't work. If it worked, I'd get a whole bunch of hash, we'd all go into a room, and we'd smoke together. But it doesn't work.' The problem is that people don't see it doesn't work because they don't understand that something else might be possible. That's the real killer—that most people will never have that conscious glimmer of real hope, or a real understanding that there's another way to be in the world. They won't even get a chance to ask the question. They will just tumble and roll until they hit the wall and die. When you really see this, this is how you develop compassion, because you see the state of things. You see how lucky you are that you know something even exists, to the tiny little infinitesimal percentage that you're able to know something. Still, it's enough to change the way we live and go through the day."[3]

As my conversation with Duncan continued, he mirrored Krishna Das's words, saying, "Why wouldn't we be completely perplexed if we were an eternal being—to some, a nonbeing, which is basically the same thing—that got stuck in the flytrap of time? You're going to freak out, and then you fall back into the nothingness. What happens is that people like Ram Dass and other great teachers have apparently been doing this loop for a while, and when they come out, they say, 'Hold on, hold on, you can do tricks. You don't have to be screaming out here.' That calms us down and lets us play around during our very brief period here. When someone exits the airport waiting room ahead of time, it's a sad moment. When friends come to stay with me and then they leave, I'm sad. It sucks. Of course I'll be able to call them, whereas I can't call somebody who's annihilated, but I can still feel the loss. When someone leaves this dimension, it's sad, but it's also the most natural thing, and every single one of us is marching in that direction. It's going to happen to every single one of us—the catastrophists seem to have forgotten that single element of reality, and because of that, any time the truth comes flashing into their lives in the form of a person dying, they freak out. It's an unnecessary freak-out. You don't have to freak out when someone goes away or when you start to go away. You can use it as an opportunity to do more tricks."

This made me think of something Eckhart Tolle said about the secret of life, when he wrote, "The secret of life is to die before you die and find that there is no death."[4] He means to die to the egoic nature, so we can see through the illusion of an individual, separate self. You then truly see that Atman or soul *is* Brahman or the ultimate reality in a direct and undeniable way. Herein lies a key to eliminating suffering. Rather than analyzing the contents of thoughts and feelings, or trying to control, change, or eliminate them, we see through the belief in a separate self who believes he is having the experience in the first place. That said, there is still suffering in life, there is still the experience of anxiety, sadness, and depression before one truly sees through this illusion.

Duncan reminded me that death is not solely corporeal. "Sometimes a relationship dies. You know how some people have brain death but are kept alive for a long time and the body is there, and they *look* like the person but *aren't* the person? That's what happens with relationships sometimes. The connection may be dead and nothing can bring it back, but we're keeping it around out of nostalgia. That happened to me with a person I'm now very close friends with. We'd been together for quite a while, and we weren't meant to be a couple. We were living in separate rooms in a house, and I was on an air mattress in the basement and depressed and scared and freaked out because a big shift was about to happen in my life. I was doing all the things that are surefire recipes for depression: pretending I was a victim, imagining that the universe was an unkind place. Everything became a noxious blur of heaviness and numbness. I was down in the basement sleeping on an air mattress, dead broke, spending hours a day playing this highly addictive video game called StarCraft II, and a real pathetic mess. Not taking showers enough. Wasting away. Somewhere in there I remembered something I'd heard somewhere about how if you give service, you do service, your life gets better." That's when Duncan started helping Raghu Markus, the executive director of Ram Dass's Love Serve Remember Foundation, create its podcast network (which, shameless plug, I'm honored to host the *Indie Spiritualist* show on). "It was the only thing I could think of to offer. And then my romantic relationship ended. I found a sublet." But things got worse before they got better. "I got cancer and then my mom died and tragedy kept happening, but it wasn't tragedy. On paper, it's tragedy, but this is where you realize the beautiful timing of things, because it was as if the Love Serve Remember people came into my life exactly when I needed it."

I wanted to return to the talk of depression, because I know for many people, psychedelics—something Duncan isn't the least bit shy about discussing—have been instrumental in healing their depression and other afflictions, including addiction. I'd talked about ayahuasca with Gabor Maté, but Duncan had been up-front about his use of psychedelics like psilocybin and LSD, so I was interested in his experiences with them. Did he ever use them in an intentional way to work through depression?

It turns out Duncan has been taking psychedelics for most of his life, so he had a lot to say. "In the old days of taking psychedelics, I was less—I don't want to use the word 'responsible,' but I would take a psychedelic for fun. I've struggled with depression throughout my life. I first experienced it while I was in college. I can remember eating mushrooms while depressed and going on a hike with some friends, and the psilocybin was kicking in but the depression was there—it was a mixture of these two things. The depression was saying what depression always says, which is, 'You're fucked. Everything is fucked. You're an awful person. You're a bad person on a bad planet in a terrible universe.' I walked out into a field, and there were flowers everywhere. It was beautiful. And the mushrooms were almost responding to this, in the most beautiful way. Suddenly raining down out of the sky and out of the earth and flowers was this: 'I love you. I love you. You are fine. You're carrying this through the world. You're carrying this heavy weight of self-judgment and guilt and all the shadows of the world. You're holding on to this.'

"The idea you get from mushrooms, on a nice day, is that you're the one piece of the universe that isn't loving you. Out of the entire universe—the cosmos, everything from beginning to end, or non-beginning to non-end—you're one little pixel surrounded by love, and the final step in this process of the universe becoming heaven is for you to surrender to the love. That's a mind-blowing thing to experience on mushrooms, or even not on mushrooms. I remember feeling much better after that trip, though. Psychedelics have successfully pushed me out of a depression, or they've at least given a little bubble of air amid depression to remember that the universe is a very loving place, which, when you're depressed, your experience is generally the opposite of that.

"Researchers are confirming that psilocybin does appear to have some antidepressant qualities. When I was younger, I was against taking prescription medications, but now I feel that anything you can use as a bit of wood to put under your tires when you're stuck in the mud of depression, use it. In my experience, I can't think of many things that are more horrible than depression. Psychedelics have helped. What psychedelics do, if taken in the right way or with the right intention in the right situation, is remind you that this is an incredibly beautiful universe, and I think the reminder comes in the form of how they bring you into the present moment. If you can come into the present moment, then the universe becomes the most excruciatingly wonderful place. If you're out of the present moment, everything sucks. When you come into the present moment, no matter what's going on, no matter what's waiting around the corner the next hour, the next day, the next year, no matter what's happened, it's the most amazingly beautiful place. It transcends all economic systems, it transcends all social constructs, it transcends all names given to geography—there's no more America, there's no more Los Angeles, there are no more names. There's a beautiful exhalation of matter into time, of which we get to be a part, and it is exquisite. That's been my experience with the present moment."

There's another side of it, though. "When you pop out of the present moment, that's where things suck. People have invested a lot of money into figuring out ways to get you out of the present moment by injecting states of need into you. Huge corporations pay billions of dollars every year to try to figure out how to trick people into thinking that there's something better than the present moment. And there are also shitty people in your life: bad bosses, bad relationships, bad friends. All of them will try to remind you of what you did some time ago, or inform you of some horror awaiting you in the future. There are many people who make a habit, whether intentionally or not, of doing this. Psychedelics can be a wonderful way to bring you back to that incredible point in time, or non-point in time is a better way to put it. That's where they get useful. How many bad trips happen because you've gone out of the present moment? How many bad trips are because you're sitting there thinking about what you should do next week, or something that happened to you in the past? That's where things get fucked-up fast. You start thinking about your death. You start thinking about your parent's death. You start thinking about whatever it may be. The answer in these situations is to surrender. Just let go, and everything will be beautiful again. The good news—because psychedelics do cost money—is that you don't need the psychedelics to get into that present moment. You don't need anything. The present moment is the great disrupter of all economic systems."

I found this fascinating. And it jibed with what I'd been researching. As Ram Dass has mentioned in many of his talks and books, his teacher, Neem Karoli Baba, maintains that psychedelics gained popularity in the 1960s because in Western culture many people needed a substance to glimpse these radical states, to taste God directly. As Ram Dass has also noted, Maharajji went on to say that while psychedelics can certainly bring you into the room where you can see the face of Christ, since you're on a substance, you'll always have to eventually leave. What's important is to learn to walk into a room from which you don't have to leave.

Duncan gave this an interesting spin. "I think about that stuff in terms of nipples, like a single nipple. Another verse in the Bhagavad Gita reads: 'He who gets attached to the flowery words of the scriptures is like a person who drinks water from a well when it flows everywhere.' In the same light, something we do probably instinctively is that when we identify a source of water, food, or happiness, we can get very protective of it and start worshipping it and pretending that it's the only nipple, when there are nipples everywhere.

"That's what can happen with psychedelics. We accidentally take up a form of pharmacological idolatry where we start worshipping the chemical structure that brought us into the holy of holies, and we forget about the actual holy of holies. It's like somebody walking you into the sanctum of some eternal temple, and instead of recognizing that the glorious joy to be found there is what's important, you find it almost unbearable to deal with the reality that you're in heaven. Imagine if Picasso, in a nonsarcastic way, said, 'Will you help me paint this picture?' and you replied, 'Fuck that! You're Picasso. Look at me. I'm this fucking guy who can barely draw a straight line.' And that's what the universe seems to be inviting everyone to do. *Paint this picture with me.* Let's paint this universe together, but that's so unbearable that we like to create the illusory idea that this state of consciousness or this experience can be accessed only via gateways that have to be unlocked using whatever our key happens to be—the right number of mantras, the right amount of psilocybin, whatever it may be—because there's something terrifyingly exhilarating about this state of wisdom that is available in every single moment."

That's so important. At some point, we need to lay aside all the drugs, books, teachings, mantras, or psychedelics; put all of it away and see that what's right here in this moment is perfect. There's no way of getting around it. It's all that's here—that is, until our thoughts arise and begin creating stories, and then it turns into a whole fucking mess.

When it comes to psychedelics, I have encountered considerable pushback from people in the recovery community because I have no qualms saying that those of us who struggle with anxiety, depression, smoking cessation, or addiction can sometimes reap benefits from using psychedelics in the proper context. There have been plenty of studies done that support this. For example, a 2015 CBS News article titled "Psychedelic Drugs as Treatment for Anxiety, Addiction," reported:

> In a carefully controlled setting, psychedelic drugs such as LSD or "magic mushrooms" may benefit patients with hard-to-treat anxiety, addiction or post-traumatic stress disorder (PTSD), new research suggests.
>
> The finding comes from a review of small-scale and preliminary studies conducted recently in the United States, Canada and Europe, all of which await follow-up.
>
> These preliminary results show that "in the right context, these drugs can help people a lot, especially people who have disorders that we generally treat poorly, such as end-of-life distress, PTSD, and addiction issues involving tobacco or alcohol," said study co-author Matthew Johnson. Johnson is an associate professor in the department of psychiatry and behavioral sciences at the Johns Hopkins University School of Medicine in Baltimore.[5]

And from a Johns Hopkins study:

> The Johns Hopkins group reported that psilocybin decreased clinician- and patient-rated depressed mood, anxiety, and death anxiety and increased quality of life, life meaning, and optimism. Six months after the final session of treatment, about 80 percent

of participants continued to show clinically significant decreases in depressed mood and anxiety, with about 60 percent showing symptom remission into the normal range. Eighty-three percent reported increases in well-being or life satisfaction. Some 67 percent of participants reported the experience as one of the top five meaningful experiences in their lives, and about 70 percent reported the experience as one of their top five spiritually significant lifetime events.[6]

Fuck reports—I've seen it with my own eyes. Ayahuasca completely turned around the life of a friend of mine who struggled with depression and drugs. However, I'm also not saying go drop acid or take a bunch of mushrooms just for the sake of doing it, either. It's all about context and purpose, and is absolutely a case-by-case scenario, where probably more of the time than not, it isn't a good idea. What works for one person may not for another, and vice versa.

Duncan heard where I was coming from. "There is a lot of superstition out there, and many people in twelve-step programs have been within inches of death. They've been resuscitated in emergency rooms, so from their subjective perspective, they know that because of the way they're wired, if they take the wrong chemical even accidentally, they're fucked. That's the reality of their situation. Those people are trying to keep themselves alive, so to roll the dice on some substance that isn't inside of their bodies already is Russian roulette. So I get it. I get the dogma. I do understand why they're like that. Ultimately we should direct our own states of ecstasy, and if we have identified any kind of exogenous chemical that enters our body and creates any kind of change in our states of experience that can lead to some cascade ending with us covered in trucker semen under a bridge with heroin needles hanging out of our arm, then clearly don't do it.

"However, we do have to give some credence to science, and we do have to give some credence to even what Bill Wilson, the founder of Alcoholics Anonymous,[7] discovered through LSD. He recognized that addiction is an incurable problem where the only hope is the transcendent entering our lives. It's such a hopeless predicament to get stuck in that, to put it in non–politically correct words, the only thing that can save your ass is God. He recognized that psychedelics are a quick way to experience the Divine. What's interesting about this is that some of the studies done using psilocybin to treat addiction found that if during the prescribed course of the psilocybin you have a mystical experience— and they've charted what makes up a mystical experience—then your odds of quitting smoking—because that's a lot of what they've been using psilocybin for, smoking cessation—dramatically increase. It's fascinating because it's not the psilocybin that's treating the addiction, it's the mystical experience that's treating the addiction.

"All problems are immediately fixed through the Divine, or whatever you want to call it, including addiction, including fear of death, including fear of anything. How are you going to be afraid anymore? There are so many ways that the light can come shining into the darkness that you've created around yourself. One of them is psychedelics. It's just one. And it's not the only one. And it's certainly not something that you should make an altar for. Make an altar for the subsequent feeling of bliss that comes when you recognize that all the horror that you thought life was composed of was a shadow—the subsequent bliss that comes from the relief of realizing that you're taken care of.

"Let's imagine you were in love with the most incredible person you ever met and you got lost in a forest, and you'd been lost in the forest for years and you assumed that this person had forgotten about you and that if you ever found your way out, you'd never be able to find that person again. But somehow you find a letter from that person and realize, 'Oh my god, they still love me. Oh my god! There's still hope.' That's what happens. You get these little rays of hope that shine in during your catastrophe, and it doesn't mean the problem is solved; it means 'Don't worry, I'm still here. You're doing fine. I still love you.' That's enough, man. That's enough to get you through about anything."

The things Duncan said struck a chord with me. I appreciated how freely he spoke about the Divine and awakening experiences. This was a pleasant rarity for me, because I do a lot of work with younger people in various settings and often find there is a very skeptical attitude not just toward the idea of God but toward spirituality in general. I can appreciate that. It's healthy to question what we've been taught and to look beneath the surface of things. That was instilled in me when I first started listening to punk rock and hardcore music at the age of thirteen, so I do understand where many of the younger people are coming from. But it often seems like the idea of God or spirituality has been written off in many cases before giving it a chance in the first place. What did Duncan have say to the cynics?

"I would say, 'Here's your predicament: You are, as far as you can tell, the only being experiencing a subjective state of consciousness.' You cannot prove that I am experiencing self-awareness. I could easily be some component in a dream you're having. What that means is that if you are using data from someone else's experiment to validate your idea that there is nothing else outside of this universe, or that there is no God, or that there is no transcendent truth or anything like that, then you're making a horrible mistake. If you were a true scientist, then you'd need to do the experiment yourself. Gather the data. Be smart about it. What's your hypothesis? Maybe it's 'There is no God.' That's a very difficult hypothesis to prove or disprove, and countless people have embarrassed themselves in either direction.

"Let's start with something like 'Does prayer work?' That's a simple experiment to run. You can run it yourself and you can create the experiment for yourself. Here's what's crazy about it: Since you're a beacon of consciousness that is being held (or not held) in a very temporary flask called your human body, maybe it's a product of the machinations of some zillion different electrochemical energies blasting through your brain. You are the only one who can do any kind of experiment on this stuff. That means you do the experiment. So start praying. Come up with a system. Maybe don't pray for a week and write down your experience every day of not praying for a week, and then start praying after that and see what happens. Is there any change at all? Does anything shift? Does it shift toward the positive or the negative? If it shifted toward the positive, then ask yourself why. Or was it a placebo effect? Okay, then great. You've discovered a placebo effect that starts transforming you. I guess the long and short of it is, do the experiment yourself.

"There's a wonderful quote often attributed to occultist and author Aleister Crowley: 'We place no reliance on virgin or pigeon: our method is science; our aim is religion.' This means that we don't care about the fucking symbols. A lot of atheists and skeptics get completely caught up in these primitive and archaic symbols that people manufactured a long time ago to try to point in the direction of the transcendent. Of course! If you get caught up in the symbols, then you're going to be one of the annoying people who say things like 'You're talking about zombie Jesus.' Really? To me, that's funny, because these very same people are not so vitriolic in dismissing Zeus. They're not going around with the other symbols of mythology and angrily shaking their fists at them. I guess they could say that there are not a lot of people who say that Zeus is the only way to wisdom, but what ends up happening is you wage a war of symbols. You're arguing over whether the symbol is valid or not, but Crowley is inviting us to rise above the war of symbols and begin to look where these symbols are pointing. Are they pointing to something real? Is that thing they're pointing to inside us or outside of us? Does it matter? *Does it matter?* If it's inside of us, if it's an embedded thing deep inside of our consciousness, some epigenetic memory encoded inside of our neurology that we can connect to in order to achieve transcendent or bliss states, fine, you're still achieving bliss states. Is it something outside of you? Even better, because now you've opened a faucet in your house that you thought didn't work, and it's going to start pouring out God stuff into your life.

"If the experiment has positive results, you've transformed your life for the better. And if the results are negative, then you've done your due diligence and now you can live in a world of skepticism, and that's fine, too. But the thing is, do you think that most of the world's population is fucking up in this way? Do you think it's all some shared delusion? Shared delusion is great, by the way. It's fun. That's the other thing about it. Why's everybody so against it?

"Let's imagine that this is a shared fantasy allowing people to experience bliss. There's an evolutionary advantage to transcendent states of consciousness if they allow you to have more energy, more focus, more charisma, more creative output. When that happens, there's a real evolutionary advantage to this, even if it's a complete fantasy. If you have groups of people experiencing heightened states of consciousness, the ability to connect with other people more, the ability to empathize with other people more, then I would imagine they are going to be more successful than groups of people who have, for whatever reason, disconnected from a potential power source.

"Just do the experiment, and if it doesn't work, it doesn't work. Don't get caught up in the symbols because a lot of people are sitting around signs that say BEACH—TEN MILES AWAY and lighting candles in front of the signs instead of going to the beach, you know?"

PRACTICE

Pee, Brush Your Teeth, and Laugh

As Duncan exemplified, one of the most important attitudes we can cultivate on our spiritual path is the ability to laugh and not take this life thing so seriously all the time. There's a very cool book called *The Dude and the Zen Master*, written by Roshi Bernie Glassman and the dude himself, Jeff Bridges. In it, Roshi Bernie offers a simple practice to help us do this.

Bernie wrote:

Wake up in the morning, go to the bathroom, pee, brush your teeth, look in the mirror, and laugh at yourself. Do it every morning to start off the day, as a practice.[8]

Yes, that's it. It's simple. Why just do it in the morning? If you want to have some real fun, why not laugh at yourself in the bathroom at work—*especially* if there's another coworker in there with you. Waiting to pick your kids up from school? Why not take those few extra minutes to sit in your car and laugh at yourself in the rearview mirror, especially if it's a busy parking lot!

All kidding aside, I've worked with this practice for a couple of years now—not daily, but off and on—and it's simple and fun and it does the trick. I mean, you're *laughing*.

I once co-facilitated a Taste of Holistic Healing workshop with my friend Laura Le, who teaches laughter yoga. In all honesty, I'd gone out of my way to avoid her classes, not because I don't like Laura—I think she's great—but the shy part of me just didn't want to laugh in a room full of other people (except in a very dark movie theater at a Seth Rogen movie—although even then I'd probably still go midday, weeks after it's come out, to avoid being in a crowded room with strangers). Laura began the yoga exercise by asking us all to start laughing. It was awkward for a couple of seconds, but in no time, all two dozen of us were sincerely laughing—at ourselves, at one another, at the sheer weirdness of the whole thing, but it was real belly laughter. Once we were finished, I felt much better.

So, my friends, take some time to laugh whenever you're able. It can be Roshi Bernie's practice, or laughter yoga (you can find instructions on YouTube), or watching *It's Always Sunny in Philadelphia*, or listening to Duncan Trussell's *Family Hour* podcast (see what I did right there?), or anything that puts a smile on your face and in your heart.

14

THOSE DARK, HORRIBLE FUCKING PLACES

CONVERSATION WITH DAMIEN ECHOLS

In the mid-nineties, I became enthralled by the media frenzy around what came to be known as the West Memphis Three—teenagers arrested, tried, and convicted for the murders of three boys in Arkansas. One of the defendants was Damien Echols, a brainy, sarcastic, metal-loving misfit who reminded me of myself. HBO aired three *Paradise Lost* documentaries over the years, which helped raise doubts about the guilt of the West Memphis Three. In August 2011, after eighteen years on death row—the last ten of which were spent in solitary confinement—Damien was released from prison due to inconclusive evidence. The real killer remains at large. Damien wrote about enduring the nightmare of his incarceration in his book *Life After Death*, which had a huge impact on me; it inspired me to find the wherewithal to carry on during my own times of crisis.

Damien practices and teaches Magick, a process of initiation designed to awaken people to higher states of consciousness so that they can manifest the lives they desire. I was beyond curious about how he used these practices to sustain himself for nearly twenty years in prison and how others could apply Magick to their lives and situations of relapse or habitual behavior that hurt themselves or others.

To start, I wanted to know more about what Magick was, as I suspected there were all sorts of misperceptions. Damien dove right in. "When I say Magick, I spell it with a *k* at the end, and that's to differentiate it from sleight of hand—pulling rabbits out of hats and sawing people in half. Magick with a *k* is like an amalgamation of Gnostic Christianity, esoteric Judaism, a lot of ancient Chinese circulation practices like Taoism, and things of that nature. It's not the free-floating, flaky, let's-all-hold-hands-and-be-friends thing that you see in many Wiccan communities right now, but it's also not the dark, evil thing some Christians portray it as."

Damien's interest and commitment to the practice of Magick led him to create an art collective called Magick Revolution, which grew out of an art collective he called The Hand that Damien and his friends David Stoupakis and Menton J. Matthews III (Menton3) formed. The Hand represented our hands as the tools we use to shape the world. "It's what we use to form our reality. It's what we use to manifest whatever it is we want to see around us. We thought there was a lot of symbolism and strength behind that image." As Damien, David, and Menton3 were working on art, they discovered they wanted to do more, to start a social awareness movement, which is how Magick Revolution originated. "In Western society, we have preconceived ideas and notions of what Magick is based on—things like cheesy horror movies and stuff we had shoved down our throats in the Bible Belt growing up. These are not the reality of Magick at all. Magick is a beautiful, deep spiritual tradition, as deep as anything you'd find in the East, but it's been neglected and demonized in Western culture. We want to tell people what Magick is, what Magick is not, and, especially for me, share some of the techniques and the practices that helped me survive almost nineteen years on death row without losing my mind. I figured if Magick helped me in there, then it would be beneficial to people out here."

While speaking with Damien, I remembered the many times I had felt locked in a prison of my own making, trapped in the cycle of addiction. In no way am I equating my addiction and Damien's prison experience, but he helped me realize that one need not be behind bars to feel imprisoned. I remember countless times when I'd be looking at a line of coke (or Ritalin) on a table or holding a fifth of vodka in my hand and sobbing because I didn't want to snort the powder or drink the poison, but couldn't *not*—I was that stuck. It wasn't a matter of being weak-willed or morally deficient. I was just caught the fuck out, and it was terrible. Like Damien, I would find a way to work more skillfully with the difficult times (at least for the most part).

The tradition that drew Damien to Magick and is the root of his teaching is called the Hermetic Order of the Golden Dawn. I did a little research and learned that it was a collective of occultists in the late 1800s. Poet William Butler Yeats was a member, as was the notorious Aleister Crowley. Pamela Colman Smith, who was an artist who did the paintings that are the basis for what we now think of as Tarot cards, was also a member. As I continued delving deeper into the Order, I came across a fascinating article in *Lapham's Quarterly* that discussed Yeats's involvement and experience, and the impact that Magick had in his life. Here's an excerpt:

> *Yeats wrote frankly about his vocation as a magician in several memoirs and in* A Vision, *a dense astrological treatise he labored over for twenty years. A Protestant Irishman in Victorian Britain, Yeats as a young man was pulled in conflicting directions, but the occult always trumped worldly concerns, because it was so deeply connected with his poetic craft. In 1892, when the Irish patriot John O'Leary admonished the twenty-seven-year-old poet for his devotion to magic at the expense of the Cause, Yeats answered:*
> *"Now as to magic. It is surely absurd to hold me 'weak' or otherwise because I choose to persist in a study which I decided*

deliberately four or five years ago to make, next to my poetry, the
most important pursuit of my life. . . . If I had not made magic
my constant study I could not have written a single word of my
*Blake book [*The Works of William Blake, *with Edwin Ellis,*
1893], nor would The Countess Kathleen *[stage play, 1892]*
have ever come to exist. The mystical life is the center of all that
I do and all that I think and all that I write."[1]

I'm no Yeats, but I've also received my share of shit for my interest
in and practice of things spiritual, sometimes even from people in the
"spiritual" community for not looking or acting the part. So I appreciated his response to O'Leary's accusations.

The Golden Dawn led Damien directly to modern-day Tarot practices. "It's an incredibly rich and deep spiritual tradition that has always been (and I mean always—ever since I was a child) the most
important thing in my life. Everything else was secondary to the practice of Magick, the study of Magick. Everything else in this world to
me is like icing on the cake. I guess some people would say that's a little
zealous, but that's what happens when you make progress in your spiritual practice—you turn inward and truly get zealous about it."

I could identify. Meditation has taught me to turn inward during the
difficult times in my life—not always, as exemplified by the relapses
I've experienced, but much more frequently than before. It's also helped
me pull myself out of relapses much sooner than in the past. Loving-
kindness meditation has allowed me to cultivate sincere love for myself:
the kind of love that doesn't want to go back down the road of full-
blown addiction; the kind of love that, even when a marriage is ending
and nothing makes sense, helps me to know I deserve better than looking to the bottom of a bottle for answers and relief.

The only time we're making any true progress is when we're going
inside and doing the kind of work that's not easy or comfortable. Ti-

betan Buddhist teacher Chögyam Trungpa Rinpoche wrote an incredible book titled *Cutting Through Spiritual Materialism*. It's been an important source for me, especially in the early stages of my spiritual exploration, and helped me get serious about what the fuck I was doing. There are so many traps we can fall into on the path. The glaringly obvious ones are things like trying to sound spiritual in the way we talk or starting to dress to "look spiritual." We learn the mantras and buy the malas—basically, we get the gear—but that's what our focus is on, the external. The clothes and accessories are fine, but when they're what we focus on instead of our practice and the inner transformational work—well, that's spiritual materialism.

Damien agreed. "It's discipline. A lot of people want to do the novelty part of spiritual practice. They want to do the fun parts. They want to wear robes and have the beads and go to the concerts and things like that, but there is a tremendous amount of real discipline required. To spend hours a day truly practicing, not just to say 'I'm a Buddhist' or 'I'm a magician' but to become a Buddha, to become the Magick itself, requires more self-discipline than most people are willing to put into those things."

That's why I keep reiterating that practices like meditation and mantra don't consist solely of love and light and rainbows. I thought I was going to sit down on a meditation cushion and my life was going to miraculously become awesome, that everything was going to be great and peaceful. That's not the case at all. A spiritual practice can reveal so much darkness. You need to be ready for it.

Damien, better than many people, realizes that no growth comes without struggle, without strife, without pain. "That's why they call it growing *pains*, not growing *pleasure*. When you're facing things in this world, that's what forces you to step outside your comfort zone. It's the confrontation and the battle. We tend to think of spirituality as entirely and absolutely about peace and peacefulness, but it's a battle. It's not an external fight or going to war to force your beliefs on other people. It's about going to battle with the things that you don't want to look at in yourself, the things you don't want to face about yourself—shining the light into those dark, horrible fucking places and wrestling with whatever it is you find there."

I couldn't agree more. Often we risk spiritualizing our egos rather than peeling away the layers. We shift one egoic identification onto another. I don't mean to sound harsh, because I have certainly done that myself, but that's where the real work, the real dedication, comes in, peeling away until we reach the core, and then peeling some more. That's why I don't look at my—or anyone else's—relapses as failures, especially if we use them as opportunities to remove more layers of what brought us back to the bottle or the needle or the poker table or the fast-food restaurant. If we use those times to explore what hurt in our lives causes us to relapse, then they absolutely were not failures at all.

Damien reminded me about all the excuses people resort to when they obscure that core. "Sometimes they'll say, 'I was acting from an ego place.' That's a spiritual cop-out. It's no different from people who used to say, 'The devil made me do it.' Now it's 'Ego made me do it.' If you're aware enough to know that your ego is influencing you, then you're aware enough to stand up and not give in to it."

How do we go about peeling away those layers? I wanted to learn a bit more about what Damien meant when he wrote about initiation when it came to Magick.

The most fascinating, sincere, terrifying, and wonderful thing about it is that it never ends. "Initiation is a process. It's similar in nature to what baptism in Christianity was *supposed* to be. It wasn't a onetime thing that symbolized something. Initiation is not a symbol; it's an actual *process*, an actual thing. For example, imagine you have a book that you like. You read that book, get a lot out of it, and then put it on the shelf. A year later you take the book down and read it again, and you get even more out of it the second time than you did the first. That's initiation. It's a constant way of going deeper into reality, deeper and deeper into the process of growth.

"That's why Magick and art go hand in hand. Art is meant to be an initiation. I work as an artist, and I've tried to take Magick and turn it into art because they're similar processes. Art was never meant to be something that you bought because it matches your couch." Damien explained that art and Magick should transform us. It could be a big transformation, a slight one, or maybe one we don't realize for years. That encounter and subsequent evolution are the initiation. "It's one of the reasons art and Magick have always been interwoven like the strands of our DNA, like the caduceus of Hermes—the snakes intertwined. Art and Magick are different sides of the same process, and when we live life the way we're truly meant to live it, everything becomes an initiation. Not just the couple of hours a day that you spend on your meditation cushion. Not just the time you spend practicing yoga. Not your rituals, if you're a ceremonial magician. Every single aspect of every single day should become about interacting with the intelligence behind reality."

I dug that—*every single aspect of every single day*. It's what I'm talking about when I say "everything mind," because everything, material or not, is imbued by spirit (or God, source, life, Buddha mind, Brahman, etc.). There's not a time or place in our experience that the intelligence behind reality, as Damien calls it, is not present. To me, this is the essence of spirituality. However, I'm also aware that if you ask a hundred people what spirituality is, you'll likely get a hundred different answers, but again, for me, spirituality imbues everything always. We must open ourselves up to it and be aware of it and make ourselves available to it. Some times are tougher than others. What role did Magick play in helping Damien survive almost two decades on death row, ten of them in solitary confinement? And what about now?

There were many different levels to Damien's answer. First he spoke about the mental realm. "Magick gave me something to focus on other than my surroundings, other than my prison environment. By the end of my time in prison, I was dedicating up to eight hours a day to Magick practice, to ritual, to meditation, to energy and breath work. During those eight hours, I would become almost oblivious that I was in prison because I was so focused on my spiritual practice. It kept me from losing my sanity."

There was also the tangible, the physical realm. "I was in a tremendous amount of pain at one point; my teeth hurt because I'd been hit in the face and severely beaten several times. In prison, they don't do caps or crowns or root canals. Your choices are live in pain or have your teeth pulled. I didn't want to lose my teeth, so I had to find a way to cope with the pain. Honestly, that pain is one of the things that drove me deepest into my Magick practice. I was forced to get better and better at what I was doing."

As with anything, when it's self-taught, Damien learned a lot through trial and error. "I found one Magick technique of working with something that pretty much every culture except for ours has a name for. The Chinese call it chi and the Japanese qi; in Hebrew it's called ruach; and in Sanskrit it's prana. Westerners seem to be the only ones who don't have a name for it, so I refer to it as energy, because that's such a nondenominational term. I began channeling this energy into healing. I'd channel as much as I could, sealing it with the intent to heal, to stop pain. When I started doing this, I experienced considerable success—if I did it for an hour, the pain in my mouth would completely go away for a week. Eventually, I had to do it for two hours to get rid of the pain for the same length of time. Then three hours of practice would get rid of the pain for only a day or so. As time progressed, I had to do it nonstop, and it was still only blunting the pain, not completely killing the pain as it was in the beginning. Then I had an epiphany, a realization that went off in me like a nuclear bomb: *Everything on the spiritual level—what we think of as the spiritual level of reality—mirrors everything that goes on the physical level of reality.* They are two sides of one coin: heads, tails. In the physical world, you don't inhale forever. You have no choice but to exhale. You can't drink water forever; eventually you pee. I realized I was taking in tremendous amounts of energy toward a purpose and not letting anything out. I began to practice a grounding technique that took maybe sixty seconds, and I felt a huge flush of energy rush out of me into the earth. From that moment on, I never had pain again. It was completely gone.

"Not only did I have physical teachers of Magick in this world—people who'd authored books, people who were widely known, people who were lesser known, who took time and energy to teach me while I was in prison—but once we reach a certain stage in the initiation process, the Magick itself becomes the teacher. It starts triggering initiations and realizations, which is what happened to me more and more as time went on."

These insights into initiation and spontaneous realization made me think of something Krishna Das has said about how life is the guru: "Don't wait for a guru. Your life is your guru." You don't need a saint or guru in the flesh. If you have one who's the real deal, then that's cool, but life is the great teacher if you're open and present to it. *If* you're ready to be taught.

Magick was first and foremost for Damien, but Taoism augmented those teachings for him and helped him reach deeper levels of understanding. "That's because Taoism is so sparse on dogma and belief and focuses almost entirely on the actual physical practices: the breath work, the visualization, the circulation of chi. Once you master those very basic practices, you can start expanding them and taking them into other areas of your life. There are no limits."

Damien has other influences as well. "While I was in prison, I had a Zen teacher who came from Japan to the prison and eventually gave me ordination in the Rinzai tradition of Buddhism. It's the same tradition that was used to train the ancient samurai. One of the things I realized from that practice is that most Westerners, especially the younger generation, aren't going to have the patience and the discipline to keep following these practices. They're not going to sit for two, three, four, eight hours a day without looking at their Facebook pages or whatever it is. The whole thing with Zen practice is that it's training you to stay in the present, to be with life from moment to moment."

Just as Zen has been diluted in the West, Damien has seen that happening in the New Age movement with Wicca. "Now it's all about flowers in the hair and the Mother Goddess and all that kind of stuff, but real, traditional ceremonial Magick can be very hard to understand, because most of the good books were written in a time when people didn't speak exactly the way that we speak now. They can be very complicated to read. You can have one book that you study for your entire life and still not get everything out of it because of the way it's written. What I discovered with Wicca is that it's basically a watered-down version of ceremonial Magick. I would read books on Wicca about rituals that were done to honor deity, honor Divinity, and break those down and compare them to what I was reading in ceremonial Magick. They would take something that I thought was complicated and hard to understand and suddenly I would have this epiphany or realization due to the simplicity of Wicca. Then I'd be able to take it and simplify it myself in a way that didn't have as much of the dogma attached to it."

Magick is the fire in his life, then Zen, Taoism, and Wicca are "the gasoline that caused it to roar. And then there's the Bible. It's probably the single greatest book on Magick ever written. You should read it for the instruction, not for the stories. For example, there's a lot about speaking in the Bible; it begins all the way back in the book of Genesis: 'God *said* let there be' this and that. There are all sorts of different things about using the voice that carry all the way from the Old Testament into the New Testament, where Jesus said things that we don't even pay heed to. In Mark 11:23, Jesus told his disciples, 'If you say to this mountain, move, it will be moved, it will be cast into the sea, it will happen.' He didn't say, 'Ask me to do it.' He didn't tell them to ask God to do it. He didn't say to get down on your knees and grovel and talk about how unworthy you are. He said to tell this thing to move, and it will be moved. It's all about how powerful our words are. That's because our words convey energy. They convey chi. Our words can take things from the more etheric levels of reality and speak them into existence in the physical world."

Damien shifted the conversation into a direction I wasn't anticipating— televangelism—and kind of blew my mind. "I used to watch this televangelist who said, 'Don't talk to God about how big your problems are. Talk to your problems about how big your God is. If you focus on the negative, you're feeding the negative energy. You're feeding chi to it, enhancing it, and strengthening it. When David fought Goliath, he doesn't step up and say, "Oh my God! This guy is a giant! What am I going to do? He's got a sword, and I've only got this sling." No. He didn't magnify the problem. He didn't say, "This guy is huge. This guy has killed a hundred people before me." None of that. He stepped up and he looked at Goliath and didn't even call Goliath a giant, because he didn't want to feed energy to that. He looked at Goliath and said, "This day I will feed your head to the birds of the air. You come against me with sword and shield. I come against you in the name of the almighty God." ' It's another illustration of using our words, using our voices, to shape reality so that we become co-creators of the physical world."

I loved that Damien used the word "God" when he spoke, because there's probably no more loaded word in our language. It's sad that "God" has so much heaviness around it. I understand why: There's no shortage of fundamentalist, hateful rhetoric that's used "in the name of God," but the beauty of that word and what it can symbolize is so important—to me, at least.

Damien got where I was coming from. "God is one of the first things I address whenever I do the Magick classes, because I want the experience to be as nondenominational and all-encompassing as possible. I want people to feel comfortable, because if you don't feel comfortable with what you're doing, then it's not going to work. I tell people, 'I might use the word "God" sometimes and other times I might not, but whatever name you want to use, whether it's God or the Divine mind or the source, whenever I'm using this word, I think of it as the source that all things came from and the source to which they will all one day return.' Strip away everything else. I'm not talking about a man floating in the clouds and judging us. I'm talking about our individual understanding of the source of all and all creation in a very nondenominational, stripped-down, nondogmatic way."

This talk of God reminded me of a quote attributed to Rumi I'd read on Damien's Facebook page: "I learned that every mortal will taste death—but only some will taste life." The passage took Damien back to when he first got out of prison after almost twenty years and a decade of solitary confinement. "Nobody in this world understood the level of shock and trauma that I was going through. People thought I was going to be happy and excited that I was out of prison, and I was, but I was also completely and absolutely destroyed to the core of my being, on every level. I was mentally alone; I could no longer read, watch television or movies. I would try to read a book and I would read the same page over and over and could no longer even remember what I was reading when I got to the bottom of the page because I'd been so psychologically devastated. I would meet a person and introduce myself two or three times because I couldn't even retain their face or their name or any of those sorts of things. I was scared all the time.

"It was a completely different world from the one I knew when I went into prison. Little things, like everyone used a debit card with a PIN number at the store—I didn't understand any of that. Things that most people took for granted absolutely paralyzed me with fear. It got to the point where I needed someone with me twenty-four hours a day, seven days a week. That's a big aspect of spiritual practice: making yourself go into things that scare you, things that you aren't comfortable with. That's tasting life, that's making yourself expand beyond your boundaries and go into new areas. If you don't do those things, you're not living."

could identify with that, because for me, that's what living a life of true recovery is all about: going into the places that scare you and boldly exploring why you're scared in the first place. It's not easy work, nor is it the quick "five steps to freedom forever" kind of thing that's so popular on blogs and in certain self-help books, but it's real, it's authentic, and if you stick with it, it will do its job of healing. That said, like everyone, I still have times when I want to turn on the TV or eat a pint of rocky road to take myself out of that moment, and as tough as it is, I also recognize that there is no way real healing or growth is going to occur unless I face this darkness, this fear, this sadness and loneliness, and sit with it. Again, in no way do I mean to compare my situation with Damien's, because there is no comparison to what he lived through, but I appreciate his being so raw and vulnerable about his experiences. He lived the truth of "the only way out is through." It's not pretty, it's not easy, but that's life; it's tragic and it's beautiful, horrific and illuminating.

There have been times when I've found myself in my own horror. Case in point, the experience I wrote about at the beginning of this book. From there, however, there's nowhere else to go but up. I think of it as "crawling toward comfortable," something the character Claire Fisher said in an episode of *Six Feet Under*. While crawling toward comfortable, the underlying experience was always one of pain, but pain can be one of the greatest catalysts for change if we're willing to work with and transmute it. As Damien said, "The number-one thing that causes us to grow as human beings is pain. The more we experience pain, the more we're able to empathize with other people, the more it cracks open our shell and forces us to let life in. What it comes down to is, the bigger the battles you face, the greater the victories you're going to have. If you go through your life seeking out little battles, then you're going to have only little victories. We should embrace the things that scare us, the things that hurt us, the things that aren't fun."

While I wouldn't advocate you go out and relapse or pick up a drug habit if you've never had one, I understand what Damien was saying, and agree (within reason). Damien and I had similar childhoods. We both grew up in rural areas (though mine wasn't as rural as his). We were both outcasts as teenagers, listening to bands like Slayer and Metallica and interested in occult symbolism and ideology. I remember that at times it felt like hell, which is why these days I'm so passionate about working with young people who've felt "other than" or who've struggled with addictions, self-harm, or depression.

Damien had some words of wisdom for the younger people who are struggling with being labeled, picked on, or bullied, or with loving themselves for who they are. "For me, spiritual practice is always about practicality, what's practical. Not about thinking good thoughts and let's hold hands and be friends. It's about what works. The way I approach things is not always the gentlest way, because I don't necessarily respond to the gentlest forms of teaching. I learn the most from the hard times. I learn the most from the times that I've experienced pain. The thing I always tell people is that you can either be a victor or be a victim—you can't be both. If you're going to sit around and cry and be all angsty, you're going to live as a victim your whole life. As harsh as it can sometimes sound, one of the best spiritual practices, the best spiritual teaching you can give somebody, is 'Knuckle up, buttercup.' This ain't no fun ride. You better dig in and get ready to fight for what you love, for what you want, or give it up. We have two choices: We can give up the things about ourselves that the world doesn't like, that the world taunts or torments us for, or we can embrace those things and say fuck you to the rest of them. It's one or the other. If you give up the things you love because of the pressure that outside sources are putting on you, then you're not alive. You're not living the life that you're going to enjoy.

"One thing I try to stress is that when people single you out, it's because you're *not* embracing mediocrity. This world loves mediocrity. This world loves football games and bars and social media and things that don't have any point or purpose or growth or anything else behind them. If you're doing something else that threatens that mediocrity, you know that you're on the right path. When someone criticizes me, I look at that person and, as unspiritual as this sounds, I say, 'If you think I'm fucked-up, I must be okay.' The minute they start thinking I'm okay, then I know I've got a problem."

It's like when I've caught shit from so-called spiritual people based on nothing more than my appearance, but I recognize that's on them, not me. If someone else wants to judge you based on your appearance or on the fact that you relapsed, that speaks volumes about *their* character, not yours, especially if you take the higher road and don't engage them. I found it interesting that Damien used the words "knuckle up," as I'd used that exact phrase just a couple of days before our conversation while writing a blog post about being dedicated to showing up for yourself and to the process of waking up. We need to knuckle the fuck up, time and time again. When we think that we don't have it in us to do it anymore, we're going to have to do it again.

Damien brought these ideas back to spiritual practice. "People have this idea that when they start a spiritual practice—whether it's Buddhism or Hinduism or Magick—life is going to be all sunshine and unicorns. I always tell people that the reason we're in this world is to grow, learn, and develop. When you take on a spiritual practice, what you're doing is accelerating your growth. Therefore, you're going to encounter more of the hard things. That doesn't mean your life is necessarily getting any harder, because you were going to have to face the same lessons anyway. It means you're getting to face them sooner than you would have had you not consciously and deliberately chosen to accelerate your growth and maturity."

Walking an honest path toward spiritual maturity, regardless of the tradition or lack thereof, is going to ask everything of us. It's not easy, but it's worth it. If I hadn't started my stumble down the spiritual path, I would be dead (that's not a metaphor). Thanks to the practices and teachers in this book and my life, I'm still fucking here.

I've continued to fall down, but I'm quicker to catch myself when it happens, and I remember that today I deserve better. You do, too.

PRACTICE

The Middle Pillar

Damien taught me a foundational practice of ceremonial Magick called the Middle Pillar. He said it was like working with the chakras, the seven energy centers that run down the center line of the body—which was something I was familiar with. Damien explained that in ceremonial Magick, there are five key points in different places in the body, each with its own Hebrew mantras.

Damien said, "I always tell people that they're a straw. Before they were born, they had a channel connecting them to Divinity that was completely open. The moment they incarnated in the physical realm, that channel began to collect gunk, because it's never cleaned out. The Middle Pillar begins to clear out that channel, clear out that straw, so more of the Divine energy, the intelligence of the Divine, and interaction with the Divine can flow through us. Think of it like doing calisthenics for your energy body, strengthening your physical body.

"When you begin this practice, it may take up to an hour, but once you've been practicing for a while, you can do it in seconds. There's no rule for how long to do the practice, but Magick is like anything else—the more effort and time you put into it, the more you're going to get out of it."

Here are the steps:

- As you do this practice, envision breathing in pure energy from the universe in the form of white light. With every inhalation, allow it to fill up a specific area of your body. With each inhalation, imagine that body part is growing brighter and brighter as it fills with white light.
- With the first inhalation, envision the white light filling your feet.
- With the second inhalation, envision the light filling your shins and calves.
- With the third inhalation, it fills your thighs.
- Continue moving from your feet to your head, filling your body with brilliant, glowing white light.
- You'll feel calm and focused, and will be ready to do whatever meditation or energy work is at hand.

15

THIS BEAUTIFUL, BROKEN REALITY
OF THE HUMAN CONDITION
CONVERSATION WITH MIRABAI STARR

Relapse has brought me to my knees (and as you know by now, I'm not speaking metaphorically) more than once, but it has also connected me to a place of gentleness. Surprisingly, at moments, this gentleness became something I could extend toward the *situation* of my suffering as well as my suffering itself—something I never could have done in the past when relapse was a full-on spiral of self-destruction. Mirabai Starr showed up for me in a big way after my last relapse. She is a tender and wonderful person, a dear friend. Her books have inspired me throughout my life, especially *Caravan of No Despair*, about the stage of her spiritual life that commenced on the day her daughter Jenny died. My conversation with Mirabai was especially meaningful because she didn't try to placate me about my addictions and mistakes, but instead bore loving witness to my situation and the pain I shared with her.

"You're showing up for your relapse and you're embracing your humanity while modeling for others how to do that, and that's all we can do." Mirabai spoke exactly the words I needed to hear! "I don't know any enlightened beings. I used to think that was the goal, but I don't think we get perfection, and I know you know that. All we can do is be present for all of it, no matter how yucky, with humility, humor, and gentleness."

She knows of what she speaks. "I come from a family of addicts and alcoholics. Everyone who was active is now either dead or in recovery. I was in my early twenties when my father went into recovery, and my brothers and one of my nephews have been very active with substances. My father, as an agnostic Jew in the first generation of Jewish families after the war, after the Holocaust, did not believe in God, and he struggled mightily with that aspect of Alcoholics Anonymous. He found ways to reconcile his lack of belief with the absolute necessity to humble himself and get on his knees and put himself into the loving arms of something greater than himself. He somehow managed, through his big brain, to talk his way into a relationship with a higher power, but it was a lifelong struggle for him. My brother is so much like him— he's another tortured artist with a huge soul. It's also an issue, but my brother uses mystical poetry, not as God, but to cultivate a relationship with a higher power that sustains him in his path of recovery.

"I believe that when we're in our darkest places of despair, we are being held in the arms of a loving presence, of a loving reality, which is ultimate reality. Ultimate reality is absolute love, and we are being held in those arms when we need it most, even though it's invisible. That's the bottom line for me. Whether we conceive of those loving arms as the arms of the mother, or the beloved, or of our own true self, we're never abandoned."

I could certainly relate to what she was saying. I've written in the past about times when I've been out running and felt held by the arms of the beloved, as Mirabai describes it. I've also felt myself in rapture with the mother while listening to bands like Sigur Rós and, believe it or not, even Slayer. Hell, even the raw and ragged writing of Charles Bukowski has brought me to that place on occasion. But just like Bukowski and his tendency toward booze and women to escape reality, even during periods of my own "sobriety" I would still find myself engaging in "little" relapse-style behaviors to escape reality (like overeating some sugary treats, or watching several hours more than I should of *Stranger Things*), though you could argue there is no such thing, and I wouldn't put up much of a fight.

Mirabai had an expansive view of relapse as well. "For you, it might be drugs or alcohol. For me, it's patterns of getting triggered by people in ways that make me hate myself for how I behave when I'm triggered. How do I approach those relapses as not being failures but being tender little moments of Mirabai-ness? I know that they don't feel like little moments, especially when you're thinking about relapses with drugs and alcohol and you can destroy relationships and a lot of damage can happen in those explosions, so it's not just having a fight with your sister over some petty thing where you end up acting out. There are degrees of relapse that have consequences. For me, as the sensitive being that I am, any kind of unskillful behavior feels like the end of the world. How do I not go to that place when I screw up? When my self-image is shattered, how do I see that as grace, as a gift? Intellectually, I get it. I can tell someone else how to do it or what they need to do." Then Mirabai shared a quote she loved from Buddhist teacher Pema Chödrön's book *The Wisdom of No Escape and the Path of Loving-Kindness*:

> *Our neurosis and our wisdom are made out of the same material.*
> *If you throw out your neurosis, you also throw out your wisdom.*[1]

"Our beauty is intermixed with our neurosis, and it's what makes us juicy, full, whole humans. I can easily explain that to somebody else, but when it happens to me, I just want the earth to open and swallow me. I don't know how to avoid those pitfalls. I'm not sure that they're anything less than perfect when they happen. How can we be humble enough to accept that there's nothing special about our failures? They're just our participation in this beautiful, broken reality of the human condition."

I knew I could count on Mirabai to take the conversation to a deep, spiritual place, and she didn't disappoint. I asked her about specific ways our spiritual practices can serve us, even during the times when we do lose it, when we relapse emotionally or to a specific substance or self-defeating behavior. "One is when things are steady. There are ups and downs, but they're not dramatic. That's when our practice comes in handy, as we deal with the small challenges like an argument with a friend or a family member and we're able to come back to presence in the moment." She went on to say that spiritual practice "also serves us well when we have extreme challenges, even traumas. Not that we can necessarily meditate our way through tragedies, but we can instinctively reach for practices like Tonglen when we're going through extreme crisis because they blow away all our attachments."

I knew about Buddhist Tonglen meditation from Pema Chödrön's teachings. The Tibetan word "Tonglen" can loosely be defined as "giving and taking." It's a way of breathing in suffering and exhaling joy that helps us develop our compassion and ability to be present for ourselves and others. Tonglen is a way to work with our most challenging experiences—relapse, heartbreak, grief—to subject them to the fire of transformation. This burns away our opinions, leaving us with the matter at hand.

Mirabai got personal—deeply personal—as she explained how meditation helped her survive her daughter Jenny's death. At first Mirabai couldn't do any formal practices. "They almost felt like an insult, but years of training in contemplative practice carved a place in my soul where the only thing that made sense was to be fully present, or as present as I possibly could be with the loss of a child. In doing so, I found my place in the interconnected web of being so that I could viscerally encounter my place in the human family, in the human condition."

Not all the things wrong in our life are huge. There's the big stuff that stands out, but there's also the whole middle range of human experience. The little stuff may not devastate us, but it still kind of sucks. Mirabai meant things like "jealousy in romantic relationships or family members giving you a hard time, or worrying about teenagers. In my case, as adolescents, my girls knew exactly how to hurt me, how to get me to lose my center. They were masterful at that." She pointed out that it is so important to engage in spiritual practice around those kinds of things—it's like training for the big race. For every crisis, there are a million aggravations, hurt feelings, rejections, or other places of discomfort that can accrue and nudge us toward self-destructive behavior when we need to treat ourselves with care and compassion to fortify ourselves for the big stuff.

Mirabai shared that "having cultivated the discipline of these practices means that even if we can't meditate or engage in mindfulness practice or Tonglen or loving-kindness or anything else when we're in the middle of a crisis, having done them has helped us with our ability to come back." This is key when we think about relapse or self-harm or any kind of damaging behavior or thought. "We can't use the practices themselves when we're on fire necessarily, and that's okay."

It's like with running or weight training—after a while, your muscles develop memory, similar in a way to Mirabai's describing "spiritual training" and its effects. Take weight lifting, for example—there have been times when I've had a cold or just been exceptionally busy and have had to take time off. Yet when I get back to it, if it's within a few days, the muscle memory is still there, and I'm not starting over from scratch. I may have to drop the weights down a few pounds, or, if I'm running, cut a couple of miles as I ease my way back into things, but again, it's not like starting over. That said, like exercise, life and love can be hard. Exceptionally fucking hard.

As Mirabai explained, "The path of the heart is a fierce path, but people want to think about the way of love as being fluffy and comfortable and comforting. To walk the path of conscious grief is not about consolation, it's about transformation. And I would say the same thing for any conscious spiritual path. It's nice when we get the goodies, when we get the moments of euphoria and the moments of epiphany and great clarity. Those are the nourishment we need to keep us moving forward on our path, but they're not the goal. The true work is to be able to show up for our lives with this sort of unconditional love and to cut through illusion. It can be messy and not pretty or comfortable.

"I think about this almost every day when I have something arise in me that I'm less than proud of, which happens continuously. It's so tempting to get away from it, to do anything I can to not feel what at first masquerades as shame. I would rather not feel that, so I have my addictions, which are the stories that I tell myself in my mind about what's going on. They're surefire ways to take me away from the experience, those little compelling narratives that I'm so good at. I must remind myself to come back to the most uncomfortable feelings, and not only to bear them but to bear witness to them in a very close, attentive way."

The little stuff of life can prepare us for the big stuff. And then, when we get to the other side of it—a relapse, say—it can provide a huge opportunity for transformation. Using my hospitalization, for example, I knew walking out of there that I was either going to die or thrive, and thanks to all the "muscle memory" of the spiritual practices I'd been using for several years, I could and did come back from that stronger than ever. Grace can be found in even self-inflicted near-death experiences. It lit a fire under my ass to look deeper at the unresolved pain I still carried inside me, to find ways to tap into the unconscious guilt and shame I've held for so many years so I could heal myself more fully. That's not to say fully heal, because I don't know if such a thing exists, but I believe in the capacity to heal *more* fully. I'm a living example of that. Maybe you are, too. It's not a selfish pursuit to heal yourself, because as you do that, your capacity to help others heal grows as well. Mirabai was a shining example of this as she held space for me in my misery, something she could do because she's endured tremendous pain in her life as well and worked with it and healed it to the extent she was capable.

By sharing a teaching that had transformed her life, Mirabai transformed mine. That teaching was the dark night of the soul based on the teachings of the sixteenth-century Spanish mystic Saint John of the Cross. It's one that is incredibly useful for people in any kind of recovery. "One of its definitive features is that we don't usually know that we've had a dark night of the soul until after it's over, until after it's passed. This would speak more to people who are on the other side of a relapse. Those are the people who will most identify with this teaching, because when we're in a true dark night of the soul, we cannot know that spiritual transformation is happening. We cannot know that there is any hope at all to see the other side of the darkness we're in. If we weren't abject, it wouldn't be an authentic dark night of the soul. At least part of it must be impenetrable darkness. This path is not for the faint of heart. It's not for people looking for prosperity consciousness or making their world better."

This summed up every bleak moment I'd experienced in my life— all the times I found myself hospitalized or in a psych unit, a detox, or a rehab, waking up in a jail cell and not knowing how I'd gotten there, or waking up the morning after a blackout drunk and seeing the self-inflicted cuts in areas I didn't know how to hide.

"The dark night of the soul is not about navigating a difficult situation in our lives. Even those powerful ones like a personal loss of some kind, the death of a loved one, the death of a relationship, or other shattering losses—those circumstances can be the catalyst for the experience of a dark night of the soul, but as we all know, a single difficult, painful life event does not necessarily mean spiritual transformation. A true dark night of the soul is often invisible, even to the person who's having one. It might have absolutely nothing to do with external circumstances. It's a private, spiritual crisis."

What are its qualities? How can we know when we've encountered one?

"According to John, there are two primary features of the 'dark night' landscape. One is that all our sensual or sensory attachments dry up and fall away. For instance, say we chant kirtan—and we chant and sing ourselves into states of rhapsody and ecstasy. Our sense of individuality begins to dissolve and we merge into this great field of love, and that's wonderful. Perhaps we've come to rely on that as part of our spiritual practice because it gets us to a state of bliss that looks like we're connected to the Divine, and I'm sure that's true. But in a dark night, that bliss doesn't happen, and the practices that used to reliably get us there fail us, including all the spiritual books that have knocked on the doors of our hearts and opened them, or whatever our methods were. Silent meditation practice has, for me, almost always been a way to feel as though I'm resting in the arms of the sacred.

"In a dark night, those connections are no longer happening. We often think that we're doing something wrong. Or, if we're believers in God, we might think that God has given up on us because we think we're so bad and fucked-up. And when we're no longer getting the juice, we're tempted to look for the juice elsewhere. It's like, 'Fuck that, this spiritual path that I've been on. It's bullshit. It's not working. I'm going to go where I know I can get the juice, and see ya later, Maharajji.' It's very tempting to do that, but according to John, what is happening is that the holy one is *weaning us from her breasts.* He uses that language. All the mystics, at some point, use the feminine and masculine interchangeably regarding the Divine. *The holy one is weaning us from her breasts* because we've grown and we're ready; we're ready to 'eat the crusty bread of the robust' and walk on our own two feet. He uses the analogy of Abraham and Sarah having a feast in honor of Isaac's weaning, which was a tradition in biblical times because it's a great and wondrous thing: This child is now ready to grow and be strong on his own and go forth. And they're all having a great time eating and drinking, but Isaac is sitting in the corner screaming his head off because he wants the breast; he's not ready to be weaned, he's having a tantrum. That's what we do in a 'dark night of the soul' experience. We throw a spiritual tantrum. We want to be fed directly. We're not ready to stand on our own, but the holy one feels that we *are* ready, and it's a great honor to enter this period of dryness, a cause for celebration, even though we don't feel it. Most people, according to Saint John, learn through their spiritual practices to endure these states and to stay with them, to quiet down the monkey mind and allow ourselves to rest in what is, even if what is, is very empty and dry. Usually, those states will pass if we can be true to them, show up for them, breathe into them, and soften and yield. Then we can get the juice back and go on our way stronger for having been through those patches of aridity and emptiness."

That has been my experience. I'm still not sure if all of it has been the holy one weaning me from her breast. It could be, and maybe I'm just not on enough of the other side to see it as such. What I do know is that these experiences have always been a catalyst for growth. The duality that I've harbored—one part of me wanting desperately to live, while another part desperately wants the pain to stop, and what better way than to die—is crazy. I've always been grateful that the part of me that wanted to live was always at least a tiny bit stronger than the part that wanted to die, because that difference was a light that guided me out of the depths of despair.

"The deeper, more advanced version of the 'dark night of the soul' experience is the *conceptual* dark night. John calls the first one 'the night of sense' and the second one 'the night of spirit.' The night of spirit is rare and harrowing, John tells us, because in the night of spirit—the deeper dark night—not only are we no longer feeling our connectedness to the sacred but we can no longer *conceive* of any spiritual reality. God, Buddha mind, the guru—none of it serves us. Even our own spiritual goals—awakening, being of service—these things lose their meaning. It's an existential crisis times ten, times a million, because the very foundation of our souls is shaken by this encounter with meaninglessness, this lack of reality regarding everything we've built our lives on as spiritual beings, spiritual seekers. The world stops making sense."

I knew what she meant. When I look back at my journals from periods of heavy drug and alcohol use, one of the main underlying themes in them was anger toward God. Let's just say the question "Where the fuck are you, you piece of shit?!" found its way onto more than a few of those pages.

"The conceptual constructs crumble in our hands, and the whole scaffolding comes tumbling down and we sit among the wreckage. Anything that we try to employ, any conceptual constructs that we reach for, even something like the teaching of the dark night of the soul, or Ramana Maharshi's teaching of neti neti in the Advaita Vedanta tradition, or anything that seems to vaguely resemble what we're going through, doesn't work. It's all empty. This, according to John, is the most powerful transformational experience—when we are truly walking through the darkness, because we have to walk blind; our eyes have failed us." We can't grasp at it or stumble our way through, because our hands and feet are useless in a dark night of the soul.

Mirabai told me Saint John liked to illustrate this with the Bible story of Jonah and the whale. "Jonah was the ultimate reluctant prophet. He was the one who tried to get away from God. God said, 'Jonah, you go to this community where the people are being abused and you tell their leader that he has to stop treating people that way.' Jonah says, 'Who, me? I'm out of here. I can't do what you're asking. It's too much. I don't have the skills. I'm not resourceful enough to do this work, God, and so I'm going to get away.' He got on a ship, hoping that if he went far enough out to sea, he could escape God. And he ended up in the belly of the great fish, and he languished there. John describes the way Jonah is suspended in the darkness as being like you're hanging, you're in a free fall, there's no ground—there's pure groundlessness in a true 'dark night of the soul' experience.

"Somehow, if we can learn to rest in that groundlessness, not only do we no longer feel a connection with the sacred, that bliss feeling we like so much that we are maybe addicted to, and not only can we not conceive of any kind of ultimate reality or spiritual truth, but we cannot feel the ground anywhere under our feet and we cannot sense any light penetrating this state. We let ourselves down into the arms of the mystery and we rest there. Or we do whatever we can to get away from it, like Jonah did. Usually that ends up causing great suffering to ourselves and others.

"A lot of people suffered because Jonah was responsible for this great storm at sea because he was trying to get away from his true calling. Afterward, when we're spit back up on the shore, we're able to see what the truth of our situation is and pick ourselves up and drag ourselves to Nineveh, or whatever the place is where we've been called to service. We step up in our broken state and say, 'Okay, how can I help?' And even then Jonah did not do it skillfully. He continued to make mistakes. It's not like after having been through a 'dark night of the soul' experience, after having endured a relapse and reentered, humbled and broken open, we're now enlightened beings who can dispense our holiness to the world. We have advanced on the path for sure if we've done it in a conscious way and we can be of service to others, but it doesn't guarantee that we're going to be masterful in how we manage our lives from then on. A dark night of the soul, when we've truly surrendered to the darkness, absolutely does change us. It transforms us: Our hearts are expanded, and we have more capacity to love."

We connect with this by allowing it to soften our heart, and lay aside as much of the protective armor we've placed over it as we can in that moment. In that place of surrender, we've relinquished control, if even for just a moment or two, and when we've let down our defenses, it's much easier for the divinity within us to do the guiding. When we come from this place of divinity, it's a state of true love not bounded by any causes or conditions. We're living from that place of unconditional love and can't help but share it freely with others. Again, this is often a short-lived experience, because as we come back from whatever hardship we've endured, we get stronger again—emotionally, mentally, physically—and that makes it easier for us to take control again. But if we can access even a small part of the softness we experienced, it can forever change our capacity to love, as Mirabai said.

"All my life I've been madly in love with a God that I don't believe in. I don't think it's about belief; it's about experience. I still have a hard time subscribing to any kind of established belief system about ultimate reality. Everything in me bristles at the effort by theologians and 'true believers' to codify mystery in any way. And many of the great mystical traditions tell us that the very effort to try to define God turns God into an idol, into a thing, and robs God of Divinity. That's the foundation of Judaism and Taoism. 'The Tao that can be told is not the eternal Tao. The name that can be named is not the eternal name.' Those are the opening lines of the Tao Te Ching, which to me is one of the greatest spiritual scriptures on the planet. Most mystical traditions affirm the absolute mystery of the Divine. Yet it's not only this transcendent, formless suchness; the immanence of the holy is available to us in our bodies. That's why we have them. That's why we're incarnated, so we can experience ultimate reality, which is love in form, and celebrate it.

"How do we establish a relationship with that when we're not even sure that there is such a thing? Particularly a personified entity called God? As you guys say in recovery, 'Fake it 'til you make it'; that's been a lot of my relationship with God. My name is Mirabai. I was named by Ram Dass when I was fifteen after the great sixteenth-century East Indian ecstatic poet who was madly in love with Krishna, the lord of love. And I've always identified with that extreme, intense bhakti quality being the path of devotion in the Hindu tradition. And even as I access in my own heart this ecstatic love-longing, which has characterized my entire spiritual path for my whole life, this yearning for union with God, with the beloved, I also have this other part of me that's drawn to the emptiness, to the formlessness, and they are equal in my spiritual being, in my soul, and they're not in conflict at all. I'm very comfortable holding these two seemingly contradictory spiritual stances. But when I'm in a place of need in my life, I go to the bhakti place. I go there and drink from that well of longing and love—it's called love-longing—to resource myself so that I can bear what's often unbearable and so that I can continue to show up in the best way."

I loved how Mirabai shared this, because it resonated with me in regard to how I approached this book in the first place, which was to offer different voices from many traditions, all guiding us on the same path.

There's no one right or wrong way to do it. The only right way is what works for you, and as Mirabai has exemplified, that's subject to change depending on what life experience you're having in the moment.

"In terms of recovery work, I would err on the side of pretending that God is my beloved and is available to me, and I would cultivate that relationship of yearning and resting, yearning and resting, that are the primary qualities of the dualistic bhakti path. And that's what I do: 'Beloved, what the fuck? Answer my prayers.' It starts with the beloved. It doesn't mean that I must believe in this beloved of mine, but it's my doorway to the numinous reality that transcends all forms. I need it. With all my heart, I need it."

PRACTICE

Tonglen

Tonglen can help us to develop our compassion and ability to be with our own suffering, the suffering of friends and loved ones, and the suffering of the whole world. It's worth noting that this practice can be rather heavy depending on the mental and emotional state you're in. You're breathing in the pain and suffering of others, and if you're already in a dark place, this may not be the best practice to undertake during that time. If you find that you are mentally and emotionally up to Tonglen, it can be a powerful practice. It's said that the Dalai Lama practices it every day. Here is the basic version.

- Begin by sitting in whatever meditation posture is most comfortable. Next, while focusing on your breath, imagine that you're breathing in and out of your heart rather than your mouth or nostrils.
- Do your best to keep the in-breath and the out-breath evenly balanced. Don't make the inhalations shorter because they're unpleasant or allow the exhalations to linger because they feel good.
- Bring a sense of stillness and openness to the experience of pain throughout the world. Our typical reaction to suffering is to try to push it away, to distract ourselves from it any way we can. With Tonglen, we learn to stop resisting. We relax our mind

and open our heart, and in the process, we cultivate a sense of trust.

- Once you've anchored yourself in this cycle, the visualized exchange begins: Continue breathing in the world's pain and suffering, and breathe out an offering of peace, comfort, and relief to all beings that are experiencing pain.
- Now, on your in-breath, breathe in a textured visualization of thick, heavy, and hot black smoke or any other image that coincides for you with pain and suffering. On the out-breath, release qualities that are light and cool, visualizing something like moonlight, a gentle stream, or a soft cloud, or whatever imagery represents light and ease for you. Continue breathing in this way for a few minutes, and embody the experience.

When we do this, we're flipping the script on the aversion we usually have toward suffering, bringing acceptance to what we'd normally reject—not just our pain and suffering but the entire world's collective pain and dis-ease as well. Breathing out, we send an aspiration of love, compassion, and fearlessness to the world. We're offering everyone, everywhere, every ounce of our own well-being, with the sincere desire that they may enjoy freedom from suffering.

16

THE GIFTS OF CRISIS

CONVERSATION WITH SALLY KEMPTON

S ally Kempton is someone I'd describe as a sought-after spiritual teacher as well as the author of an incredible book, *Awakening Shakti*, in which she gives readers a path for accessing the transformative power of the sacred feminine. When I worked with her, I found her approach to integrating meditative experiences within the framework of the practical to be life-changing. I was especially eager to hear how the energy of the Divine feminine can be accessed within the context of self-defeating behaviors and how to work with them and find true healing, but first, I'd read an article Sally wrote in *Yoga Journal* several years ago and I wanted to discuss her take on resilience:

> *The very sound of the word resilience captures its bouncy, rubbery quality.* Webster's Collegiate Dictionary *defines it as "an ability to recover from or adjust easily to misfortune or change"; psychiatrist Frederick Flach describes it as "the psychological and biological strengths required to successfully* master *change [emphasis added]."*
> *Resilience lets a writer like Frank McCourt turn the pain of a*

difficult childhood into a compassionate memoir. It carries a leader like Nelson Mandela through years of prison without letting him lose heart. It shows an injured yogini how to align her body so that her own prana can heal the pinch in her groin. Resilience is essential; without a basic supply of it, none of us would survive the accumulated losses, transitions, and heartbreaks that thread their way through even the most privileged human life.

But there also exists a deep, secret, and subtle kind of resilience that I like to call the skill of stepping beyond your edge. This kind of resilience has less to do with survival than with self-transformation. It's the combination of attentiveness, insight, and choice that lets some people tune in to the hidden energy lurking within a crisis and use it as a catalyst for spiritual growth. Though psychologists can list the qualities that resilient people have in common—insight, empathy, humor, creativity, flexibility, the ability to calm and focus the mind—this deeper resilience transcends personality traits.[1]

That seemed to me like as good a place to start as any. How do we find that resilience to bounce back during the difficult times in our lives?

Sally believes that resilience is something we develop throughout our lives—it's not instantaneous. What I found fascinating was that she saw resilience in our most tender of places: our *vulnerability.* "Everybody is vulnerable. Everybody is screwed up. Everybody is recovering from something. Everybody is addicted to one thing or another. Every one of us is subject to having everything we've relied on taken away. We need to be able to say 'Okay, I'm a vulnerable human being. My mind is subject to the same pain and despair and confusion as any human being's. So let me just admit my vulnerability.' From that place of recognizing our humanity, we can begin to develop what I consider real resilience: the ability to take one step and then another step and then another step toward a new way of being. For true resilience, we need to avoid putting on new armor, which means that we stop trying to escape from life's natural pain.

"If we keep returning to the heart and we keep returning to the vulnerable self, we discover the amazing miracle of vulnerability. It's the doorway into the sacred essence of ourselves. We find God inside ourselves by entering through the doorway of our vulnerability. Of course, there are lots of qualities that make us resilient. One of them is the ability to keep on truckin', to keep on doing it, even when we're knocked on our ass and we don't want to get out of bed. At some point, we must get out of bed. It's the ability to be strong without being brittle, without being masked, without being armored that is real resilience. It's very hard to find our deep strength, our unshakable strength, unless we've been through losses, unless we allow ourselves to be vulnerable."

Sally was preaching to the choir—I'm sure anyone reading this can relate. I loved that she said "keep on truckin'." I've experienced no shortage of guilt, shame, and pain with my relapses. As I became more serious in my practice and path, I learned that part of what kept me reverting to drugs and alcohol was that I wasn't going to those raw and tender places within myself and becoming vulnerable. Once I started to do that and lean into the pain, my life didn't get perfect, but my relapses began to happen less often, and were more surmountable in the sense that they were less difficult to come back from. I would look at myself and ask, "What the hell am I doing?" as well as recognize that I deserved better. I could do that because I was learning to have compassion, gentleness, and care for myself. I was applying the resiliency Sally spoke of. I would be in a terrible mess, but I'd be able to call myself on my own shit and say, "Look, I have a decision to make here. I'm in a bad place, and I'm either going to keep going down that road or pick myself back up." Sink or fucking swim—the choice was mine. I chose to stand back up and—to the best of my ability in that moment and in the ones that followed—be vulnerable with my thoughts, emotions, and feelings as they happened. I found my way through them by holding space instead of giving in to them. Then I could begin to gently look deeper at what was inside that brought me back to drinking and drugs. I'd explore what wasn't healed (the material that was conscious to me, at least) that was still causing me so much pain and sent me tumbling back down that dead-end road.

Accessing that vulnerability requires a certain amount of compassion. I wanted to learn Sally's views on compassion in general, especially within the context of the current divided and angry political climate in the United States. How would Sally suggest we practice compassion rather than anger in these situations and in general?

She recommended "looking past the physical person and trying to see what their story is, what their pain is, what's behind their mask, and also what is the human being behind the ideas I may not agree with. Where is the pain in these people? And, especially, what is their goodness?

"I tend to be judgmental about people who are smug about what they have, who feel that they deserve it but are afraid that if others have more, what they have will be taken away. So in that case, I'd try to consider what it would feel like to lose everything I worked for, to feel hopeless about things getting better for me. And I realize that almost all human beings experience that at some point." Sally reminded me about the way the Dalai Lama speaks of compassion, to realize that every human being wants to be happy, and that every human being is suffering in one way or another.

Sally took it beyond compassion. "The thing that I've been seeing recently is how much everybody needs to be respected. As much as we need compassion, we need to have respect for other people. People know when they're not respected or taken seriously, and I find that this is one of the things that makes us most resentful. I think that's what so many people in our country are feeling."

absolutely resonated with that. I thought about all the nights I'd lie awake, sick and suffering, mad at God, mad at everything, or perhaps more accurately, *scared* of everything. There was so much fear in me. I would think about that and how the expression "Hurt people hurt people" made so much sense. By remembering that place of fear and pain in my own life, I began to think about how much fear and pain must be inside people in hate groups and how, at the heart level, I could relate to that. That took some of my anger toward them away because I saw they were hurting very much like I've hurt. We express our pain in very different ways, but it is pain and fear that underlies all of it—for myself, for members of hate groups, and for all human beings, period.

Sally grokked what I was getting at. "A lot of us confuse compassion with pity. It's because we are naturally experiencing *me* here and *you* there and not necessarily feeling the true connection between *us*. During the times in my life when my heart was open completely and I experienced what I would call 'true' compassion, I felt a literal oneness with other people. It's not 'I'm over here feeling compassion for you' or 'You're there feeling compassion for me'—it's a realization that there's no difference between *us*. That we're all threads in one fabric. Our hearts ache for others. We rejoice with others because they are part of our own being.

"Admittedly that's an ideal, a high state. I've experienced that kind of compassion at a few wonderful peak times in my life, though I'll freely admit that it's not my daily experience. Yet remembering those moments, recognizing that those feelings are the true ones, shows me that there is no way I can separate myself from you or my heart from your heart or my pain from your pain or my happiness from your happiness. To remember that allows a feeling of compassion, which is not 'I feel sorry for you' or 'I'm going to try and empathize with you,' but is more like 'I *am* you. There's no way I can't be you.'"

I related what Sally was saying to my own direct experiences of this nondual oneness. I sat with that for a minute, and then began to wonder who there is to even be compassionate in the first place, since there's just this one compassion occurring that involves all of us. I hoped Sally could connect this to her wisdom rooted in the tantric Shaivism school of yoga—a tradition that originated after 850 CE in Kashmir. She helped me understand how the Divine feminine can reconnect us with nondual awareness, which was the basis of her book *Awakening Shakti*.

She started by sharing her understanding of the Divine as nondual. "We can't understand the Divine feminine without recognizing its relationship to the Divine masculine. In the Shaiva tradition, Shiva Shakti—empowered consciousness—are two sides of the same truth, the same sacred reality. Tantra describes reality as having two main qualities: It's still, unchanging, and transcendent, and it's also playful, creative, and completely present in the physical and subtle worlds. The tradition of nondual Shaivism also takes it for granted that there are many subtle realms between that absolute transcendent reality, the ever-present awareness-love, and the physical world. Of course, most of us aren't aware of these levels of reality, just the way we can't hear some of the frequencies that dogs hear. But the Tantras say that there are subtle, powerful energies who occupy a very subtle sphere of reality but who also function as energies throughout the physical world and within the human personality. In tantric Shaivism there's a recognition that the human being contains all worlds, all powers, all planes of existence. Everything is accessible within us, which is part of the allure of meditation.

"Deity energies, whether they are the Hindu deities like Durga or Krishna or the Buddhist deities like Manjushri or Vajrayogini or the ancient Western deities, are specific vortexes of energy. We experience these energies around us—as weather, as emotional energies, as particular resonances that we pick up in nature or in groups. We exist inside our own energy systems. This is something that more and more of us are able to recognize, especially now that traditional forms of healing, Chinese medicine, and so forth are becoming more familiar." Sally took it even further. "What is more difficult for us postmoderns to accept is that there is also a level at which deities actually appear in forms, which can be felt or even seen in meditation or dreams. The images of deities function as meditation aids that eventually can lead us to an actual experience of the deity energy, often in a form. Similarly, mantras related to specific deities can supercharge our bodies and our consciousness with unique forms of presence. Deities then can be experienced as helpful presences, protectors, vehicles for receiving grace from the infinite. There's an entire science of what is sometimes called deity yoga in which we practice enlarging our capacity for experiencing our own divinity by invoking deity energies through visualizations and mantras, and eventually coming to see that we have these energies within ourselves."

I wanted to know more about that! Could Sally use the Hindu goddess Kali—the Divine mother and Shiva's consort—as an example of how we can work with deity energies?

"Kali is a great goddess to talk about. One of the questions that comes up when we Westerners are talking about Hindu goddesses is 'Why Hindu goddesses? Why Hindu deities?' They're obviously not a part of our tradition. But over the past century or so, Westerners have been immersing themselves in Indian culture. In some cases, it's clearly a kind of spiritual tourism or cultural appropriation. But I believe the deeper draw that serious practitioners experience is because these deity forms are alive. Because they are invoked and loved every single day, by millions of people, they are accessible with not too much effort by anyone who approaches them with a degree of openness. It's not so different than the way, say, the energy of Jesus or Mary can be felt in certain churches. Because so many people have been calling on these energies in such a concentrated way, a pathway is formed. Then the mantra of a deity or a prayer can serve as a doorway into what I would call light realms.

"Kali, of course, has become a catalytic icon in the West. Her form is highly psychoactive, especially for women. To many Western women, Kali's image can summon the inner archetype of the untamed feminine, the woman who is not hiding her audacity, her intensity, or her sexuality. Yet ultimately Kali is a goddess of spiritual liberation— the dissolution of all thought forms into pure awareness. In the iconography, she's shown as a more or less naked young woman. Most of the icons of Kali show her being about sixteen years old, with full breasts, wearing a necklace of skulls, which represents the letters of the Sanskrit alphabet—that's a long story. She classically carries a bloody meat cleaver in one hand and a severed head in another (that represents the ego, severed by her sword). In the traditional story of Kali, she's a bloodthirsty warrior who manifests out of the warrior goddess Durga, while Durga is battling a horde of demons and conquers thousands of demons.

"What's interesting to me about Kali is that she has so many faces, as a true goddess should! She started out in the Hindu tradition as a scary, marginal figure to whom you prayed if you were looking for the power to kill your enemies. She gradually came to be seen as the full-spectrum Divine mother. Great sages like Ramakrishna called Kali 'Ma' and extolled her compassion and her beauty. She's both a goddess of life and a goddess of death. She's the goddess of dissolution and destruction and also of the violent creativity of the birthing. Of all the feminine deities, she's the one who can most powerfully take a sword to your obstructive tendencies, and ultimately to your false self-identification. Kali is the force that dissolves your masks and false ideas and shows you what you are at the very core. She melts you down to the bone, then shows you the vastness of what you really are. In her most esoteric form, Kali is the great void into which all forms dissolve. She's a multilayered goddess who can kindle radical ecstasy inside you. And if you call on her, you need to be prepared for some radical transformation!"

Sally's take on the Divine feminine was so much more expansive and inclusive than any I'd encountered. I mean, right there, you hear the word "feminine" and many people assume it's about gender, but what she was talking about incorporated the relationship between the Divine masculine and the Divine feminine, as well as the importance of all of us realizing the full potential of our energy.

"In India, Divine feminine practices are called Shakta, meaning that they invoke Shakti, the cosmic, dynamic energy that is the source of everything in the universe. The basic understanding behind tantric understanding about reality is that the Divine masculine and the Divine feminine are utterly intertwined. On the cosmic level, there's no gender separation. There's only a vast, androgynous, transcendent beingness. Once there are forms—once the big bang has happened—you are in the realm of Shakti. What that means is that men as well as women are Shakti. Our gender identities operate only at certain stages of consciousness. In the tantric tradition, the qualities of the Divine masculine are pure awareness, detachment, freedom, stillness, and unchanging existence. The qualities of the Divine feminine in the tantric tradition are energy, power, love, the capacity for knowing and acting, and, critically, the power that both binds you to the experience of limitation and also reveals unity. In fact, a Shakta practitioner will tell you that all forms of success are actually gifts of the goddess. Anything you want in life is in the hands of Shakti or the Divine feminine.

"In the tradition, men as well as women—in fact, as far as I can see, men *more* than women—invoked the Divine feminine as a loving mother and giver of boons. The idea was that for mastery of life, you need to have a relationship with goddess. Most of the literature about goddesses that we have from the Eastern traditions seems to have been written by men. So traditionally in India and Tibet, there isn't much written by women about goddess practice, and that is one of the things that are changing in modern times.

"When I started giving goddess classes, I was teaching mainly in yoga studios, and there would be fifty women there and maybe three men. Usually the men would be either the studio owners or maybe the husbands or boyfriends of the women attending. What would happen is that the men would come up to me afterward and they would say, 'Gosh, I thought this was going to be one of those female empowerment things that I don't relate to, but it turns out that I could identify the goddess as a part of my own energetic experience.' In fact, what happens once men recognize the feminine as a Divine quality in themselves is that they realize that these archetypal energies that we identify as goddess energies are actually very intimately a part of their own psyche. Men *and* women realize how much of their strength, their skill, their capacity for intuition and creativity are connected to Divine feminine energy itself.

"Sacred feminine energy is naturally a part of everyone's psyche, and it is both nurturing *and* strong, even aggressive. What the tantric view points out is that a man doesn't have to depend on a woman for nurturance and acceptance, nor does a woman have to go to a man for strength. It is such a transformative, integrative understanding to take in this view of masculine and feminine. When you recognize that all of us are actually powered by the feminine energy, not only does it engender more respect for women, which is always a good thing, but also more comfort with men's vulnerability and the connection between inner strength and vulnerability."

There was that word again: "vulnerability." Meditation has helped me soften to my own vulnerability. Learning to stay with the memories and visions of the shitty things I've done in the past rather than get up off the cushion and walk away is a humbling experience, as is bearing as much loving witness toward the experience as I can muster. Thinking about that, I wanted to bring it from the theoretical to the personal. What role had goddesses played in Sally's life? How had they transformed her?

Her teacher, the great Indian guru Swami Muktananda, was a kundalini master. "Although he was not a 'form' guy, his teaching was very much that 'the Divine lives within you and as you, so don't worry about external forms.' Nonetheless, he always referred to kundalini—the inner transformative energy—as a goddess. He would invoke the names of the great Indian goddesses to describe kundalini and help us understand the sacredness with which he viewed the awakening energy. He had built a gigantic statue of the goddess Durga in the back of his ashram, and after he died, his successor began to hold celebrations of the yearly autumn Durga festival, which is called Navaratri. These celebrations became more and more elaborate, which is customary in India.

"My own journey with the goddesses began during one of these celebrations. I was telling a mythic tale about the goddess when I actually felt her presence inside and around me as an explosion of love and ecstasy. Ecstasy, by the way, is one of the qualities of goddess. She *is* ecstasy. You don't know ecstasy until you have connected to the Divine feminine. From that time on, I began to experience the natural world—the trees and the mountains and the ocean—as having consciousness, sentience. I could feel trees and rocks and plants as literally being aware. Over time, I began to realize that this shift in my vision was a new kind of awakening, and that it had something to do with the forms of the goddesses. A couple of years later, I started teaching classes on the Hindu goddesses, on the iconography, and I would find that when I thought about them, when I thought about the goddess Kali, when I thought about the goddess Durga or Lakshmi, I would feel the unique energy signature of that goddess, and experience a kind of transmission about what their energy does in the world.

"It's very beautiful to look for goddess energies as they express themselves in the natural world. Storms and lightning connect with Kali. The beauty of a garden is very connected with the goddess Lakshmi or the goddess Lalita. The whole realm of inspiration is the realm of the goddess Sarasvati, who is the goddess of learning, language, and music. If you start to see the Divine activity, the sacred activity, in your inspiration, your capacity for speaking, your appreciation of music, and if you realize that these are not ordinary capacities, they are tinged with a kind of Divine allurement, then you can start to see your own gifts and capacities as sacred gifts, as goddesses acting through you. In my experience, this gives a new kind of sweetness and beauty to whatever you do, and also a growing capacity for surrender. There's an intimacy that one can have with inner worlds that comes through looking at the world as the play of the Divine feminine. Then you can also find the Divine masculine as that unmoving stillness that is present no matter how crazy the play gets."

PRACTICE

Lalita Tripura Sundari Guided Visualization

Understanding that the Divine feminine is an entire path unto itself, I asked Sally to take me through a practice that anyone—male or female—who is interested in connecting with their Divine feminine could try. She suggested we work with the goddess Lalita, who in the form of the powerful, great mother goddess is beautiful and erotic, and has the power to slay demons as well. She's an aspect of the feminine that is both playful and protective. Sally described her as "the love energy that draws molecules together and creates wholeness."

Here is what she taught me:

- Begin by closing your eyes. Imagine yourself in a beautiful garden. See the trees, the sunlight. Smell the fragrances and feel the breeze. Take a moment to center yourself and focus on your breath.
- Picture an exquisitely beautiful woman—a goddess, whose name is Lalita Tripura Sundari, which means "playful beauty of the three worlds." She is smiling and walking through this garden toward you. Her skin is the color of the sunrise. She has large, luminous eyes. She's carrying a sugarcane bow in one hand, and in the other, five arrows made of flowers. The

bow represents the mind, and the arrows represent the senses. In the middle of her forehead is a third eye, which is open, showing that her awareness is fully awakened to the truth of unity.

- As you gaze at this being, realize that a rosy pink light is emanating from her heart and flowing into yours. It's healing the emotional wounds that you may have carried for lifetimes. Allow yourself to absorb this light through your heart. Feel it flowing through your body.
- Imagine that a beam of pale blue light flows from her third eye into yours. Let it move into the very center of the head and bathe your brain in illumined awareness.
- Now you feel that from the belly of this goddess, from the area below the navel, flows a deep red light directly into your own belly chakra. Let it cleanse the whole lower body of wounds, of sexual abuse and shame, of disempowerment, of insecurity, of the feelings of rootlessness or disconnection.
- Sit feeling the goddess's energy as light filling your head, heart, and lower body for a moment.
- Now imagine the goddess dissolving into a point of light and being drawn into your own heart. As you continue to invoke her, accept the gifts she brings—awareness, love, and strength, all of which are in the hands of the Divine feminine, of Shakti, the power who awakens us and teaches us love.

Sally shared the mantra that goes with this visualization:

Om Aim Hreem Shreem

She followed it with an invocation to Lalita:

Om Aim Hreem Shred Lalitambikayai Namaha.

"*Om* is the primordial sound. *Aim* is the mantra of inspiration. *Hreem* is the seed mantra that is said to bring forth the power to manifest anything, and indicates the goddess's unlimited power to create. *Shreem* carries with it auspiciousness, foundational goodness, and beauty. These are the qualities of the goddess you invoke as you invoke Lalita."

17

TRANSCEND AND INCLUDE

CONVERSATION WITH KEN WILBER

A uthor, philosopher, and cosmic storyteller Ken Wilber has written numerous books, many of them on integral psychology. He's also the creator of integral theory, a pioneering four-quadrant grid that views all human wisdom and experience through lenses of the intentional, behavioral, cultural, and social. He has been a mentor to me since the start of my spiritual exploration, and we've spoken about a lot of things over the years. I was especially touched by his book *Grace and Grit*, a memoir of his short but profoundly beautiful and life-changing marriage to Treya Killam Wilber (which Ken candidly shares a bit about later in our conversation).

I wanted to begin this conversation with Ken's perspective on the causes of trauma and addiction. How can we heal ourselves from substances, destructive behaviors, and emotional wounds?

Ken shined a light on the matter. "There are various levels of being and awareness, and the way they unfold is in developmental stages. The evidence for this is overwhelming. I wrote a book called *Integral Psychology*, and in it I included charts of over one hundred different developmental models. You could see in all these models that there were six to eight major stages of development that continued to appear repeatedly.

"Development is a real process. Some developmental models have been tested in over forty different cultures, including Amazon rainforest tribes, Australian aborigines, and Harvard professors, and no exceptions were found in any of those. The stages are real. That's what's so astonishing. These are stages that we find throughout nature, so we look at the most common holarchical stage of unfolding in nature.

"It's quarks to atoms to molecules to cells to organisms. Each level transcends and includes its predecessors. "Transcend" means it goes beyond, it has a bigger truth, more expansive. Molecules transcend atoms, they go beyond them, but they also include them. They enwrap them. Atoms are the ingredients of molecules. Molecules don't hate atoms—they include them. Transcend and include is the primary nature of evolution itself. To negate is to move beyond something and its limitations. That's what evolution does, and that's what all the developmental lines in a human being do—they transcend and include." This really resonated with me. The only way we'll truly evolve is by including and integrating what came before into something great—into a greater good. Not by wiping it out. I just did a day-long workshop with my friend JP Sears out at Alex Grey's Chapel of Sacred Mirrors (CoSM) facility, and during that workshop JP made the point that if you cut a tree, you'll see all of its rings—from one to a hundred of them (if it's lived that long). As he spoke, I remember thinking to myself, "Wow, what a perfect example of transcend and include." It also reminded me of an old Curl Up and Die band poster I used to have hanging in my apartment. On the poster was a big tree—half alive, half dead—and the text read, "But the past ain't through with us." So true. That shit still kinda haunts me to this day, so I no longer hang the poster (definitely a cool-ass band, though).

"That means at any of the stages of human development, because there are two components—transcend and include—something can go wrong with either one. When that happens, you develop a pathology. You develop a sickness. You develop something wrong. When something goes wrong with the transcend part, it means it doesn't get to fully move beyond or let go—it remains fixed at the previous stage. You're stuck in it in some way. What that means is it can become an addiction. The individual is going to be addicted to some component of that stage that it should have let go of, and that addiction is going to show up in all sorts of ways. The person is going to be addicted to anything that reminds them of the original fixation, the original addiction, and that's going to be a very real problem."

"Could a lack of self-worth or self-loathing be an addiction?" I thought to myself. Sure it could! In fact, these have been two of the great lessons I wish I could say I've chosen to work with in my life, but it was much more that they crashed down full speed ahead in a "holy shit, I've really gotta do something about this" moment (or moments would be more accurate—there have certainly been plenty of them). There are still times I look in the mirror and have to glance away quickly as I shudder at what's reflecting back at me, remembering exactly how I got here and struggling with my worth. I look at the belt notches in my shorts and will often judge my sense of physical health by them. Not entirely unrealistic, but still, physical health should be judged by much more than a fucking hole in a piece of leather (or pleather or canvas, for my vegan/veggie friends). And here I am writing this book and feeling as inadequate as ever. Two books written on healing and spirituality and I still relapsed. I still went through phases of eating terrible food. I still lost my marriage. I almost died. Ah, life. If there's one thing above all else that's become clear to me, it's that a spiritual path *will not* save you. What it can do, however, if you're lucky (and committed), is help you make it through those "oh shit" moments by the skin of your teeth (and this is on a good day, of course). In fairness, the path wouldn't be worth undertaking if a better quality of life didn't come along with it as well. So fine, positive spiritual experiences/results, here's your moment to shine: greater sense of well-being, spontaneous bouts of joy and gratitude, a deeper reverence for the simpler things in life (sunsets, good coffee, health, family, friends)—all right, all right, enough already, we get the picture.

"The person is going to find themselves, for reasons that they can't understand at all, obsessing about these things. They want to chase after them." Ken was talking about things like drugs and food. "They want to repeat experiences.

"Here are some very simple versions: food, sex, power, love, achievement, harmony, wholeness, unity. Even writing. You could say I was addicted to writing at the time I met my wife, Treya. I had been writing since I was twenty-three, about a book a year for almost ten years. It was my persona, it was who I was. You can get addicted to food by overeating. The person is looking to stuff himself with food. There is now a very large portion of the American population that's overweight, many of them clinically obese. This is serious. You can have an addiction to sex. This used to be made fun of, but then as we looked at it more and more, we found that men and women could get addicted to the release that sexual orgasm brought. You can become addicted to power and become a power-mad, crazed, insane person. You can become addicted to love. Wherever we have these developmental unfoldings, we can have these fixations and therefore addictions to some component that we should have been letting go of. We should have transcended and included.

"We should have very healthily let go of it, included it in a general, loose way, and then moved on. But we get these extreme versions, and that causes nightmares. On the include side of things, if you fail to do that correctly, then you fail to integrate the previous stage. You fail to embrace it, include it. It's like molecules refusing to include atoms in their makeup. It's sick, it's a pathology. All the way back to the Big Bang, the universe has transcended and included, on and on and on, and when that goes unhealthily, it can make addictions and allergies, and on and on, and those are truly problematic. They're very common. They happen all the time. They're part of what we need to be paying very close attention to."

Ken's extraordinary take on development and addiction segued into another thing I love discussing with him—what Swiss psychiatrist and psychoanalyst Carl Jung called the shadow self. I wanted to understand how humans repress and disown various aspects of themselves and the repercussions of this repression when it comes to all sorts of addictions, acting out, stress, and neuroses in the context of addiction and relapse.

Ken dove right in. "The shadow is a general term for those aspects of the self that are truly part of the self, belong to self, but that the person has become out of touch with, has become unaware of. Often—because it's not that we forget them, but that we don't want to know we have them—we disown them. We push them out of awareness. It's an actual active repression." Ken experienced a profound repression from who he knew himself to be during the very difficult time his wife was fighting cancer. He said that she had as profound an impact on his life as anything that ever happened. It's still hard for him to talk about her death even twenty years afterward, and we'll learn a little more about what he calls a "sheer withdrawal of actions" later.

An example that came to mind from my life was an experience I had on a Little League baseball team when I was roughly eight or nine years old. I'd suppressed this experience for many years until it came flooding back one day while I was sitting in meditation. The coach was handing out our new team jerseys to all the players. We excitedly put them on, and mine was a size too small (and I was a husky kid). The coach took notice and made a comment in front of the entire group of children and parents, saying, "Looking good, Crisco!" That was the first time I became conscious of my weight and physical appearance; up until then, who gave a fuck? As a kid, all I was interested in was having fun playing with Transformers and Super Mario Bros. and shit. From that point on, I struggled with my physical appearance and weight, and while I know that this was in no way the only factor that led me to addiction, I'm certain it was part of it. At some point, I disowned that material, repressing it into my unconscious for many years while it wreaked havoc on my well-being. That's one of my shadows.

Ken was just getting started. "Shadow stuff is essentially if you look at the basic stages of growth that humans can go through, from the initial fusion state where the infant is one with his physical environment and he can't tell where the body stops and the chair starts, through the impulsive stage and then through a self-protective, safety, or power stage. Then it moves into a conformity stage, and then it moves into the emergence of reason and the capacity for hypothetical, deductive thinking, scientific thinking, third-person world-centric notions, and so on. From there into postmodern pluralism and multiculturalism and multiple perspectives, and from there to the integral stages, which are all inclusive. But at any one of those stages, you can take some aspect of that stage, and because you have a great deal of judgment about it or a great deal of negativity about it or because you're afraid of it, or because it triggers anxiety or fear in you, you can repress it. You push it out of awareness. It's the defense mechanism that the human mind has, which is that it can cut off an awareness of something and pretend that it's not there and 'I don't own that. That's not me.'" But unfortunately, repressing something—dissociating it and pushing it out of awareness—doesn't make it go away. "At the time my wife was ill, I was writing all of these books. It was the first time in my life I was really adapting to this new profession and new persona, but I couldn't continue doing it. Treya's illness forced me to really drop that persona of the writer, of my work, of making things okay. And of course this is an extremely common problem that men have, as we tend to identify with our doing. And so this was just a sheer withdrawal of actions that, if you want to, you can think of as an addiction. I had to drop something I had done literally every day of my life for the last ten or fifteen years. And stopping that was one of the single most difficult things I have done. It just ate me up, and as much as I had a Zen practice and Christian contemplative prayer, all these tools to help me accommodate to these changes—well, the changes were really overwhelming, and it became a profound learning lesson for me to simply drop that and give my life to this woman. And because I loved her enormously, I found ways that I could do that, but it was still eating at me.

"Once you push something into an unconscious state, it continues causing problems. The most common thing that happens with it is that is gets projected onto other people. If I'm having trouble with expressing anger and I repress that, then I can project that anger onto people in the environment. Instead of me being angry at my boss, I'll think my boss is angry with me and I'll start reacting to it. That will make the situation bad, because I'm reacting to something that's not there. Or at the same time, if I have a positive quality and I don't give myself credit for it and I repress that, disown that, and project that onto others, then I'll tend to hero-worship them. I'll tend to think, 'Oh, they're the greatest.' Now, they may be great, but when you take their greatness and add your projected greatness, you get a double greatness. That turns them from being very admirable people into superheroes. Then you completely do whatever they say, whatever they want, completely worship them—hero worship and so on."

I could absolutely relate to what Ken was saying about projecting the good and the bad repressed shadow material within myself onto others. Spending time doing shadow work helped me recognize how I projected so much shit onto other people, whether old friends or complete strangers—again, both good and bad. Let's use bad as an example. A simple one that comes to mind is that I've often mentally judged men's haircuts, especially when they're fancy. But why the fuck should I even care? I shouldn't—except the thing is, I do, and it is beyond jealousy. It's shadow material I repressed for a long time during my adult years about how I started balding in my early twenties. My hair began to thin as early as sixteen, but the full-on balding started in my early twenties. Luckily for me, I was heavily into punk/hardcore, where you could easily get away with a shaved head or a baseball cap. But as the years went by and I began going to fewer shows, I couldn't hide behind that as much, and the projection onto others grew. To this day, I'm still super self-conscious about the no-hair thing. I mean, I look decent with a shaved head, but I still struggle with it, and yes, at times I still judge those damn sexy-looking-man haircuts because I can't have one.

As I've come to learn with shadow work, virtually anything we project onto others is a form of shadow. Sure, sometimes a person is a dick, there's no way of getting around that, but more times than not, if we take a minute to trace back whatever thoughts we're projecting onto others and do a little exploring within to see what they're saying about us, we'd be quite surprised (until we work with shadow for a while and it becomes like riding a bike).

Ken continued with his intriguing point of view, saying, "In the same way, if you happen to be very controlling and critical and you repress that and push that out of awareness and you project it onto somebody in the environment—it very likely might be your mate, for example—you then feel that that person is constantly criticizing you, is constantly trying to control you. Now, they *might* be controlling, but when you add their controlling tendencies to your controlling tendencies, then they get a double dose of controlling. You feel completely overwhelmed by their attempt to control you. That is very common. When we project a negative onto people in the environment, we often will project it onto somebody who already has some of that trait, because we'll see it and then go, 'Oh, that's who has it. That's the controlling son of a bitch. I know somebody is being controlling as hell, but that can't be me. Ah, it's them.' Then we get a double dose of that shadow material. That's where people react wildly to that kind of perception. That's a real shadow tip-off.

"If something simply informs you in the environment (and it can be negative), that's the tip-off. You see it and say, 'Okay, I got it, I understand it.' But if something wildly affects you, if you get extremely emotional and reactive and upset in either a negative or a positive way— hating something or outrageously loving or adoring something—then it's likely you're projecting. It's people who end up shadowboxing their way through life or shadow hugging, but either way they are crippling their own potential, because every time you push shadow material out of your awareness, push it into the unconscious—let alone project it entirely out of your system and onto somebody out there—then you lose that amount of consciousness for your own self."

Ken provided an interesting example. "Let's say the average person is born with the equivalent of a hundred dollars' worth of consciousness in their system. At the first stage of growth and development, they repress 10 percent of their psyche—say they had a bad childhood, and they repress 10 percent. Now ten dollars is taken out of the conscious bank account and put into their unconscious account, and now they have access to only ninety dollars. Maybe they go another stage or two and then they hit some difficult times, and maybe a third stage, fourth stage, and then use another ten or fifteen dollars. Now they have only seventy-five dollars left in their conscious bank account and twenty-five dollars in their unconscious account. They can't use the money in the unconscious account, they can't access it, so it doesn't add anything. All it's doing is causing problems. It's causing pain and neurotic suffering, and they are likely projecting it onto the outside world, and that's causing problems. Any time you project shadow into a relationship, you won't see that relationship accurately, and you'll end up giving wacky and idiotic feedback to the partner in the relationship. They know it and they don't like it, so sooner or later that relationship is going to end in trouble. Of course they're likely doing the same thing to you to some degree, but you're headed for trouble if you're doing that. Now they've got seventy-five dollars in their conscious bank account; maybe they're seeing the world through more inclusive, integral eyes. Now they're working, trying to get to the next level, and they want to become enlightened or awakened or something like that. Maybe at that integral level they lose another five bucks. Now they have only seventy dollars in their conscious account. It turns out that to get to that next level, the level of transcendence, they need eighty dollars. It takes that much consciousness to get into that, and you don't have it.

"The fact that you simply push shadow out of awareness doesn't mean that it goes away and stops causing problems—it causes an enormous number of problems, particularly if you project it and see it in somebody else. It distorts reality around you. It also distorts your own self-concept. You get a false self-concept or persona; you have a false self. Now, there was a year or year and a half during Treya's illness when it was very, very difficult, and at one point I even got almost suicidal. And I remember driving to a gun store, frankly, and walking through, looking for a gun to buy. I looked at shotguns and thought of Hemingway, and thought, 'Well, maybe I'll try a Hemingway,' and then I looked at other types and thought, 'Well, okay, that was another famous author who ended his life that way,' and it was just a devastatingly difficult time for me. And we'd also been facing the one difficult characteristic that Treya had, which was, when you have cancer, that kind of becomes your trump card for every argument you have. So no matter what argument we ended up having, it always ended with her saying, 'But I have cancer.' And that just ended anything I could say. I just couldn't see how to get around something that horrible. And whatever problems I had were minuscule compared to hers. I didn't make them go away, so I was still facing these incredibly difficult issues.

"At any stage of development from bottom to top, you can get into trouble with that level's needs or drives or motivations or characteristics, and you can either remain in fusion with them as the development continues or let go of them. As I mentioned earlier, you're supposed to transcend and include each level. But if you don't transcend, part of you remains infused with it or stuck to it; then you have an addiction to that quality, and your shadow is an addiction shadow. If, on the other hand, you push too hard, you don't let go of it, you disown it, you shove it into the basement, then that's a shadow allergy. Both involve losing track of aspects of yourself and creating a false self, because it's an inaccurate self-image, an inaccurate self-concept. You're not being truthful with yourself about what is in yourself, what you are actually like. What are the real qualities and characteristics and aspects that define you, so there's no untruthfulness or lie? The shadow is the locus of the lie. It's where we have a self-deception. Once that happens, all our interactions with others and the world out there and the environment are going to be distorted, because we're interacting with a false image of what we are. We're never being truthful in any of our interactions with the world. That always causes some sort of problem, because most people will be able to detect that something's not right. You're either overreacting or underreacting, or you say things about yourself that make most people roll their eyes, thinking, 'There's no way he's that.'

"One of the irritating things about shadow material is almost everyone else can see it except you. That's why they're always called blind spots, and blind spots are just that: something you can't see. You can't see what you can't see. That's what causes so many problems in life and in our interpersonal relationships: You're running around doing all this stuff, and people are spotting this stuff and every now and then somebody will sit down and try to give you feedback. Unless you're used to working on this and can lower your defenses and open up to this kind of stuff, you'll become reactive. You'll get defensive. You can always tell when someone is getting defensive. You try to bring something up to them and you can see the hackles rise. They get scrunched over and fold their arms and cross their legs and glare at you, all these sorts of standard defensive moves, so it's a constant problem. It's a problem that comes mostly from the complexity of being a human being."

This has happened to me on a number of occasions. In retrospect, I see how most of the time it was out of care and concern, but when an individual is locked into a particular state, whether it's addicted to drugs, alcohol, or any other activities or substances that they associate with the safety of their own life or well-being, more times than not, they'll be put on the defensive. Early on in my own addiction experience, I remember my parents pressuring me to stop. In their defense, they had not taken the time to learn about what addiction actually consists of (mentally, biologically, neurologically, etc.) and couldn't understand why I couldn't just stop. I have a vivid memory of being in a psych unit in Middlesex Hospital and my dad being outwardly pissed off at me for "doing this again." If he had understood the complexities of addiction at the time, I'm sure he would have responded differently (which he has since). But in that moment, he was like so many other families struggling to understand and navigate working with their loved ones' addictions or self-defeating behaviors. Through the years, my dad has gone on to learn and love me in a way that I still at times almost don't feel worthy of, but in the beginning it was hard for everyone involved.

"As I've said, we are comprised of so many parts, from quarks to atoms to organisms. We contain every one of those in our body to this day. Every single one. Atoms don't tend to have shadow elements, because you must have one part of you that's pushing the other part out, and then you must have a place where you can push it—an unconscious— and then that's something that your consciousness is going to do, and then you must have a defense mechanism. Atoms don't have that, molecules don't have that, and cells don't have that specific kind of thing. It's only when you start getting up to organisms and then at least early mammals, because they have a cortex and they have a limbic system and they have a reptilian brain stem, so these things should be unified and integrated.

"Any time something is built like that, there's something that can go wrong with it. Whenever that many things are put together, there's always a chance you can do it wrong. That's what happens. It's the price humans pay for the complexity that we have. What each stage is supposed to do is transcend and include the previous stage. By transcend, it means you let go of the previous stage. You drop it and move to a higher stage. There's something, this emergent reality. Something new comes into being. It isn't present in the previous stage. That's what an emergent is. You move up to this higher level, which is partially an emergent, and so there's a newness there, but to do that, you should let go of that previous level. If you let go of that in a healthy way, then you've transcended it. If you don't let go of it, if some part of you remains attached to some part of that previous level, then you're addicted to that part of that level but in an unconscious way; you're not facing it consciously, so you don't know what's causing it. Suddenly now you find yourself drinking or shooting heroin or whatever you're doing, but you have an addictive behavior now because you didn't transcend that previous level correctly. But then you're also supposed to include it. You transcend *and* include—include means that you embrace it. You integrate it. If you don't do that right, if you fail to integrate it, then you are disowning it. You're dissociating it. You're repressing it. Now that's an allergy, because evolution is built out of transcend and include. You can break down in either one of these, either by remaining addicted to parts of it or by becoming allergic to parts of it. That's the breakdown of the transcendent part or the breakdown of the include part, the integrate part.

"If everything goes right and we transcend and include, we move beyond all our previous levels but we also include them. We embrace them. We no longer exclusively identify with them. The whole point of going through an entire growth process is that by the time we get all the way to the highest level, we've transcended all the previous levels. This means we've let go of all of them, we're exclusively identified with none of them, it's truly neti neti. I'm not this, I'm not that. The pure witness, the pure self, big mind, is all that's left, and you have no attachments, no addictions, no grasping in any part of your being. But you also embrace them; you have also included them, you're no longer exclusively identified with them. But you're including them the same way you're including everything else that's arising in the universe moment to moment. You're identified with them, but no more so than you're identified with everything else that's arising moment to moment.

"There was one very low point with Treya and me, and it was from this low point that we all of a sudden realized that things could get that bad. We knew we had to really work to change. Fortunately, both of us had a great number of tools to help us. We had both been meditating for fifteen years, and I knew an enormous amount of psychotherapy and how to use and apply it. Slowly things started turning around. That's the point where we started to learn lessons, really powerful lessons, daily. And we grew and grew. We had an authentic love for each other, and that's why it worked. We never stopped loving each other, no matter what happened. Although her cancer got worse and worse, our bond just got better and better.

But any part of those two components can break down. Most people break down to some degree. Almost nobody gets out of childhood without losing at least 10 percent, and with some people it's 15 or 20 percent, but by the time it gets to 10 percent, you have some moderately significant neurosis. By the time you get to 15 percent, you have some very noticeable problems. You know it, and so does everybody around you who interacts with you for any amount of time; they all start to know it. When it gets to 20 or 25 percent, you almost always come to the attention of the authorities, one way or another. Either you yourself will feel so bad that you'll go seek professional help, or if it's bad, you might end up briefly incarcerated or institutionalized.

"It's a widespread problem that nobody fully escapes. It's weird because we know a fair bit about how shadows are created and what causes them, and there are a lot of different schools and there are a lot of disagreements as well. There's a fair amount of general understanding of what this stuff is, but we don't seem to apply it on a culture-wide level at all. Most people can get through high school without any understanding of shadow material—how to spot it or notice it in themselves, let alone simple ways to deal with it. There are a handful of very simple techniques."

So how does the shadow work in regard to relapse, whatever the substance is? Once we become aware of that, how can we use this to begin to truly heal and change these patterns that we're caught in?

Ken said, "I discussed this in 1980 in a book called *The Atman Project,* and a few years later, Robert Kegan brought out a book called *The Evolving Self,* in which he said the same thing. Part of the key to growth in general, including therapeutic growth, is that we can use the chakras. When someone steps up to the second chakra and identifies with it, then that's the subject, that's what they are. They're looking at the world from that second chakra. They're using it to see the world, so it's become their subject. It's their self, they're identified with it. When they let go of that and move up to the third chakra, then they have let go of their identity with the second chakra, so now they can see it as an object. They're free of it. But now they become identified with the third chakra, and they can't see that; that's where their self is and where they are now acting from. If they're doing that, they're stuck at acting from power and the self they can see. Now they must wait until they turn that power into something they can see, make it an object of aware-ness. Unless they do that, it tends to let go. They are free of it. They have transcended it. It's one of the reasons that mindfulness works so well with things like this, because you keep seeing things as objects and then letting them go. See it as an object and let it go. If you can't see it as an object, it remains a hidden subject. That means it can be split off as a sub-personality—that's a subject that can't be seen.

"When you have a sub-personality, you don't know it. It's looking at the world. You can't look at it. If you could forget it, you wouldn't be identified with it. It would be an object. It would no longer be your-self. The whole trick to development is that the subject at one stage be-comes the object of the subject of the next stage. Then the subject of that stage becomes the object of the subject of the next higher stage. You're dis-identifying with, you're getting rid of all those until you get all the way up to pure subjectivity that can never become an object, and that's generally known as Purusha." He was talking about the San-skrit term meaning cosmic self or consciousness. "Or the pure self. It's a vast, open emptiness, because you can never see it as an object. It's the pure seer. It's pure awareness itself, without any content of awareness. When you fall into that, you're radically free of all content, so you're resting as the witness. I see the mountain. I'm not the mountain. I have these sensations. I'm not these sensations. I have these feelings. I'm not these feelings. I have these thoughts. I'm not these thoughts. I'm the pure witness of all of them. The discovery of that freedom is known as the great liberation; that's how you become free of these things. That becomes central. That's a real part of an overall development. It takes us into wider and wider and wider expanses of pure freedom and pure awareness. That's what's wild."

I could dig this, because in that stage, who's left to be addicted or to have these struggles? We're left as what Ken calls I-am-ness. That being the case, though, how can we take working toward that, or working with that, and use it in a way for those who have or struggle with any form of addiction, from drugs to workaholism to whatever, so that we can heal? Not a quick-fix Band-Aid healing, but deep healing?

"Part of what happens, unfortunately, with an addict is that it starts generally with something in the interior awareness (upper left quadrant) of an individual and ends up fixated to some aspect that it can't let go of. As the next stage emerges, in this hidden, underground way, there's an obsessive lust for this thing that we're identified with. We don't want to let go of that. That becomes a seed that gets more and more thirsty, more and more hungry for whatever it is that it's lusting after. Then what starts happening in the brain (upper right quadrant) is that these things start to get hooked up. Whenever you're producing addictive thrusts in your interior, it starts to have a correlate in the brain; the brain starts to release hormones, dopamine, serotonin, any of these hypercritical, hyper-pleasure-releasing events. Part of the problem becomes that you have this unbelievably intense pleasure release connected with these facets in your psyche that you can't let go of. We've invested them with an enormous amount of attention and drive and desire and identification, and when that hooks up with this corresponding brain release, that forms a kind of dual unit that can become incredibly hard to break into. That's the start. Because something went wrong developmentally to hook somebody this way, and then the brain starts responding to a release of drugs, which themselves are incredibly addictive. Now you must also consider the relational and social constructs (lower left and right quadrants of the brain) as well, and those start to come apart fast as the addict needs more and more money and starts to rearrange his world.

"Over time, addicts cut out almost all friendships, work, most forms of relationship. They start to center their human interaction around a group of people they share the drugs with, and whether they love them or not, they're attracted to them because that's where they get to do this activity. This group forms an intensely real part of the addict's life, and the person becomes attached to that group. All of a sudden you have the person's interior, brain, and relational and social aspects of life (all four quadrants) that are activating the addiction. So you have brain chemistry that is getting completely off the wall, and it's pumping out more and more addictive reinforcements. Your work relations are becoming disastrous. It's tragedy after tragedy after tragedy. Eventually, dozens of relationships have been reduced to maybe four or five. The addict is left with 'Where do I get my next hit? How do I pay for it? Where am I gonna crash? What am I going to do for something resembling friendship?' That becomes secondary as the addict is brought up in this new world that they find themselves in. When you have that many different areas of your life so aggressively aiding the addictive act, it's the worst possible thing you can think of, preventing any sort of sensible response. It's part of something so wired as to make it almost impossible to do anything about it.

"What starts to happen at some point—which is horrifying—is that there's more and more confrontation with death. The person nearly dies, has a near-death experience. At some point, it's the last opportunity. They say, 'If I do this again, I'm going to die. Or I can try to recover and maybe I'll have a chance.' Sometimes that can be the one slow, small step that they take to start to get their life back. But the incredibly hard part about that is that getting their life back now means getting everything back. You must learn to brush your teeth again. You must learn how to dress again. You must learn how to eat cereal, you must learn how to drive, you must learn what friendship means. How do you treat people? You must learn what love means. It's probably one of the most horrifying and cruel things that can happen to human beings. It's nightmarish. I know I don't have to tell you any of this. But isn't it a sort of suffocating feeling, this experience?"

could see how this would leave an individual feeling completely imprisoned—a slave to their substance of choice. I wrote about this earlier, but there have been times when I've had a bottle in my hand or been looking at a line of coke on the table and have wept because I did not want to do it, but it was beyond my capacity at that point to stop myself. This is what a lot of people who've never been in an addict's shoes don't understand, and they write people like me off as weak-willed or morally deficient. Honestly, I understand why someone might say that. Maybe they lost a loved one to addiction or currently have a family member struggling, and they're hurting and scared, so they project that fear onto those who also struggle with addiction as though it is a matter of wills and morals, which it's not. This is an opportunity for me to try to cultivate compassion for people who look at addiction in that way. I know they're scared and hurting, and my heart aches for them.

And therein lies so much of my gratitude for Ken, his work, and his personal impact on my life, especially in regard to working with my shadow, for staying ignorant of my shadow self has kept me stuck in a place of living life and treating others unskillfully. It's often not me. It's my repressed bullshit projecting itself onto the situation rather than the real me showing up and meeting each moment, each person, each situation, from a fresh and truly present perspective.

PRACTICE

Three, Two, One Shadow Process

Ken cautions that all obstacles can't be overcome with mindfulness. "Because these traditions don't know about what happens when you repress and project something, they don't catch that kind of flip that can occur. You're stuck with a reactive emotion that you have, which is a false emotion. The false, reactive emotion is fear. Meditation doesn't help with shadows. Again, that's the problem. Cleaning up and waking up are very different processes, but both are important."

Ken turned me on to something called the Three, Two, One Shadow Process. "It's a method to reverse the interior process that creates shadow material. It's a way of noticing something in our environment or even in a dream, anything that upsets us or creates problems, by looking at it from the third-, second-, and first-person perspectives—kind of like a stripped-down loving-kindness meditation in that we take steps toward our challenges and break down the boundaries that separate *them* from *us*."

I try to use this practice whenever I notice myself having a strong personal emotional experience or projecting one onto someone or something else (or both). This can be something in life or even something from a dream. (This can be used for positive emotional experiences as well.) For example, there was a time when I was presenting a talk at a conference and watching one of the other presenters and found myself having a deep, emotional repulsion toward their presentation, so I worked through it using the Three, Two, One Shadow Process:

- After the presentation, I went back to my room and sat contemplating why I was so affected by this talk. It's not that the material was anything emotionally heavy, nor was it that the presenter did a bad job. This is where I started to recognize my own thoughts I'd been projecting onto the presenter during the talk. Things like "Yeah, right" or "You're full of shit" or "You're only in this for the money," which unfortunately is often the case in the spiritual marketplace. The thing was, in my gut, I didn't get that vibe from the person, so I was baffled as to why I was having such a visceral reaction toward him.

- I imagined myself having a dialogue with this person, expressing everything that was coming up for me, and that's when it hit me. I was projecting my own feelings of inadequacy as a public speaker and presenter onto him. I've seen plenty of "good" public speakers, but often the message is so watered down or so lacking in integrity that I'm not affected at all. This person wasn't doing any of that, so again, it just came down to the fact that he was good and delivered a strong message—I was just fucking jealous. I began to see how my old, deeply rooted feelings of self-loathing and my lack of self-confidence were very present in my unconscious, which is where the shadow material resides. I looked at the situation and the problem as separate from me, as *him*.

- As I finished saying all that I had to say to this person, the next step in the practice was to take on the role of the other person speaking back to you. Picture yourself *as* him, sitting in his chair and looking at you—which *yeah*, feels kind of weird at first, but this can be a very revelatory practice if you keep an open mind. I listened as this person expressed simple truths—you're always your own worst critic; being jealous of others only harms you; use that negative energy to continue honing your craft; and statements of that nature.

- The final step was to recognize that jealousy and feelings of inadequacy are part of me, a shadow, which is why it was a problem in the first place. As I identified, the *them* progressed to *you* and then *I*. In doing this, I re-owned or re-associated the otherwise unconscious and repressed material. *Huzzah!* A shadow-work miracle!

18

THIS SHIT ACTUALLY WORKS

CONVERSATION WITH NOAH LEVINE

Hardcore Buddhist teacher, author, and punk rocker Noah Levine has been a friend in dharma and recovery for many years. I knew he'd be up for a no-holds-barred discussion about the myriad addictions that people struggle with in life. I wanted to dig into what happens when we have a good thing going and we sabotage it. It might be recovery, accomplishments at work, relationships, or even school. In other words, why can people be their own worst enemies?

For Noah, the key to self-sabotage is *intolerance*. "If we had to boil it down to an answer, I'd say intolerance for discomfort. Whether that's the intolerance for pain, intolerance as in lack of compassion, intolerance for some painful experience, emotions, or losses, stressors, or intolerance for the mind's craving and the body's craving. Sometimes it's intolerance for success. Sometimes people are sober or are healing and are breaking into a new level of happiness and freedom, and they find that hard to tolerate because their self-view and self-esteem don't match up with the success they're experiencing."

He also linked it to being too much in our heads. "We're so identified with the mind and taking things personally and believing our thoughts when they say, 'You should suffer.' The mind is so tricky in that way, especially in a relapse, because it will show up as Mara [the demon of temptation] and say, 'If you have a drink [or whatever the relapse is], you will get free from this pain, and it will be a *compassionate* act to get high,' or to overeat or whatever it is. The mind tricks people into thinking, 'I'd be acting in a loving way toward myself if I got out of the pain that I'm in.'" That's how he saw most relapses, but there was an exception.

"Sometimes it's just that people have had enough and can't take it anymore." This can be more complicated. "The only time I'd meet a relapse with some kind of approval is if it came down to someone either killing themselves or getting high. I mean, truly planning to kill themselves or get high. Don't kill yourself. You can do the work if you survive." Still, much of the time, people need to sit with the impermanence of the difficulty that's happening in the now.

If people have tools to sit with the impermanence—things like meditation, prayer, twelve-step programs, or other support—why is it that instead of getting on their knees or their yoga mat or their therapist's couch, they step over the help that's right in front of them and return to self-destructive, uncompassionate actions?

Noah's answer surprised me but made a lot of sense: "All spiritual practice on some level is counter-instinctual, because we're not fleeing pain." *Whoa*—think about that for a minute. "Especially Buddhism, because it's asking us when we're in pain, the natural thing to do is to hate it, that's our survival instinct—hate the pain, avoid it, suppress it—and the practice is asking us to tolerate it, to turn toward it, to sit with it, to tend to it. Because of this, it makes perfect sense that people don't practice, that real sitting with compassion is rare. It also makes sense that even those of us who have a lot of practice under our belt will come to a place where we don't utilize the practice. That is a kind of relapse."

Noah turned me on to the Buddha's teaching called "The Simile of the Cloth," or the Vatthupama Sutra:

> Suppose a cloth were dirty and dull, and a dyer dipped it in some dye or another—blue, yellow, red, or pink. It would take the dye badly and be impure in color. Why is that? It is because the cloth wasn't clean. So too, disciples, when the mind is defiled, an unhappy destination may be expected.
>
> But suppose a cloth were clean and bright, and a dyer dipped it in some dye or another. It would take the dye well and be pure in color. Why? It is because the cloth was clean. So too when the mind is undefiled, a happy destination may be expected.[1]

The Buddha lists seventeen "defilements of the mind" that need purifying. As Noah put it, "Most of the list is greed-based stuff—craving for pleasure, jealousy, envy, hatred, resentment, ill will, self-centered stuff, arrogance. The last thing on that list that we need to clear away in our hearts and minds is negligence. When we neglect our practice, we'll never get free. If we're overlooking what needs to be done or procrastinating, we're turning toward a sensual or material solution rather than an internal healing modality.

"*Of course* it's hard for anyone to do deep, transformative practice. Even people who have been meditating for a while are going to find themselves in a place where they'd rather plug back into the Matrix than continue to face painful reality. Others will feel so overwhelmed by the pain that in the moment, compassion doesn't seem to be accessible." Noah connected this to the six different Buddhist realms—heavens, humanity, angry gods, hungry ghosts, animals, and particularly "the hell realm state of mind. Compassion in those places is generally inaccessible because the pain is overwhelming, but it's important to remember they are impermanent." The inspiring thing about the hell realms in Buddhist cosmologies—unlike theistic cosmology—is that hell is not eternal. We don't have to stay stuck there. "You might find yourself in a hell realm when your child is in the middle of a lot of suffering, and it may feel so painful that you can't access your practice in that moment, but it will be impermanent and it will pass, and you will come out having tolerated that very painful experience. Then you can return to the human realm where you can actually practice."

While we're heading into our hell realm of relapse, when we're obsessing over a drink or lighting that cigarette, what's going on with us physically, psychologically, and spiritually?

It's not always what you might think. Noah pointed out that there is a spectrum, and sometimes people relapse because they feel *good*. "When they're feeling the best they've ever felt physically, they're feeling emotionally elated and invincible and they're in a joy state." Of course, other times "it's because they are in physical pain or depressed."

Then there are the times when someone looks like he's doing okay but is on a self-destructive path. "People relapse when they're disconnected from community, when they're disconnected from having accountable relationships, whether they're amid joy or sorrow, even if they are continuing to show up and be of service to others and be accountable to teachers and sponsors and mentors and all that kind of stuff. Especially in the twelve-step world, there's an understanding that stopping participation precipitates the relapse. I agree with that, and Buddhism works so that sangha is important, having community is key. I'm not sure what's going on physically, mentally, spiritually, when people disengage from the community—insecurity, resentments, judgments."

That reminded me of something I'd learned from Gabor Maté, but Noah put his own spin on it: "I'm seeing treatment and addiction more and more as an attachment issue—an attachment *disorder*, if you want to use that kind of language. Relapse is about when we're detaching or disconnected; recovery is about reattaching."

I thought about how I went about reattaching and rebuilding my relationships after relapse. I had to repair some relationships and terminate others because I knew they were potentially toxic and could lead me back down roads I had no interest in traveling. What about our relationships with ourselves? How could we rebuild those?

As Yoda put it, "Patience you must have, my young padawan." Noah stressed that any kind of healing is a process. "It takes time to rebuild an internal sense of trust and well-being. Meditation is a sense of internal intimacy that we've disconnected from because of the drugs and alcohol and behaviors, and meditation is coming back into ourselves. That doesn't always feel good and safe. It takes a while to build that sense of internal connection with ourselves, and it's going to take a while to do that with others.

"Forgiveness meditation practice—self-forgiveness, offering forgiveness, and making amends or asking for forgiveness from others—is a key part of rebuilding relationships. I've been a bit critical of the philosophy that says all you must do is make amends to others and you're done. There is so much internal work. Making amends does not equal forgiveness. I had to do the meditation training in my heart and mind to dislodge resentment and to at least have the potential of feeling reconnected with some people."

Then Noah spoke a truth that resonated with my experience of genuine healing. "When it comes to forgiveness, it's not always about reconciliation or reconnecting. Sometimes it's about good boundaries that say, 'I'm going to forgive you, but we're not going to reconnect, because it was an unhealthy relationship and I'm going to put a boundary around it.'"

This made me think about how I've been terrible with boundaries throughout my own life. As far back as high school, I would always put my friends' needs before my own, taking on their pain and difficulties rather than my own. This, however, was also a means of avoidance, a way not to have to look at my own internal shit show. This continued into relationships with girlfriends and then into my work life—not being able to say no, not being able to respect myself and my needs enough to draw some lines—and it resulted in plenty of negative consequences, from toxic relationships to poor mental and emotional health from being stretched too thin with work obligations, and much more.

Boundaries or no, I believe forgiveness is crucial. My personal forgiveness practices revolve around loving-kindness meditation. (If you've forgotten what this is, go back to the Sharon Salzberg conversation. I'll wait. I've got the patience of a statue over here. Okay, that's not entirely true. On a good day I can come close, though, so at least there's that.) While it's not a specific forgiveness practice, I find cultivating an attitude of kindness and compassion is an integral part of softening my heart, which then allows forgiveness to flow more freely. But no matter how much I work with loving-kindness meditation, I will still often get stuck on offering forgiveness to myself. What kind of practices had Noah seen work in terms of forgiving ourselves, both for relapsing and in general?

"The key understanding is that it's impossible to forgive, because we don't have that kind of control over our mind. Saying 'I forgive you' and meaning 'I'm never going to allow resentment to arise within my mind again' is like saying 'I will no longer have any fear ever again.' We have nervous systems that react to danger with fear. I have a sensitive mind and heart that hate pain and are going to resent the ways I've caused pain to myself and the ways others have harmed me, but I'm also going to regret the ways I've harmed others. That's how the mind works. Forgiveness is an ongoing process . . . *an ongoing practice.* Even genuine moments of forgiveness (like everything else) are impermanent. It's not 'I forgive you, and now I'm done forever.' But rather, 'I forgive you in this moment. I forgive you right now because I'm not feeling angry about the pain.'

"Another key understanding is that forgiveness doesn't get rid of the pain. Sometimes there's a sort of 'I forgive you' or 'I forgive myself' and now you're not going to be in pain about what happened, but painful stuff happened in your life. When you consider things like abuse, betrayal, neglect, abandonment—there are always going to be unpleasant sensations around them, no matter how much compassion, no matter how much forgiveness is done. Those things are going to carry painful memories, and that's the appropriate reaction and understanding. I have a practice I like called 'The Three Directions of Forgiveness' that I use to work with this. It's a way of offering self-forgiveness, asking for forgiveness, and offering forgiveness, and training our minds."

Noah reminded me of the neuroscience involved in forgiveness—how neurons that fire together wire together. Repetition creates "new neural pathways, and it changes our relationship to internal and external pain. Often it will lead us from a place of shame about the past to a place of healthy regret. Sometimes we believe that if we have forgiven ourselves, we won't have any regret about the past, but the people who have no regret about the harm they've caused are called sociopaths. That's the spiritual bypass. When we've caused harm—I have as an addict—regret is healthy. That's compassionate, that's empathetic. It's healthy to say, 'I fucked up over and over in my life, and I regret all of the harm that I've caused.'

"Forgiveness doesn't get rid of regret, but it does get rid of the shame that says 'I'm a bad person.' Or the guilt that says 'I'm unworthy' or 'I'm wretched.' It enters a place where we can realize that we're good people even though we've done some unskillful things in our lives—not bad, but unskillful. Then we can heal, recover, and begin a lifelong process of self-forgiveness."

I appreciated his perspective on regret. I once had a conversation with someone who insisted that having regrets was pointless and that it's not "spiritual" to have regrets. I didn't see it that way. Not for me. I've done some fucked-up things in my life, and I do have regrets about them. And that's a launching pad for my growth.

Noah shared his insights into a Buddhist teaching from the Pali

Canon that translates as "a healthy sense of shame." He dislikes the use of the word "shame" because of the connotations of being good or bad or unworthy. "A healthy sense of *regret* is a spiritual concept, and it's a necessary one. The twelve-step programs teach 'We will not regret the past,' and I get it, because sometimes I feel that way, where everything has worked out well. Through all that confusion, I came out on the other side desperate enough to start meditating. If I hadn't caused all that harm, then I wouldn't have gotten the willingness to dedicate my life to trying to help others. I get that 'don't regret it, because you wouldn't be here without it' phenomenon of the grateful recovering addict or alcoholic, and I am grateful that I was an addict, which led me to dharma practice at such a young age. Nevertheless, I can hold that gratitude *and* the regret for the ways that I hurt people to get where I am."

I wanted to talk about that. What got Noah to where he is today? Where did it come from? In recovery programs, we're taught to connect to a higher power. For me, it's always been about acknowledging that I can't recover alone. Like the saying in the fellowships goes, "I can't. We can." But I also believe in a power, a source greater than myself. Whatever label is slapped onto it means little to me because it's just that, a label, and could never do justice to what my direct experience of it has been. What about Noah?

He didn't see the necessity for believing in any kind of external power. "We recover based on our own actions and our own efforts. I understand that some people's belief in God helps them to take wise actions, and it's a useful belief system because sometimes it inspires the positive, but as a Buddhist, I don't believe that at all. It's unnecessary. What is much more important is the commitment to practice and the commitment to relational practice—in sangha, community, satsang."

Noah brought up an interesting point: Even people's belief in God could lead to a relapse. "If people are taught that there is a loving, caring higher power that's going to take care of them, and then they find themselves in a difficult situation, they might feel betrayed by God and the philosophy that said that God was going to take care of everything if they just showed up and believed. For example, their son is suffering and relapses, and they feel betrayed by that, asking, 'Where is my higher power now?' or when a relationship ends or a child is sick. On some level, being told that God will remove your shortcomings, God will restore you to sanity, can be processed as a betrayal." When it doesn't happen, when people say the prayers and make the amends and they're still experiencing suffering and shame, it can lead to disappointment or worse, and that can lead to slipping. Noah thinks that "a lot of people have probably relapsed out of a loss of faith, a crisis of faith."

I hadn't finished with the idea of a higher power yet. What about spiritual community? I know that for me, as Noah and I have already discussed, community and not trying to go it alone is of paramount importance. At times, I've experienced that as a power greater than myself. What did Noah think about working with a sangha with regard to a power greater than ourselves, since it's a group effort, a group support?

Noah encouraged me to let go of the "higher power" terminology. "Most of my feeling—most of Buddhist practice—is internal. It's training your mind and developing internal well-being and compassion. A core refuge is sangha, and what we're doing is relational. It's about living together, working together, having the forgiveness, the tolerance, the compassion, and helping each other. In Buddhism, there's an internal meditative training and an ethical way of speaking, livelihood, and action, so it's all about relationships. I wouldn't call it a higher power, but I would call it a core part of the treatment process or the recovery process."

I liked that, because if there's no higher power, then there's no *lower* power either, but we're still better off not trying to go it alone. In that sense, it's all about community. According to Noah, the Buddha was passionate about this. "Whether it was the monastic community or the lay sangha of non-monastics, it was as if he said, 'You guys must practice together. You have to learn to work together. You have to learn to forgive each other, because this is where the healing and awakening is.'

And when it's real, when there's conflict and disagreement, when there are different views, *can we still come from a place of kindness, even when we're disagreeing?* That's where the rubber meets the road."

Cool. If we can apply that to ourselves as well as others, we have a better chance of not falling back into self-destructive behavior. But what else can we do to protect ourselves from relapsing?

"Most of what comes to mind is the pretty simple stuff, like staying engaged in the community even if you're bored with it, even if you're no longer inspired, even if you're the person in the room with the most time sober. It's important to say, 'I'm going to remain a part of this community. I'm going to keep going even when I don't want to.' It's like with meditation practice. I don't feel like meditating every day, but I do it. And I don't feel like going to meetings or being a part of community all the time, but I do it."

Noah says it's important to have that balance in one's life and recovery—serving and helping others, but also places of allowing ourselves to be served, of seeking out people who inspire us. "I'm with my teachers and I'm accountable to them. And then there are the people who are accountable to *me*. There are upper-, lower-, and peer-based relationships—making sure we have teachers, mentors, sponsors, peers, and that we have people who are in the earlier stages where we are that teacher/sponsor/mentor for them as well.

"I like staying engaged long-term, but I don't think it needs to mean that you're required to attend a meeting every day for the rest of your life. It certainly hasn't been that for me, but what has happened is that I've stayed in spiritual communities for almost thirty years now. Sometimes those have been twelve-step groups, and now it's much more Refuge Recovery and Against the Stream—my Buddhist communities—but I'll still go to a twelve-step meeting when I need it. I like going to them because those are my people. I don't like some of the philosophy, but those are my people, so I stay connected.

"This applies to meditation as well. Deep, long-term, internal meditative training is going to do something to ensure that we get through the difficult times that are coming, whether that's death or some sort of loss or illness—those core preparations people often use as excuses for relapse or that lead to relapse. For example, saying, 'Well, this is painful. I'm getting high.' If we have a deep meditative training, we can say, 'This is painful, but I know how to meet it with compassion. I understand impermanence. I understand the importance of forgiveness, and I'm going to apply that in this moment.' We have that ability.

"Sometimes we get to a place where we don't have that ability. I can remember my first trip to India twenty years ago. Some of the time I was so lonely and suffering. I couldn't sit, and so what I would do was blast loud music as a distraction. I couldn't access my practice, but I had enough wisdom to at least avoid the deep, unpleasant, afflictive emotions and give impermanence time. Twenty years later, when I returned to India, a part of my trip was looking at that. I got divorced this year; my father died a couple of months ago. I could sit with difficult emotions and loss and reflect on midlife experiences and see that twenty-eight years of meditation practice makes a difference. I have much more space, much more tolerance for sadness, loss, loneliness—for all that stuff. Not that emotions don't come, but after almost three decades of meditation, I'm able to meet them. There's been a lot of progress. This shit actually works."

PRACTICE

The Three Directions of Forgiveness

Noah taught me a powerful forgiveness meditation that has worked for me when I find myself struggling with forgiveness—for myself or others. Who, *me*? Of course—this shit still happens to the best and the worst of us and always will, because we're human beings. What else would you expect?

The practice is divided into three parts:

PART ONE

- Start by naming a person you have harmed. Reach within yourself to a place of humility and acknowledge, "At times in my life, I have been the one causing harm." Reflect on that and ask yourself:

1. Why did I lie?
2. Why did I not show up?
3. Why did I cause harm in the ways that I did?

- Connect to how you were in pain, confused, scared, or filled with craving or addiction. Then begin asking for forgiveness, perhaps reciting, "Please forgive me for having caused you harm, whether it was intentional or unintentional. Whether it was through my words or my actions, I ask for your forgiveness."

- Sit with that request, and then move on to the next individual you have harmed. And then the next . . .

PART TWO

- After asking forgiveness, we strive to understand that all harm comes out of confusion. We reverse the direction of the practice, offering forgiveness to the people who have harmed us.
- We say, "I forgive you as much as I can in this moment for having caused me harm, whether it was intentional or unintentional, whether it was through your words or your actions, whether it was out of anger or fear or greed or delusion. I offer you forgiveness *as much as I can* in this moment."
- Noah says, "The importance of saying 'as much as I can' is to remind ourselves that we don't get to control this but, rather, it's our aspiration, it's our intention to forgive, but perhaps it's not going to all be done right now. This is a process."

PART THREE

- After asking for forgiveness and forgiving others, we turn toward ourselves and say: "I forgive you as much as I can in this moment for all the ways that I've caused myself harm through my judging thoughts, through my actions, through my speech. Whether the harm was done intentionally, unintentionally, out of anger or fear, greed or ignorance, I offer myself forgiveness."

I'm grateful to Noah for this one. Genuine forgiveness can be such a challenge for so many of us, but if we take Noah's advice and forgive as much as we can in this moment, whether that means forgiving ourselves or others, it's a start, and that's what matters most—taking that first step.

19

WE'RE ALL WE'VE GOT

CONVERSATION WITH DERON DRUMM

Deron Drumm writes and speaks about the need for a more holistic and compassionate way of supporting people experiencing emotional distress. He is the executive director of Advocacy Unlimited and the founder of Toivo, a wellness center in Connecticut focused on mind-body-spirit healing that provides statewide and national classes, workshops, and conferences. At its home base on Franklin Avenue in Hartford, Toivo is a center where people can engage in expert-facilitated yoga, meditation, fitness and strength training, creative writing, expressive art, walking/running groups, nutrition workshops, qigong, drum circles, and more! Toivo represents a celebration of the human experience in all its forms and believes in the unfathomable power of looking within for direction. The organization also believes that no one should be denied the benefits of healing modalities because of socioeconomic standing, psychiatric history, or experiences with addiction.

Deron and Toivo hold a very special place in my heart. The organization's core intent is to meet people where they are in their recovery and help them learn how to go more profoundly and realistically into that process and ultimately thrive. My connection to and respect for Toivo grew over the years as I taught workshops and created a web series exploring the ways people experience pain and the means and methods with which they can recover.

After my last relapse, I returned to my hometown in Connecticut. About a week later I received a call from Deron. He was checking to see how I was doing. Then he asked about my plans. "Are you staying in Connecticut for good now?" I knew exactly why he was asking, and *he knew* I knew exactly why he was asking! We both chuckled, which was a good thing, because at that point in my life I needed all the laughs I could get. I told Deron I was indeed back for good.

Toivo provided the perfect place for me to heal and grow into this new stage in my life. I still host the web series and teach workshops at Toivo's home base in Hartford, and now I also visit prisons, rehabs, psychiatric units, and more with the Toivo team—Deron, Hilary, Annette, Laura, Linda, and Kali (as well as our extended family at Advocacy Unlimited)—and bring meditation to those who wouldn't otherwise have access to it. It's a group effort built on hope and a commitment to helping others turn their lives around.

Along with these duties, I'm working with Deron and the team to create a holistic health coach certificate program based on the highly successful and celebrated teachings that Toivo offers. So that's where I am as I write this book. It's been a tremendous blessing, one that affords me the opportunity to serve my community. It's incredible how this life thing can align itself if you're simply willing to show up, put one foot in front of the other, and do the damn work. To close this book, I wanted to introduce you to Deron and shine a light on some of the things I've learned from him and the rest of the Toivo crew as they've developed into a point of focus and passion for me.

One thing I'd seen brought to light in so many ways during our work—from sessions in psychiatric units to community lectures—is the toll emotional pain takes on us all. It's obviously part of the deal of being human. There's no way to escape it, and yet the Western mind-set encourages us to escape feeling our feelings, rather than using pain to heal and teach us. I've seen time and again that turning escape into big business—from liquor to video games, social media to Big Pharma—has become a way to reduce levels of awareness of what is happening in our society and to keep us in check.

Deron had tremendous insight into this. "The human experience is painful by nature. Yet our society has normalized the need to run from and seek relief from distress rather than find ways to navigate and heal. The medical-disease model has reduced emotional suffering to biological problems in people's brains to be treated with diagnoses and drugs. This reductionist standard is far better at generating revenue than healing. I've heard it said that Western medicine 'mops the floor without turning off the faucet.' Clearly, we need a cultural shift away from the disease model. Holistic approaches like the ones we use at Toivo aim to focus on root causes, not on symptoms."

The folks at Toivo believe that focusing on symptom abatement is shortsighted and ultimately makes experiences worse. This approach ignores the roots of emotional distress: things like trauma, poverty, racism, gender discrimination, bullying, and one-size-fits-all educational systems. Healing and self-awareness are about facing pain and suffering with openness and curiosity and seeing distressing experiences as opportunities to grow and heal.

There's no doubt that people are reaching out for support in dealing with their difficult emotions, but in many cases they're given a "diagnosis" of mental illness, and along with that often come prescriptions for psychiatric drugs, which can further the societal inclination to institutionalize escape. I was impressed by Deron's thoughts about how we can begin to change this paradigm both locally and nationally.

"Toivo uses a two-pronged approach. First, we compassionately raise awareness of the outcomes of the medical-model approach—such as the people who enter the mental health system dying at an average of twenty-five years younger than their peers.[1] Second, we create healing communities—places where people can be seen, heard, and connected with others. We offer ways for those who are suffering to soothe their nervous systems through yoga, qigong, meditation, sound healing, and creative expression. We believe that to be of healing service to others, we must embody the practices we teach."

Sounds like my kind of people, right? I wondered what Deron thought about the role that things we can't sell and doctors can't prescribe—like love and compassion—play in the recovery process. How can we make sure we're not deadening our hearts to those who are hurting?

"Love and compassion are *everything* when it comes to healing. When we numb ourselves, we may mask our pain, but we also anesthetize our Divine emotions, like love, compassion, and joy. It's important for us to be embodied practitioners—to make sure we have adequate tools to clear ourselves so we are present for those we're serving. Daily mind, body, and contemplative practices are crucial to staying heart-centered in our work."

I asked him to break down his understanding of holistic healing and give some insight into what Toivo's approach offers that indiscriminate use of medication doesn't.

For Deron, it was "about tapping into the body's natural ability to repair itself. The body has tremendous healing resources when the nervous system is relaxed. External solutions to inner strife and struggle at best deaden the fight-or-flight response without engaging the parasympathetic nervous system, which is essential for healing. Our approach is also about raising awareness—self-awareness is the key to transformation. It's about looking at the whole person, not a quick fix, and helping people make a lifelong commitment to living better. Holistic healing considers all areas of our lives—the physical, emotional, energetic, social, and spiritual—to be connected. *It's about transforming pain, not transferring it.*" That's how we can move away from the mechanical approach—treating our bodies as machines—and toward a holistic view, one recognizing that if one is out of balance, then all are out of balance.

During my work with Toivo, I'd observed that the body self-heals when the nervous system is relaxed. I was hoping Deron would speak to this relaxation response as opposed to the stress response. What causes them? Can we learn to spend more time in the relaxation state than in the stress state, and if so, how?

Toivo's collective goal is to support people in moving from a state of protection to a state of growth and healing. "The body has an amazing ability to protect itself from threats. When we sense a threat, the sympathetic nervous system goes into action. Blood flows to the muscles. Stress hormones are released. The body is ready to move fast. This is great if a bus is coming at us—the fight-or-flight response can allow for a quick reaction. The problem is that the body cannot tell the difference between an abstract threat (worrying) or an actual threat (the bus). Many people spend far too much time in a state of protection. In this state, the immune system is suppressed (the body is worried about surviving the immediate threat, not healing), access to creativity is decreased (it's hard to write and create in fight or flight), and access to our intelligence is decreased (blood that would go to the brain goes to muscles)." I got where he was coming from. For example, have you ever said anything you didn't mean when you were angry?

Deron went on to say that when we are in a fight-or-flight situation, our access to our hearts—love, compassion, and empathy—also decreases. Many people are chronically in a stress response. This explains so many of the struggles people have. "Interestingly, pharmaceuticals may numb fight or flight, but they do not elicit the relaxation response (within the parasympathetic nervous system). When the relaxation response is elicited with things like breath practice, meditation, qigong, or yoga, the immune system works at full capacity; we are also more intelligent, more creative, more compassionate, and more able to respond consciously to stressors rather than react impulsively. Stress response also impacts the body's ability to take in nutrients. Digestion is far more efficient when the body is relaxed—in 'rest and digest' mode. Fight or flight narrows our focus; the relaxation response broadens our focus."

This made perfect sense to me from the perspective of relapse. I certainly wasn't in a "rest and digest" space when I decided to pick up the bottle or snort a line of powder up my nose. I was in the fight-or-flight space, and regardless of the specific circumstances that had led me to that place, I was undeniably there. However, I wasn't involved with a therapeutic community such as Toivo, or actively engaging in the numerous mind-body practices mentioned in this chapter, and in this book as a whole. I was isolated. I was caught in self-pity, as Michael Taft put it earlier. I was in that place of "Fuck it, I just don't care anymore and don't want to feel this shit." As I've come to learn, truly the only way out is through. We don't—no, we *shouldn't*—have to go through any of it alone. Support networks are invaluable to the healing process—any healing process.

A book a lot of us at Toivo refer to regularly is Dr. Bernie Siegel's classic *Love, Medicine & Miracles*. Siegel was a pioneer in popularizing the mind-body connection, pointing out that doctors can kill their patients with the information they convey or neglect to convey. Hearing the words "There is nothing more I can do" or "Put your affairs in order" can seal a patient's fate. Some prognoses cause fear and put people in a perpetual stress response, thereby shutting off their natural healing abilities. There's a lot of research[2] on the placebo and nocebo effects regarding what information is conveyed to people receiving treatment. People must be given honest information in a way that leaves room for hope and healing. There is no "false hope" when it comes to healing. Dr. Siegel wrote, "All patients must be accorded with the conviction that they can heal, no matter what the odds."[3] What did Deron think about this?

"I believe it all comes down to the nervous system. When people are given negative outcomes, their bodies go into a state of protection. When they are given hope, their bodies go into a state of growth and healing. I believe the nervous system's role in healing is far more important than what most Western corporate medicine acknowledges. We need to respect the power of the mind to manifest outcomes."

As I've learned through my work with Toivo, if you can do only one thing to empower yourself and your healing, to begin to create a space between yourself and the possibility of relapse, it's to use any tool that helps elicit a relaxation response. It might be the mindfulness body scan taught by Michael Taft that helps us to become more in touch with our bodily emotions. Maybe it's the practice of loving-kindness from Sharon Salzberg's chapter that teaches us not only to love ourselves more but also to love and be kinder to others in the process. Or maybe it's Tara Brach's practice of RAIN, which helps us work with our difficult experiences in real time. Whatever the practice (or practices) are, I ask only that you begin incorporating them into your life starting *today*! Especially if your life and way of living is/was anything like mine, tomorrow is not guaranteed, so please don't take today for granted. *Please.*

As Deron says, "If you're going through an emotional storm in your life, find the eye of the storm; there is always an eye. When you find it, cultivate a higher vibration by focusing on love and compassion."

I'm incredibly grateful for the opportunity to practice altruism, compassion, and interconnection through Toivo; it takes me further and further from relapse, one breath at a time. I'll say it one more time: It's crazy how life can align in your favor if you show up, put one foot in front of the other, and do the next fucking right thing. Toivo is one of those blessings not just for me but for the myriad others the organization serves. My wish is that more organizations like Toivo begin popping up throughout the United States and the world. If you're interested in learning about how you can work toward making this change in your own community, I encourage you to email us at www.toivocenter.org /contact.

We're all in this life thing together, so why not start acting like it? Let's show up for ourselves and for each other. Let's fucking rise above and do this thing *together*. We're all we've got.

AFTERWORD

ONWARD AND INWARD

I was going to close with one more practice, but I changed my mind. Instead, I'll direct you to the practice so you can dive in and out at your convenience. For the Rise and Thrive practice, go to http:// theindiespiritualist.com/2017/08/22/dead-set-on-living-bonus-practice -rise-and-thrive/.

What I want to talk about here is what we can do the next time we find ourselves on the brink of returning to self-defeating behaviors— which can be in the moment you find yourself twisting the cap off a bottle of vodka or making the excuses and self-destructive choices that will lay the groundwork for a relapse weeks or months or even years from now.

In my own case, as I look back at the relapses in my life, I can re-member several occasions when, months before I'd pick up a bottle, I'd start noticing things. I'd pay attention to how late liquor stores were open, or I'd take an extra-long look at the drink on someone's table while I was eating at a restaurant. Things like that are cues we're start-ing to slip, even if it's just slightly, back into old patterns.

This isn't about relapse prevention specifically, because there are al-ready a hundred and one books out in the world about that. Instead, this is about how we are going to be sure we've set ourselves up in a safe enough way to either call bullshit on ourselves, have someone we trust call bullshit on us, or a combination of both. Again, not just about slipping back into drug and alcohol use, but about heading off *all* types of self-defeating behavior!

I figure I may as well do what I do best here and use myself as an example by sharing what I've done since my last relapse. Some of this will be obvious—perhaps all of it will—but for the benefit of those for whom it's not, please bear with me.

First and foremost, I had to set up a small network of friends I know I can count on to be there for me, to listen to me, to support me, and to do so nonjudgmentally, whenever I need them. That's been incredibly huge, having some people I can bare my soul to who will listen or bear loving witness to whatever it is I'm going through, yet stay judgment-free. It's a cathartic release to be able to talk with friends, mentors, sponsors, and family members in that respect.

Another huge part of my well-being is having a community of like-minded folks to help encourage me on the spiritual path. This doesn't mean everyone along the way is going to be your best friend or confidant, but they, like you, have an interest in spiritual development, and if there's at least one thing you can count on them for, it's being there to walk with you, side by side.

Finding some sort of physical activity helps replace the negative behavior. I've seen countless people relapse because after putting down the bottle or pills or needle or chocolate cake, they didn't replace it with something positive. Running, hiking, gardening, weight lifting, kayaking, swimming, dancing to Le Butcherettes (my editor's input, and I'll respectfully leave it in here for her)—anything that gets your blood flowing is a tremendous complement to integral well-being. Bonus points if you're able to do these activities outdoors in the sunshine!

Take up a meditation practice. As you've seen by now, there are so many ways to meditate, some of which have been presented to you in this book, and many more that haven't. I believe there is a form of meditation for everyone; you've just got to take the time to find what works for you. Remember, though, meditation—like any other practice or sport or program—doesn't yield results overnight, so do your best to bring patience to your practice.

Speaking of patience (and I know I addressed this in an earlier chapter, but I believe it bears repeating, so here goes), I've often been asked if there was one thing I wish I'd done differently on the spiritual path. What would that be? My answer every time is that I wish I had learned to cultivate more compassion and softness toward myself in the process. Dedicating yourself to sincerely working with difficult emotions, life experiences, and spiritual practices that will help you heal and grow as a person is no easy thing, so please, please, *please* be as gentle with yourself as you can, while still staying dedicated and willing to push yourself as much as you're able to in the moment (with the understanding that there are always variables).

Get a fucking sense of humor. If you already have one, do whatever it takes to keep it. Laughter is such potent medicine, especially the ability to laugh at ourselves. I can't even begin to tell you how many times I've found relief in watching shows like *Curb Your Enthusiasm*, *Impractical Jokers*, *The Office*, and *Chappelle's Show*. Taking a break from being so earnest and laughing at inappropriate shit can sometimes be one of the most compassionate things you can do for yourself. At least I've found that to be true, but hey, what do I know? That said, go laugh at some dumb shit for a little while, okay? I think you'll thank me for it later.

For a complete listing of the contributors and their bios, please go to http://theindiespiritualist.com/2017/08/22/dead-set-on-living-contributor-bios/.

ACKNOWLEDGMENTS

Brenda and Lawrence Grosso; Jason, Catie, Addison, and Eleanor Grosso; Steve Harris; Alice Peck; Michele Martin, Diana Ventimiglia, and the rest of the family at Simon & Schuster; Michael Geres; Deron and Carrie Drumm; Hilary Bryant, Laura Le, Annette Medero, Kali Farrell, Linda Lentini, and the rest of my Toivo and Advocacy Unlimited family (there are just too many names to include, but you and I know exactly who you are—thank you!); Harriet Cianci; Michael Taft; JP Sears; Jen Taylor, Justin Vood, and The Sanctuary at Shepardfields; Eben and Rachel Sterling and *Thrasher Magazine*; Jessica Pimentel; Kelly and Jess Margera and CKY; Bam Margera; Dana Sawyer and Stephanie; Alanna Kaivalya; Lauren Seder; Breeze Floyd; Ram Dass, Rachel Fisher, Raghu Markus, Mirabai Bush, Kelly Rego, JR Morton, Corey Leonard, and everyone else at the Love Serve Remember Foundation; Ken Wilber, Corey DeVos, Colin Bigelow, and everyone at Integral Institute; Rachel Sclare and Joey Marsocci; Michelle Jean and Asher; Jessica Durivage; Jenn Lui and Morgan Walker; Keli Lalita; Erica Lynn; Justin Mehl; Cheryl Guertin; Amy Scher; Patrick Rivera and my Hartford Refuge Recovery Family; Raghunath "Ray" Cappo; Jamison Monroe and Newport Academy; Alex and Allyson Grey, Jon Ohia, Joness Jones and everyone at COSM; Lissa Rankin; don Miguel Jr. and Jose Ruiz; Bartolotta; Sera Beak; Lisa Braun Dubbels; Jessica Durivage; Belle of the Fall; Ben Grippo; Amy LaBossiere; Patricia Mahmarain;

Chris and Jenny Hinman; Laci-Ann Mosher; and every single person who's supported me and given a shit about my work. My heart is sincerely humbled. And, of course, all of the contributors in this book who took the time to share their wisdom and experience. I'm forever grateful!

NOTES

I. THE TRANCE OF UNWORTHINESS

1 Tara Brach, *True Refuge: Finding Peace and Freedom in Your Own Awakened Heart* (New York: Bantam, 2013).
2 Nicholas Bunnin and Jiyuan Yu, *The Blackwell Dictionary of Western Philosophy* (Chichester, UK: Wiley-Blackwell, 2009), p. 362.
3 http://ho-oponopono-explained.com/tag/dr-hew-len.

3. GOD IS NOT YOUR BITCH

1 Lissa Rankin, MD, *The Fear Cure: Cultivating Courage as Medicine for the Body, Mind, and Soul* (Carlsbad, CA: Hay House, 2016), p. 11.
2 Walter B. Cannon, *The Wisdom of the Body* (New York: W. W. Norton, 1932).
3 Tina Fossella, "Human Nature, Buddha Nature: An Interview with John Welwood," *Tricycle*, spring 2011.

4. DRINKING, DRUGGING, OVERSPENDING, AND SEXCAPADES

1 https://www.ncbi.nlm.nih.gov/pmc/articles/PMC1494926.
2 https://www.ncbi.nlm.nih.gov/books/NBK207191.
3 Terence T. Gorski and Merlene Miller, *Staying Sober: A Guide for Relapse Prevention.* (Independence, MO: Herald House/Independence Press, 1986).

4 Anne Wilson Schaef, *When Society Becomes an Addict* (San Francisco: Harper & Row, 1987).

5. I DON'T BELIEVE IN ANYTHING

1 https://www.ramdass.org/selfhood-spirit-personality.
2 https://www.drweil.com/videos-features/videos/the4-7-8-breath-health
-benefitsdemonstration.

6. THE PLACE WHERE THE SWEETNESS HURTS

1 Michael W. Taft, *The Mindful Geek* (Kensington, CA: Cephalopod Rex Publishing, 2015), p. 5.
2 Ibid., p. 70.
3 Michael W. Taft, *Nondualism: A Brief History of a Timeless Concept* (Kensington, CA: Cephalopod Rex Publishing, 2014), p. 3.
4 Bill W. and Dick B., *Alcoholics Anonymous: The Original 1939 Edition*, Dover Empower Your Life Series (New York: Dover Publications, 2011), p. 70.

7. THE LOVE THAT ROLLS UP ITS
SLEEVES AND GETS MUDDY

1 Paul Brunton, *The Short Path to Enlightenment: Instructions for Immediate Awakening* (Burdett, NY: Larson Publications, 2014), p. 40.
2 Ken Wilber, *The Integral Vision: A Very Short Introduction to the Revolutionary Integral Approach to Life, God, the Universe, and Everything* (Boston: Shambhala Publications, 2007), p. 201.

8. A LONELY CONSCIOUSNESS IN A BAG OF FLESH

1 http://intentblog.com/how-i-went-from-58-pounds-nearly-dead-to
-healthy-happy-loving-life.
2 https://www.ncbi.nlm.nih.gov/pmc/articles/PMC3599773.
3 https://www.nimh.nih.gov/health/topics/eating-disorders/index.shtml
?utm_source=rss&utm_medium=rss.
4 https://www.cdc.gov/violenceprevention/acestudy.

9. A HAPPINESS THAT ISN'T GOING TO SHATTER

1 http://thesunmagazine.org/issues/439/sunbeams.
2 Sharon Salzberg, *Lovingkindness: The Revolutionary Art of Happiness* (Boston: Shambhala Publications, 1995), p. 18.

10. WRITING AND FIGHTING FOR FORGIVENESS

1 J. Ivy, *Dear Father: Breaking the Cycle of Pain* (New York: Atria/Beyond Words, 2015), p. 19.
2 Ibid., pp. 207–8.

II. RISING FROM THE WOUNDEDNESS

1 http://www.isr.umich.edu/williams/All%20Publications/DRW%20 pubs%202000/racism%20and%20mental%20health.%20the%20 African%20American%20experience.pdf.
2 Nelson Mandela, *Long Walk to Freedom: The Autobiography of Nelson Mandela* (New York: Back Bay Books, 1995), p. 622.

12. A TINY BIT MORE

1 Chris Grosso, *Everything Mind: What I've Learned About Hard Knocks, Spiritual Awakening, and the Mind-Blowing Truth of It All* (Boulder, CO: Sounds True Publishing, 2015), p. 14.

13. THE INEVITABLE CATASTROPHE

1 https://astis.com/6/37.html (copyright © 1972 by His Divine Grace A. C. Bhaktivedanta Swami Prabhupada).
2 C. S. Lewis, *The Screwtape Letters* (New York: HarperCollins, 2001; originally published in 1942), pp. 37–38.
3 https://beherenownetwork.com/krishna-das-ep-20-gotta-go-in-to-get -out.
4 Eckhart Tolle, *The Power of Now: A Guide to Spiritual Enlightenment* (Vancouver: Namaste Publishing, 1999), p. 46.

5 http://www.cbsnews.com/news/psychedelic-drugs-as-treatment-for
   -anxiety-addiction.
6 http://www.hopkinsmedicine.org/news/media/releases/hallucinogenic
   _drug_psilocybin_eases_existential_anxiety_in_people_with_life
   _threatening_cancer_.
7 https://www.theguardian.com/science/2012/aug/23/lsd-help-alcoholics-theory.
8 Jeff Bridges and Bernie Glassman, *The Dude and the Zen Master* (New
   York: Blue Rider Press, 2012), p. 29.

14. THOSE DARK, HORRIBLE FUCKING PLACES

1 http://www.laphamsquarterly.org/magic-shows/w-b-yeats-magus.

15. THIS BEAUTIFUL, BROKEN REALITY OF THE HUMAN CONDITION

1 Pema Chödrön, *The Wisdom of No Escape and the Path of Loving-
   Kindness* (Boston: Shambhala Publications, 2001), p. 17.

16. THE GIFTS OF CRISIS

1 http://www.yogajournal.com/article/health/bouncing-back.

18. THIS SHIT ACTUALLY WORKS

1 http://wisdomquarterly.blogspot.com/2010/12/simile-of-cloth-mn-7.html.

19. WE'RE ALL WE'VE GOT

1 https://qz.com/863196/why-are-americans-with-severe-mental-illness
   -dying-25-years-younger-than-their-peers.
2 Primavera A. Spagnolo, Luana Colloca, and Markus Heilig, "The Role of Ex-
   pectation in the Therapeutic Outcomes of Alcohol and Drug Addiction Treat-
   ments," *Alcohol and Alcoholism* 50, no. 3 (2015): doi:10.1093/alcalc/agv015.
3 Bernie S. Siegel, *Love, Medicine & Miracles* (New York: HarperCollins,
   1986), p. 39.

ABOUT THE AUTHORS

CHRIS GROSSO is a writer and public speaker. He is the author of *Indie Spiritualist* and *Everything Mind* and writes for *ORIGIN Magazine*, *Huffington Post*, and *Mantra Yoga + Health Magazine*. Chris speaks frequently at conferences and festivals and is passionate about his work with people who are in the process of healing or struggling with addictions of all kinds. He is a member of the advisory board for Drugs over Dinner and hosts *The Indie Spiritualist* podcast on Ram Dass's Be Here Now Network. Visit Chris at www.indiespiritualist.com.

ALICE PECK is drawn to finding the sacred in everyday things. Her books include *Mindful Beads*; *Be More Tree*; and *Bread, Body, Spirit*, among other titles. Her writing has appeared in *Center for Humans & Nature*, *Spirituality & Health*, *Rewire Me*, *Prime Mind*, *Daily Good*, and *Mountain Record*. As an editor, she focuses on mind and spirit, collaborating with Zen teachers, Tibetan Buddhist psychotherapists, and mindfulness instructors.